CW00953299

A LAKE DISTRICT
MISCELLANY

A LAKE DISTRICT MISCELLANY

TOM HOLMAN

FRANCES LINCOLN LIMITED
PUBLISHERS

For Ceri and Beth

A LAKE DISTRICT MISCELLANY
Frances Lincoln Limited
4 Torriano Mews
Torriano Avenue
London NW5 2RZ
www.franceslincoln.com

First Frances Lincoln edition: 2007

ISBN 978-0-7112-2851-1

Printed and bound in Singapore

2 4 6 8 9 7 5 3 1

THE LAKE DISTRICT IN NUMBERS

Some facts and figures about the Lake District National Park.

41,831 . . . . permanent residents
28,931 . . . . hectares of woodland
17,937 . . . . household spaces
5,724 . . . . miles (9,158 km) of watercourses
2,225 . . . . miles (3,560 km) of public footpaths and bridleways
1951 . . . . year the National Park was established
1,744 . . . . listed buildings and churches[1]
885 . . . . square miles area (2,292 sq km) of the national park
275 . . . . scheduled monuments
253 . . . . square miles area (654 sq km) of cultivated farmland
132 . . . . sites of special scientific interest
80 . . . . parishes
58 . . . . square miles area (151 sq km) of bracken
51 . . . . square miles area (131 sq km) of coniferous forest
47 . . . . residents per square mile
40 . . . . miles length from north to south
33 . . . . miles width from east to west
23 . . . . square miles (58 sq km) of still water
21 . . . . conservation areas
18 . . . . officially recognised lakes
9 . . . . registered parks and gardens of historic interest
8 . . . . national nature reserves
3 . . . . settlements with a population of more than 3,000[2]
1 . . . . World Heritage Site (Hadrian's Wall)

[1] 31 Grade I; 120 Grade II; 1,593 Grade III
[2] Windermere / Bowness, Keswick and Ambleside

CHARLOTTE BRONTË ON THE LAKE DISTRICT

*'The Lake Country is a glorious region, of which I had only seen
the similitude in dreams, waking or sleeping.'*

DIARY ENTRY

THE HIGHEST MOUNTAINS

The heights of the Lake District's peaks and what actually constitutes
a mountain are matters of lively debate among walkers. What is a peak
in its own right, and what is merely an annexe to another mountain?
This list of the 20 highest mountains is based on the popular 'Nuttalls'
classification, which defines a mountain as being over 2,000 feet high
with a rise on all sides from immediate surroundings of at least 50 feet.
It therefore includes fells that some walkers might consider to be
sub-peaks of other host mountains, such as Helvellyn Lower Man and
Bowfell North Top. By the Nuttalls classification, the Lake District has
the ten highest mountains in England. All heights are as recorded by
Ordnance Survey.

1	Scafell Pike	978m	3,209ft
2	Scafell	964m	3,163ft
3	Symonds Knott	959m	3,146ft
4	Helvellyn	950m	3,117ft
5	Ill Crag	935m	3,068ft
6	Broad Crag	934m	3,064ft
7	Skiddaw	931m	3,054ft
8	Helvellyn Lower Man	925m	3,035ft
9	Great End	910m	2,986ft
10	Bowfell	902m	2,959ft
11	Great Gable	899m	2,949ft
12	Pillar	892m	2,926ft
13	Nethermost Pike	891m	2,923ft
14	Catstye Cam	890m	2,920ft
15	Esk Pike	885m	2,904ft
16	Raise	883m	2,897ft
17	Fairfield	873m	2,864ft
18	Blencathra	868m	2,848ft
19	Bowfell North Top	866m	2,841ft
20	Skiddaw Little Man	865m	2,838ft

THE WETTEST PLACE IN ENGLAND

Anyone who has visited the Lake District for any length of time would
probably have no problem agreeing with the Met Office's suggestion
that this is the wettest part of England. Rainfall varies enormously from

town to town and valley to valley, but some places in the central region get around 2,000mm of rain a year. That's two metres or more than six feet of rain a year, more than twice the national average and three times the measures in flat areas such as East Anglia. The Met Office reckons that it rains in England on about one day in three on average—an estimate that soggy walkers might feel is on the optimistic side in the Lake District.

Several places lay claim to the title of England's wettest inhabited location, but Seathwaite in Borrowdale usually takes the dubious honour. This tiny cluster of houses and a farm typically receives around 3,250mm of rainfall a year—an inch every three days, and in some years much more. Another reason why Seathwaite is usually considered England's wettest place is because Sprinkling Tarn, about two miles to its south, holds the record for the most rainfall in one year. In 1954 it received 6,528mm, or more than 21 feet, of rain.

FROM THE LAKE DISTRICT TO AUSTRALIA IN DRY STONE WALLS

A 1996 survey by the Countryside Agency estimated that Cumbria has around 9,400 miles (15,000 km) of dry stone walls. That's more than an eighth of England's total of 70,400 miles (112,600 km), and of the English counties only Yorkshire has more. The total is also enough to stretch continuously from the Lake District to the western coast of Australia, or to the middle of America and back again.

LIES, LIES, LIES

The Lake District has a rich heritage of storytelling, and the tradition is taken to its logical conclusion in an annual contest to find the world's biggest liar.

The competition celebrates the life and lies of Will Ritson, the 19th century landlord of what is now the Wasdale Head Inn in the western Lake District. Ritson earned himself the title of the world's biggest liar by regaling his customers at the remote inn with amazing stories, told with such enthusiasm and conviction that many listeners believed them. His tales of local heritage and legend included a theory that turnips grown in Wasdale Head were so large that they were quarried for food and turned into sheds for Herdwick sheep; and a claim to own a crossbreed golden eagle and fox hound that could both jump and fly over dry stone walls. Evidence for his stories was always elusive, but it should also be added that Ritson was regarded as a sincere gentleman and a good friend to many—albeit one who was at times economical with the truth.

Ritson's tall stories live on in the annual World's Biggest Liar competition, no longer held in the Wasdale Head Inn but at the Santon Bridge Inn at the opposite end of Wast Water. Staged every November, it is now an established and popular event that attracts sponsorship from local brewery Jennings, a sell-out audience, widespread media interest and liars from all over the world. Participants get up to five minutes to tell the most outlandish, humorous and convincing lie they can, without the use of props. For fear that they would start at an unfair advantage, politicians and lawyers are barred from taking part.

The winner receives a cash prize, a trophy and the right to bill themselves as the world's biggest liar for a year. Competition is now quite fierce, which means that participants' tales become taller by the year. Winning stories have included reports of floating hotels, one-legged mountain rescue teams, a network of cable cars across the fells and a theory that the geology of the Lake District is the result of activities of moles and eels. The 2006 winner was TV comedienne Sue Perkins, who theorised that Lake District sheep breaking wind had created a hole in the ozone layer. The event has inspired similar competitions in other pubs in the UK and abroad, but Cumbria can always lay claim to the original and best liars.

WATER, WATER EVERYWHERE

A glance at maps of the Lake District reveals that there is plenty of water wherever you go—and the Lake District National Park Authority calculates that it has 5,724 miles of watercourses in addition to the lakes and tarns. It's just as well, then, that there are plenty of different terms to describe it. Here are ten of the more unusual names for watercourses in the area.

Beck A mountain brook or stream, eg Newlands Beck.

Burn A small stream, more commonly found in Scotland, eg Wyth Burn.

Dub or **dubs** 'Dub', Celtic for dark or black, lends itself to pools, usually in rivers, eg Buttermere Dubs.

Gill or **ghyll** A stream along a ravine, eg Sour Milk Gill.

Grain Fork of a stream, eg Howe Grain.

Gutter Any stream that runs along a channel, eg Quarry Gutter.

Nick A small chasm or steep valley, usually cut into the hillside, eg The Nick.

Pot or **Pots** Deep, roughly circular pools, eg Flag Pots.

Sike A stream, usually thin, eg Greenup Sike.

Sough A whistling or rushing sound from winds or flowing water. eg Whythemoor Sough.

LITERARY LAKELANDERS – WILLIAM WORDSWORTH

No poet is more closely linked with the Lake District than William Wordsworth—and few people have done more to open up the area to the rest of the world.

Unlike most famous literary names associated with the Lake District, Wordsworth was actually born in Cumbria—in Cockermouth in 1770. He went to grammar school in Hawkshead and had a generally happy childhood, although his parents died while he was young. He had his first poetry published at the age of 23, and soon afterwards met Samuel Taylor Coleridge, with whom he wrote *Lyrical Ballads, with a Few Other Poems* (1798), a pivotal work in the Romantic movement in literature. In 1799 he and Coleridge passed Dove Cottage in Grasmere while on a walking tour, and soon afterwards he settled there with his sister and lifelong companion Dorothy. They lived there for nine years, and William married Dorothy's friend Mary Hutchinson, with whom he had five children.

Wordsworth did much of his best work at Dove Cottage, before moving with his family to nearby Rydal Mount in 1813. A comfortable income as 'Distributor of Stamps for Westmorland' funded his continued writing, and he was poet laureate from 1843 until his death in 1850. He was enormously prolific, compiling about 70,000 lines of poetry in his lifetime, substantially more than any other poet of high standing.

Wordsworth's poetry is characterised by intense imagination, a love of nature and thoughtful reaction to the social and political upheaval of the time. He was inspired by the Lake District throughout his life, writing a popular guide to the area as well as numerous poems about it. His deep affection for the Lakes encouraged other visitors, both literary and non-literary, and he was alarmed by the influx of tourists as the 19th century wore on. He continues to be a major tourist attraction more than a century and a half after his death.

Wordsworth is buried in St Oswald's Churchyard in Grasmere. There are a number of places with Wordsworth associations across the Lake District, but the most popular one is Dove Cottage, attracting around 70,000 visitors a year. It is looked after by the Wordsworth Trust, which also runs an excellent museum and study centre, as well as exhibitions and events. His birthplace in Cockermouth is now called Wordsworth House and has been recreated as a 1770s home by the National Trust. Rydal Mount is also open to the public.

FROM HIGH TO LOW

The western Lake District is home to both the highest point in England—Scafell Pike, at 978m or 3,209ft—and the deepest below water—the bed of Wast Water, at 79m or 258 feet down.

WAINWRIGHT'S SIX BEST FELLS

In the conclusion to his seventh and final *Pictorial Guide to the Lakeland Fells*, Alfred Wainwright revealed what he thought to be the finest of all the mountains he had covered, based on his criteria of height, appearance, view, steepness and ruggedness. 'After much biting of finger-nails', the six he picked were:

Scafell Pike
Bowfell
Pillar
Great Gable
Blencathra
Crinkle Crags

In a footnote to his list, Wainwright picked Scafell as runner-up, and gave honourable mentions to the Langdale Pikes, Place Fell, Carrock Fell and, 'most of all', Haystacks—where his ashes were scattered after his death in 1991.

THE FIRST LAKE DISTRICT GUIDEBOOK

Tourists to the Lake District today have dozens if not hundreds of guidebooks to choose from, covering every patch of the Lake District and all the possible things to do. But back in the late 18th century they had just one—Thomas West's *Guide to the Lakes in Cumberland, Westmorland and Lancashire*.

Published in 1778, the book was not the first about the Lake District—writers had covered the area since Celia Fiennes recorded her thoughts on it during a journey across Britain in 1698—but it was the first to call itself a guide. It was an immediate success, having coincided with increased interest in the Lake District, particularly among the literary set and those who had already conducted grand tours of Europe, and its release is often said to mark the birth of tourism in the area. West was working on a revised edition of his bestselling guide when he died in 1779.

THE LAKES OF THE LAKE DISTRICT

Contrary to its name, the Lake District actually has only one area of water called a lake—Bassenthwaite Lake—but plenty of meres and waters. The definition of a lake is open to question: some consider Wet Sleddale to be a reservoir, for instance, and other candidates such as Devoke Water and Hayeswater are actually classified by the Lake District National Park and mapping agencies as tarns. The 18 'lakes' of the Lake District are generally agreed to be:

Bassenthwaite Lake	Grasmere
Brothers Water	Haweswater
Buttermere	Loweswater
Coniston Water	Rydal Water
Crummock Water	Thirlmere
Derwent Water	Ullswater
Elter Water	Wast Water
Ennerdale Water	Wet Sleddale
Esthwaite Water	Windermere

WHO OWNS THE LAKE DISTRICT?

The majority of land in the Lake District National Park is under private
ownership, though the relaxation of access rights means that most of it
is open to walkers. Bequests to and purchases by the National Trust
have made it the biggest single landowner in the park.

Private ownership 58.8%
National Trust 24.8%
United Utilities 6.8%
Forestry Commission 5.6%
Lake District National Park Authority 3.8%
Ministry of Defence 0.2%

TEN LAKE DISTRICT LITERARY HOMES

The Lake District is steeped in literary tradition and has dozens of
cottages and country houses that were once home to writers. These
places fill a long and excellent book—Grevel Lindop's *Literary Guide
to the Lake District* (Sigma Press)—but here are the homes of ten of the
most important Lakeland writers.

Brackenburn Derwent Water. Home of Sir Hugh Walpole as he
wrote *The Herries Chronicle*. Now privately owned and available to
rent as self-catering accommodation.

Brantwood Coniston. John Ruskin lived here and developed
the house and estate. It is now a museum dedicated to the man and
his works.

Dove Cottage Grasmere. Home to William and Dorothy Wordsworth
and later Thomas de Quincey. Now one of the busiest tourist
attractions in the Lake District.

Greta Hall Keswick. A home and inspiration to Samuel Taylor
Coleridge and Robert Southey. Now a family residence offering bed-
and-breakfast accommodation.

Hill Top Farm Sawrey. Beloved home and inspiration of Beatrix
Potter, now a mecca for the author's fans and looked after by the
National Trust.

The Knoll Ambleside. House built by the renowned writer, journalist, feminist and philosopher Harriet Martineau. Now privately owned.

Lanehead Coniston. Home of writer, artist, musician and Ruskin associate WG Collingwood; about a mile from Brantwood.

Low Ludderburn Cartmel Fell valley. The favourite home of Arthur Ransome, and where he worked on *Swallows and Amazons*.

Mirehouse Keswick. Historic country house where Tennyson, Wordsworth, Southey and Carlyle all stayed and worked. Now full of literary memorabilia and open to the public at limited times.

Nab Cottage near Rydal Water. Home to Hartley Coleridge and, before that, to the future wife of Thomas de Quincey. Now a guesthouse. Original features including Thomas de Quincey's opium room have been preserved.

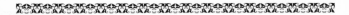

WORDSWORTH ON... THE FELLS

'Their forms are endlessly diversified, sweeping easily or boldly in simple majesty, abrupt and precipitous, or soft and elegant. In magnitude and grandeur they are individually inferior to the most celebrated of those in some other parts of this island; but, in the combinations which they make, towering above each other, or lifting themselves in ridges like the waves of a tumultuous sea, and in the beauty and variety of their surfaces and colours, they are surpassed by none.'

FROM *GUIDE TO THE LAKES* BY WILLIAM WORDSWORTH

JOHN RUSKIN AND THE FIRST MOUNTAIN RESCUE

In between writing, painting and thinking, John Ruskin was an enthusiastic walker in the Lake District fells, and in 1859 was involved in what is possibly the earliest recorded mountain rescue. Ruskin recorded the incident in his *England's Lakeland: A Tour Therein*, and his thoughts on poorly-equipped walkers and the brave volunteers who rescue them will be familiar to mountain rescue teams and the people they have plucked from the fells a century and a half later.

'Coming over from Borrowdale to Wastdale, over Sty Head, in our walking costume, we overtook a young gentleman attired as though for a lounge in Bond Street; shirt-collar had he, an umbrella-parasol, and (if we do not exaggerate) straps! Yes, he was bent upon ascending Scafell Pike in straps! After that little walk, he said, he hoped to have the pleasure of meeting us that evening at William Ritson's, one of the excellent farm houses at Wastdale; whereto we replied something civil, but very much doubted in our inmost heart of the events coming off. When we told one of the dalesmen what this superlatively dressed person was about to attempt, he pulled his pipe out of his contemptuous lips, and said "t' lad el dee"—meaning that it would be the death of him.

When mist came on that evening, in such thick folds that Wastdale might have been Salisbury Plain for all that we could see of the mountains, the good dalesman and some friends of his started to feel their way up those pikes. They found poor Straps, dead beat, but upon the very summit of the hill, lying down breathless upon his back, and watching the awful curtain of night and death descending upon him. It was so dark that even the dalesmen themselves lost their way in coming down, and carried the poor young gentleman into Eskdale. The Wastdale folk will do any kind thing for any body.'

THE SOUNDS OF THE LAKE DISTRICT

What are the most distinctive sounds of the Lake District? Cumbria Tourism has chosen seven gently evocative noises to bring the area to mind for callers to its 'Lake District Escape Line'. They are intended to comfort people pining for the Lake District while a long distance away during the dark winter months, and were also produced as sound files for download to computers and music players, to be listened to during times of stress. The seven sounds of the Lake District are:

The water of Windermere lapping against a jetty

The gush of Aira Force waterfall near Ullswater

Fresh air blowing across Scafell Pike

The crunch of autumn leaves on a walk

Birdsong and peacefulness in a Lake District valley

A reading of William Wordsworth's poem 'Daffodils' by Eric Robson, broadcaster and chairman of Cumbria Tourism

The sizzle of Cumberland sausages in a pan.

The Lake District Escape Line can be reached on 0870 224 2856. Sounds can also be accessed at www.golakes.co.uk/lakesescapeline.

LAKE DISTRICT POEMS – 'THE WANDERER RETURNS' BY ROBERT SOUTHEY

Once more I see thee, Skiddaw! once again
Behold thee in thy majesty serene,
Where like the bulwark of this favour'd plain
Alone thou standest, monarch of the scene:
Thou glorious Mountain, on whose ample breast
The sunbeams love to play, the vapours love to rest!

Once more, O Derwent, to thy aweful shores
I come, insatiate of the accustom'd sight;
And listening as the eternal torrent roars,
Drink in with eye and ear a fresh delight:
For I have wander'd far by land and sea,
In all my wandering still remembering thee.

And now am I a Cumbrian mountaineer;
Their wintry garment of unsullied snow
The mountains have put on, the heavens are clear,
And yon dark lake spreads silently below;
Who sees them only in their summer hour
Sees but their beauties half, and knows not half their power.

BRITAIN'S BEST PLACE FOR WILDLIFE

Cumbria is the best place to live in Britain if you like wildlife, according to an environmental study by *BBC Wildlife* magazine. The county was chosen for its variety of mountains, moorland, woodlands, meadows, valleys, lakes, farmland and coastline. *BBC Wildlife*'s survey was based on the amount of land protected by law, variety of habitat and environmental factors like pollution and water quality.

CUMBRIA INDUSTRIES – SLATE

Slate has probably been used in the Lake District ever since prehistoric times when men found copious quantities of it on the surface. It was certainly retrieved and used in an organised way by the Romans at Hardknott and other settlements, and has been employed in building ever since.

The slate industry began to thrive in the 18th and 19th centuries, primarily because of rising demand for roofing in industrial northern England. Slate used to be collected by hand from open quarries, but gunpowder was used to retrieve it from the early 1800s, and drills were employed from the early 1900s as miners began to look underground for new sources. Even with developing technologies, slate mining was massively hard and dangerous work. Sledgehammers, knives, chisels and saws were variously used to cut and shape the slate once it had been retrieved, and accidents were common. Treated slate would be transported to the coast by cart over packhorse ways such as Moses Trod at Honister, named after an infamous quarryman. The advent of the railway made life a lot easier, though the remote locations of some slate mines meant transportation was still a challenge.

The slate industry now is a fraction of its size in the boom years, but there is evidence of the mining of centuries gone by, both in the open quarries on fellsides and the slate buildings across the Lake District. Demand for Lake District slate keeps several companies in business and it is still mined at Honister, where an excellent visitor centre and guided underground tours outline the history of the industry.

WESTMORLAND, CUMBERLAND, LANCASHIRE, YORKSHIRE – AND CUMBRIA

Although Cumbria is a name that has been used for centuries, the county was only officially created in 1974. In a shake-up of local government and boundaries, it was formed from the ancient counties of Cumberland and Westmorland, together with the county borough of Carlisle, the Furness part of northern Lancashire and a slice of the West Riding of Yorkshire.

Even though the government of the time insisted that the new county had been created for administrative purposes only, the redrawing of the boundaries caused plenty of controversy. Many people in what were previously Lancashire and Yorkshire still identify themselves far more strongly with those counties than with Cumbria, and the old county names of Cumberland and Westmorland live on in many aspects of life—in newspapers like the *Westmorland Gazette* and the *Cumberland News*, for instance.

The reorganisation of boundaries has made Cumbria the second largest county in England by area at 2,630 square miles (6,800 square kilometers). But it is only the 41st largest by population with just short of 500,000 people, making it one of the emptiest counties in the country.

LITERARY LAKELANDERS – BEATRIX POTTER

Of all the literary heroes of the Lake District, no-one has sold more books nor built such a following around the world than Beatrix Potter.

Like many people, Potter fell in love with the Lakes while visiting on holiday. She was born in London in 1866, and spent many summers at country houses in the area. In 1882 her family was introduced to the local vicar, Canon Hardwicke Rawnsley, whose opinions on the conservation of the area had a lasting influence on Potter. She later became housekeeper to her family and was discouraged from taking up any sort of career, although she had written diaries and sketched from an early age.

Encouraged by Rawnsley, Potter incorporated her love of animals, drawing and storytelling into her first book, *The Tale of Peter Rabbit*, but she could not find a publisher for it until Frederick Warne & Company took it on in 1902. The book picked up a substantial following, and Potter followed it up with 22 more tales in the series, the bulk of them published over the next decade. Potter was engaged to be married to her publisher Norman Warne, but he died suddenly, leaving her devastated.

As royalties from her books started to pour in, Potter purchased Hill Top Farm in Sawrey, in and around which many of her stories were set, and she acquired further Lake District properties and pieces of land over the years. Her purchases were guided by local solicitor William Heelis, whom she married in 1913, and soon afterwards Potter's interests turned from her writing to domestic life and the Lake District countryside. She became a respected farmer, dedicated in particular to preserving and promoting the Herdwick breed of sheep, and she helped Rawnsley preserve the natural beauty of the Lake District after he co-founded the National Trust.

Potter died in 1943. Her ashes were scattered around Sawrey, and the bulk of her property and 4,000 acres of land was bequeathed to the National Trust. Her tales have gone on to sell tens of millions of copies around the world, and her popularity has created what is probably the biggest single tourist industry in the Lake District. Properties and places connected with her can be found across Cumbria, but the most popular is Hill Top Farm, looked after by the National Trust and attracting around 65,000 visitors a year—more than half of them from overseas.

BRITAIN'S OTHER NATIONAL PARKS

The Lake District was the second part of the country to be designated as a National Park in 1951, since when a dozen more areas have been awarded the status. The Lake District is the second largest of the 14, and the most populated.

	Founded	Area /sq miles	Population
Peak District	1951	555	38,000
Lake District	**1951**	**885**	**41,800**
Snowdonia	1951	840	25,480
Dartmoor	1951	368	29,100
Pembrokeshire Coast	1952	240	22,800
North York Moors	1952	554	25,000
Yorkshire Dales	1954	685	19,700
Exmoor	1954	267	10,600
Northumberland	1956	405	2,200
Brecon Beacons	1957	519	32,000
The Broads	1989	117	5,700
Loch Lomond and the Trossachs	2002	720	15,600
Cairngorms	2003	1,467	16,000
The New Forest	2005	220	34,400

A 15th National Park, the South Downs, was due to be designated after a public inquiry in 2007. It has an area of 1,020 square miles and a population of around 115,000.

THE SHEEP OF THE FELLS

As much as the lakes, fells and dry stone walls, Herdwick sheep are emblematic of the Lake District. The breed is native and peculiar to the area, thriving high in the mountains where few others could survive.

Although plenty of other theories for their arrival abound, Herdwicks are thought to have been introduced to the Lake District by Norse settlers, and the name derives from *herd vic*, Old Norse for sheep farm. However they got to the area, they have taken to the fells and made them their own. Quite literally, in fact, since Herdwicks' mysterious 'heafing' instinct provides them with a remarkable sense of direction that helps them keep to their familiar ground and return to it even after being moved miles away. This instinct stretches through the generations, meaning that Herdwicks graze on, and become heafed to, the same patches as their ancestors.

The half-smiling, half-doleful white faces of Herdwicks make them instantly recognisable. They are immensely hardy sheep, capable of living and lambing in extremes of weather at 3,000 feet that would soon see off other breeds. Their resilience and foraging agility mean they do not give much meat, and the conditions they live in mean they do not produce as many lambs as other breeds. Their profitability for farmers is therefore low, though the uniquely flavoured, succulent meat that lambs do offer is becoming more widely enjoyed. And while the coarse, hardwearing wool produced by Herdwicks has declined in popularity and price, this too is now enjoying something of a renaissance.

One of the greatest champions of Herdwicks was Beatrix Potter, who took on 16 sheep when she bought Hill Top. She soon became captivated by the breed and devoted much of her farming life to it, using her book royalties to acquire thousands more sheep. Her friend Canon Rawnsley founded the Herdwick Sheep Breeders Association to promote the breed, and the group is still going strong today. Potter bequeathed her flock to the National Trust, which has continued her work to promote and protect Herdwicks via the farms it manages.

The catastrophic outbreak of foot-and-mouth disease in 2001 threatened to wipe out Herdwicks in the Lake District, but farmers' dedication to the breed has ensured that stocks gradually recovered. About 150 farms now breed Herdwicks in commercial numbers, and the Herdwick Sheep Breeders Association promotes co-operatives of farmers selling their meat direct to consumers. It also champions the use of the wool in knitwear, carpets, rugs and even thermal insulation. But perhaps the greatest contribution of Herdwicks has been to the landscape they have helped to shape. Sheep have enormous environmental benefits, keeping bracken and scrub under control and prompting the enclosed fields, dry stone walls, drove roads and intake land on the slopes that are all so familiar to visitors.

Herdwick lingo

Draft ewe A ewe past her productive life

Ewe Female after mating

Geld Female without lambs

Gimmer Young female

Hog or **hogget** A young sheep between the ages of weaning and shearing

Inbye Sheeps' land fenced between fields and open fells

Intake Sheeps' pasture fenced from the fells

Lug and **smit** Distinguishing marks to identify a sheep's owner – a small hole made to the ear and chemical dye on the fleece respectively. The different marks are recorded in Shepherds' Guides.

Ram Male sheep of one year or older

Shearling A young sheep after first shearing

Tup Mature male. Tupping is the practise of breeding

Wether A castrated male

CUMBRIA'S PEOPLE IN NUMBERS

Some figures about the county's population, as compiled by Cumbria County Council.

498,900 . . . . .Cumbria's estimated population in mid-2005

209,021 . . . . .Number of households

51.1 . . . . .Female percentage of population

16.6 . . . . .Percentage of the population aged 14 or under

25.4 . . . . .Percentage of the population aged 60 or over

0.7 Percentage of the population from black and minority ethnic groups

51.6 . . . . .Percentage of the population living in rural areas

0.7 . . . . .Persons per hectare of land in Cumbria

10 . . . . .Live births per 1,000 people in 2004

11.4 . . . . .Deaths per 1,000 people in 2004

43.2 .Percentage of total population working

1.9 . . . . .Unemployment rate in percentage

TEN STATELY HOMES

There are historic houses all around the Lake District; here are ten of the most interesting that are open to the public.

Abbot Hall, Kendal. Fine Georgian home, now used as an art gallery with an extensive 18th century British collection. Tel 015397 22464 or online at www.abbothall.org.uk.

Brantwood, Coniston. Magnificent house above Coniston Water developed and filled by John Ruskin. Tel 015394 41396 or online at www.brantwood.org.uk.

Dalemain, near Penrith. Medieval, Tudor and Georgian manor house with a striking pink façade. Tel 017684 86450 or online at www.dalemain.com.

Holker Hall, Cark-in-Cartmel. Neo-Elizabethan mansion home, with substantial gardens and year-round events. Tel 015395 58328 or online at www.holker-hall.co.uk.

Hutton-in-the-Forest, near Penrith. Built on from the 14th to the 19th centuries, with a striking peel tower and interesting collections inside. Open April to October. Tel 017684 84449 or online at www.hutton-in-the-forest.co.uk.

Levens Hall, near Kendal. Elizabethan mansion with interesting panels, Jacobean furniture and lovely gardens. Tel 015395 60321 or online at www.levenshall.co.uk.

Mirehouse, near Keswick. House built in the 17th century that has been passed on through inheritance ever since. The ground floor is open to the public, and showcases the house's connections with Wordsworth, Southey and other poets. Tel 017687 72287 or online at www.mirehouse.com.

Muncaster Castle. Built on Roman foundations and restored by the architect Anthony Salvin in the 19th century; the Pennington family has lived in the castle for 800 years. The rooms, large gardens, owl centre and maze are open to the public. Tel 01229 717614 or online at www.muncaster.co.uk.

Sizergh Castle, near Kendal. Medieval house originally built in the 14th century for the Strickland family, who still live there. The castle's rooms and large landscaped gardens are looked after by the National Trust. Tel 015395 60951 or online at www.nationaltrust.org.uk.

Swarthmoor Hall, near Ulverston. Sixteenth-century house that is usually held to be the birthplace of the Quaker movement. Now offers holiday accommodation and conference facilities, but guided tours are available from March to October. Tel 01229 583204 or online at www.swarthmoorhall.co.uk.

THE LAKE DISTRICT WALKER: 18TH CENTURY v 21ST CENTURY

How modern walkers on the fells look compared to their predecessors two or three hundred years ago.

	18th century walker	**21st century walker**
Clothes	Breeches, shirt, topcoat	Breathable fleeces and trousers
Weatherproofs	Umbrella	Waterproof jacket
Footwear	Buckled shoes, hobnails or Wellington boots	Lightweight hiking boots
Transport	Foot or coach	Car, bus, train
Navigation	Road-books	Ordnance Survey maps, guidebooks, satellite navigation
Packed lunch	Cold meats, water from streams	Sandwiches, Kendal mint cake, energy drinks
Accommodation	Inns, private homes	Hotels, B&Bs, campsites, caravans
Communication	Letter	Mobile phone, email

ROCKS OF THE LAKE DISTRICT

The bulk of the fells in the Lake District are formed by three great zones of rock—the Skiddaw Slates in the north, the Borrowdale Volcanics in the centre and the Windermere group in the south.

The Skiddaw Slates. The Lake District's oldest visible rocks, they collected 450 to 500 million years ago and are found in the north and west of the area. The slates make for long, smooth, bare slopes like those of Skiddaw, from which the group gets its name.

The Borrowdale Volcanics. Formed about 100 million years later from a mixture of lava and ashes after violent volcanic activity. The thickness of this series of rocks—around 10,000 feet—means the fells they underlie are typically steep, craggy and dramatic, and include the highest peaks in the central Lake District.

The Windermere Group. Formed about 400 to 440 million years ago, these mostly limestone rocks from the Silurian period make for the rolling and more gentle fells that characterize the south of the Lake District.

Other rock types include a strip of carboniferous limestone, which runs around the north, south and east edges of the Lake District, and patches of granite and sandstone.

A FELLS GLOSSARY

The Lake District's hills and mountains have a language all of their own. Here are some of the most common words in use on maps and in the fellwalker's lexicon.

Band Tract of land that divides two areas that are lower in height, eg The Band between Mickleden and Oxendale.

Barrow Small hill, eg Stybarrow, Whitbarrow.

Beck Mountain brook or stream, eg Newlands Beck, Aira Beck.

Bield Shelter for humans or sheep, usually found in remote mountain areas, eg Nan Bield, Fox Bield.

Both or **Bothy** Shepherd's hut, sometimes used now as a mountain refuge, eg Holme Wood Bothy.

Buttress Projecting part of a hill, usually a rock face, eg High Crag Buttress.

Cairn Pile of stones on the summit of a fell or marking the way up to it.

Cam The crest of a hill, eg Catstye Cam.

Col Dip in a ridge between peaks.

Comb or **Combe** A hollow enclosed by hills, eg Black Combe, Combe Head.

Crag Rocky cliff, eg Ill Crag, Broad Crag.

Dale Valley, lending itself to many names in the Lake District, eg Borrowdale, Langdale.

Dodd Rounded top, eg Great Dodd, Stybarrow Dodd.

Dore or **Door** Gap between walls of rock, eg Mickledore.

Edge Narrow ridge, eg Striding Edge, Sharp Edge.

Fell Derived from the Old Norse *fjall* meaning hill or mountain, eg Harter Fell.

Fold Hollow among hills, eg Skelwith Fold, High Fold.

Force Waterfall, usually powerful, eg Aira Force, Taylor Gill Force.

Garth An enclosed space or piece of land, eg Gatesgarth.

Gill or **Ghyll** Small ravine, or a stream that flows down it, eg Sour Milk Gill or Dungeon Ghyll.

Gully Wide, steep cleft in a cliff, eg Central Gully.

Hause The head of a pass or ridge, often a meeting point of paths, eg Esk Hause, Honister Hause.

How Low hill, eg Silver How, Gummers How.

Knott Craggy, rocky hill, eg Symonds Knott, Hardknott Pass.

Lad A cairn or pile of stones, derived from the Old Norse *hlaed*, meaning pile, eg Lad Stones.

Man Cairn on a summit, often used to differentiate a peak from another summit close by, eg Helvellyn Lower Man.

Moss Fairly level area, usually marshy, eg White Moss.

Nab Promontory of a hill, eg Nab Scar, Ferry Nab.

Needle Tall, thin, pointed rock or peak, often used for climbing, eg Napes Needle.

Pass Narrow passage between mountains or valleys, eg Hardknott Pass, Kirkstone Pass.

Pike Sharp, rocky, prominent peaked mountain, eg Scafell Pike, Nethermost Pike.

Raise Pile of stones, eg High Raise, Dunmail Raise.

Rake Path through rocks or in a gully, eg Lord's Rake, Jack's Rake.

Rigg Ridge, eg Bleak Rigg.

Scar Bare, rocky face, eg Nab Scar, Walna Scar.

Scarth Gap in a ridge, eg Scarth Gap.

Scree Loose stones, or a slope covered with them, eg Red Screes.

Slab or **slabs** Broad, thick piece of rock, eg Seathwaite Slabs.

Slack Hollow between two higher points, eg Deepdale Slack.

Steel or **stile** Steep, eg Steel Fell, High Stile.

Stickle Sharp peak, eg Pike o'Stickle, Harrison Stickle.

Sty Steep path, eg Sty Head.

Tarn Small mountain lake, eg Innominate Tarn.

FERRIES ON THE LAKES

Passenger ferries run on four of the Lake District's 18 lakes.

Windermere Lake Cruises is the busiest of all the ferry companies, carrying more than one million people each year. Services run from Lakeside at the south end of the lake to Bowness halfway along it to Waterhead near Ambleside at the north end. There are up to 20 services a day in peak season. A car and passenger ferry also crosses Windermere from the east near Far Sawrey to the west near Bowness.

The Coniston Launch runs year-round solar electric ferries in all directions across **Coniston Water**, plus Swallows and Amazons themed cruises. The National Trust also runs the Gondola, a steam-powered yacht from April to October.

The Keswick Launch Company runs cruises from Keswick's boat landings to seven jetties around **Derwent Water**.

Ullswater Steamers have been running services around Ullswater since 1859. The steamers run all year round.

ENGLAND'S BEST DRIVING

The Lake District has the most picturesque scenery in England to drive around, according to a survey of about 2,000 motorists by Direct Line Insurance. The drive along the A592 by the shores of Ullswater was also voted the second best scenic drive in the country, just behind a drive from St Just to St Ives in Cornwall. The route by Ullswater takes in spectacular fell-side scenery and runs close to the cluster of daffodils that inspired William Wordsworth's most famous poem.

LAKE DISTRICT FOOD – KENDAL MINT CAKE

Kendal mint cake is the friend of walkers, the scourge of dentists and one of the Lake District's biggest food exports.

Like many great recipes, the cake was created by accident. At Joseph Wiper's confectioners in Kendal in 1869, the contents of a pan of ingredients for glacier mint sweets was left unattended and began to cloud and harden. When the mixture was poured out, cooled and found to taste good, Kendal mint cake was born. It was sold at first mostly to locals, but its reputation gradually spread and other manufacturers tried to recreate Wiper's recipe.

The cake received some excellent free publicity when it was supplied to Ernest Shackleton's Antarctic voyage of 1914 to 1916, and to Sir Edmund Hillary's expedition to Mount Everest in 1953. After Hillary and Sherpa Tenzing Norgay reported that they had nibbled the cake at the summit, it soon established itself as the original energy boost, long before the advent of isotonic and hypertonic drinks. Kendal mint cake provides around 380 calories per 100g, making it one of the most effective energy boosts around—and one of the worst for your teeth.

Manufacturers of Kendal mint cake now include Romney's, which bought the Wiper name in 1987, and Quiggin's, which has been producing it since 1880. Versions include chocolate-topped cake, though purists don't like the idea of tampering with the original recipe. There have also been complaints that the confectionery is a sweet rather than a cake—not least from the US customs department, which ruled in the 1950s that Kendal's export could not be admitted because the lack of eggs and flour meant it did not constitute a cake. The cargo had to be sunk in the Atlantic.

The ingredients of Kendal mint cake are simple: sugar, glucose, water—sometimes milk—and peppermint oil, all brought slowly to the boil in a copper pan. The trick to the recipe is pouring the contents out at the right time—at the 'soft ball' stage, when the sugar syrups. The mixture is then poured into shallow tins and cut into slices as it cools. Kendal mint cake makes a good accompaniment to chocolate mousse, ice cream or strong after-dinner coffee—but is best eaten, of course, after a long slog to the top of a fell.

THE CHRISTENING OF THE LAKE DISTRICT

Calling this particular corner of the country the Lake District is a relatively modern development. Until the 19th century, large lakes would more likely be called meres or waters, and the collective description of the Lake District was probably only used for the first time in 1829 in the title of Parson & White's Gazetteer. William Wordsworth gave a crucial endorsement by using it in 1835, and the Lakeland derivation soon followed. There may be earlier usages.

FARMING IN THE LAKE DISTRICT

Farming in the Lake District has changed dramatically over the last half-century. Pressure on prices means farm incomes are falling, substantially in some cases, and more and more medium-sized farm holdings are being amalgamated or sold off. The number of large farms is therefore increasing—but so too is the number of small farms, often specialising in niches. After the foot-and-mouth crisis of 2001, many farms were forced to diversify into services like bed and breakfast, cheese making and selling direct to customers. Some are thriving as a result; others are struggling to adjust to the changing market.

Here are some facts and figures about farming in Cumbria. Most of the data is based on the 2005 agricultural and horticultural census for the Department for Environment, Food and Rural Affairs (Defra).

7,991 farm holdings in Cumbria (a holding is defined as land farmed in one unit, and farms can have more than one holding).

These are made up of:
2,977 . . . . .less than five hectares in size
1,170 . . . . .from five to 20 hectares
1,096 . . . . .from 20 to 50 hectares
1,324 . . . . .from 50 to 100 hectares
1,424 . . . . .more than 100 hectares
1,786 . . . . .square miles (4,627 square kilometres
or 462,674 hectares) of farmed area
5,510 . . . . .full-time farmers (13,140 full and part-time labour in total)
16,596 . . . . . . .average income in pounds per farm in the north-west
of England in 2004-5—a fall of 22% on the previous year
2,641,095 . . . . .chickens on farms in Cumbria

2,049,539	.sheep
444,277	.cattle
78,492	.pigs
5,966	.ducks
1,827	.geese
1,788	.goats

Cumbria is home to more than one in every eight farm sheep in England, and nearly one in every 12 cattle. Sheep outnumber Cumbria's human population by more than four to one.

DAVID BAXTER'S FAVOURITE LAKE DISTRICT VIEWS

David Baxter is a photographer and founder of Dane Stone Cards, a postcard company specialising in the north of England. His cards combine landscapes with traditional local recipes, and he has brought many of them together in a book, *The Lake District in Recipes and Photographs*. David has travelled the length and breadth of the Lake District to take the pictures for his cards, and here are his ten favourite views, together with the season or weather that suits them best.

Brothers Water on a perfectly still morning, reflecting autumn colours

Crummock Water from the Buttermere end

The Furness fells from the top of Brow Edge above Backbarrow in early autumn

The Langdale fells, from either Crinkle Crags or Loughrigg, with snow

Orrest Head near Windermere, when showers are driving in from the west

From **Place Fell**, across Ullswater and to the south

The River Derwent near Grange-in-Borrowdale, with the summer sun catching the green of the stones

The Scafell range from Border End, in summer

St Bees Head on one of the first hot sunny days of the year around nesting time, looking down on the thousands of seabirds and out to sea

Wast Water, with the sun setting across the screes.

LAKE DISTRICT POEMS – 'CALM AFTER HURRICANE AT PATTERDALE' BY ELIZABETH SMITH

The storm is past; the raging wind no more,
Between the mountains rushing, sweeps the vale,
Washing the billows of the troubled lake
High into the air; the snowy fleece lies thick;
From every bough, from every jutting rock
The crystals hang; the torrent's roar has ceased—
As if that Voice that called Creation forth
Had said 'Be Still.' All nature stands aghast
Suspended by the viewless power of cold.

THE LAND OF THE LAKE DISTRICT

The Lake District National Park Authority breaks down the 885 square miles of land in the park as follows:

Grassland, moorland and heathland 48%
Cultivated land 31%
Woodland and forest 12%
Water 4%
Rock and coastal 3%
Developed land 2%

TEN PLACES FOR AFTERNOON TEA

Whether it's to follow a long walk in the fells or just to keep you going until your country house dinner, afternoon tea is taken seriously in the Lake District. Here are ten of the best tearooms, hotels, farms and cafés to get your fill of tea, sandwiches, scones and cakes.

The 1657 Chocolate House, Kendal. With a choice of 18 chocolate drinks and 14 chocolate cakes, this is not the place for a light tea. All served by waitresses in 17th century dress. Tel 015397 40702 or online at www.chocolatehouse1657.co.uk.

Grange Bridge Cottage Tea Shop, Grange-in-Borrowdale. Tea, scones and homemade cakes in the beautiful Borrowdale valley. Tel 017687 77201.

Hazelmere Café and Bakery, Grange-over-Sands. A winner of the Tea Guild's 'Oscar' for the 'Top Tea Place' in Britain, Hazelmere's menu has dozens of different teas from across the world. Tel 015395 32972 or online at www.hazelmerecafe.co.uk.

Low Sizergh Barn Farm Shop and Tearoom, near Kendal. The tearoom on this working farm looks down on the cows' milking area, so you can watch them supply the (organic) milk for your tea every day at 3.45pm. Tel 015395 60426 or online at www.lowsizerghbarn.co.uk.

Miller Howe Hotel, near Windermere. Afternoon tea is a major event here, with great views over Windermere and top-notch sandwiches, scones and cakes. Tel 015394 42536 or online at www.millerhowe.com.

Rothay Manor, Ambleside. Renowned buffet-style afternoon tea, rated one of the 50 best in the world by the *Guardian*. Tel 015394 33605 or online at www.rothaymanor.co.uk.

Sharrow Bay Country House Hotel, Ullswater. The archetypal country house afternoon tea—a meal in itself, with wonderful accompanying views across Ullswater and the fells. Tel 017684 86301 or online at www.sharrowbay.co.uk.

Syke House Farm, Buttermere. This pretty farm sells its own Buttermere Ayrshires ice cream as well as tea and cake. Tel 017687 70277.

The Tea Garden, St John's-in-the-Vale. Tea and homemade cakes in the grounds of Low Bridge End Farm with picture-postcard views. Tel 017687 79242 or online at www.campingbarn.com.

Yew Tree Farm, Coniston. The tearoom here was originally furnished by Beatrix Potter and helped to sustain the farm through the 1930s depression. Tel 015394 41433 or online at www.yewtree-farm.com.

CUMBRIA INDUSTRIES – COAL

The coalfields of west Cumbria have been mined since at least the 13th century, when monks at St Bees Abbey near Whitehaven dug for coal at Arrowthwaite.

There were also seams in the north Pennines in the east of the county, but it was in the west that the coal industry triggered the greatest changes. Coalfields here stretched from Whitehaven to

Maryport, reaching several miles both inland and out to sea. They employed thousands of men, women and children, whose work was extremely hard and, with the constant risk of methane and explosions, notoriously dangerous. At least 1,200 men, women and children are thought to have been killed while mining in Whitehaven alone, and 136 died in Cumbria's worst single mining disaster at the Wellington Pit in 1910. Mine-owners on the other hand, led by the powerful Lowther family, became very rich from coal, which transformed the local economy. The Lowthers built up the harbour at Whitehaven to transport the coal, and new railways sprang up to move it within and beyond Cumbria.

As coal seams were exhausted and falling prices wrecked the economics of the industry, the mines gradually closed. It was a hammer blow to the towns of west Cumbria, and the last deep coal mine, Whitehaven's Haig Pit, shut in 1986. Some of the pit's machinery, including the winding engine house, has since been restored by volunteers, and the Haig is now an excellent mining museum, open seven days a week. Remains of other pits and memorials to those killed in them can be found in and around Whitehaven.

SOME PLACE NAMES AND THEIR MEANINGS

Ambleside Pastures by the river sandbanks, from the Old Norse *melr* and *saetr*, meaning sandbanks and pasture.

Backbarrow The ridge shaped like an animal's back.

Boot The bend in the valley, from the Middle English *bouzht* meaning bend.

Bowness The bull's headland, from the Old English *bula* and Old Norse *nes*, meaning bull and headland.

Brantwood Burnt wood.

Cartmel The sandbank by the rocky ground. From the Old Norse *kartr* and *melr* meaning rocky ground and sandbank.

Clappersgate The path over large flat stepping stones, clappers.

Coniston The king's settlement. From the Old English *cyning* and *tun*, meaning king and settlement.

Finsthwaite Finn's clearing. Finn is an Old Norse name. Thwaite, meaning clearing, is found across the Lake District, in Rosthwaite, Crosthwaite and Stonethwaite among many others.

Glenridding The valley full of bracken. From the Welsh *glyn* and *rhedyn* meaning wooded valley and bracken.

Grange-over-Sands and **Grange-in-Borrowdale** A grange is an outlying farm or granary.

Hawkshead Haukr's shieling or abode. Haukr is an Old Norse name.

Ings Meadows or outlying pastures.

Kendal Formerly known as Kirkby Kendal, meaning the village with a church in the Kent valley. From the Old Norse *kirkja, byr* and *dalr*, meaning church, village and valley. Kirkby also lends its name to Kirkby Stephen and Kirkby Lonsdale.

Keswick The cheese farm. From the Old English *cese* and *wic*, meaning cheese and farm.

Millom The settlement by the mills. From the Old English *mylnum*, meaning mills.

Penrith Either 'the main ford'—from the Welsh *pen* and *rhyd* meaning chief and ford—or 'the red hill'—from the Old English *read* meaning red.

Portinscale The harlot's hut. From the Old English *portcwene*, meaning a harlot, and the Old Norse *skali*, meaning hut.

Rydal The valley of the rye. From the Old English *ryge*, meaning rye, and Old Norse *dalr*, valley.

Sawrey Muddy places. From the Old Norse *saurar*, meaning muddy.

Shap Pile of stones. From the Old English *heap*.

Staveley Clearing where staves are found. From the Old English *staef* and *leah*, meaning staves and wood clearing.

Troutbeck The trout stream.

Ulverston Ulfr's farmstead. Ulfr was an Old English or Old Norse name, and *tun* is Old English meaning farmstead.

Witherslack Wooded hollow. From the Old Norse *vithr* and *slakki*, meaning wood and shallow valley.

CUMBRIA'S TOP 20 TOURIST ATTRACTIONS

Of the myriad of attractions in Cumbria, it is perhaps appropriate that the most popular is water-based. Windermere Lake Cruises, operating from Bowness, Waterhead near Ambleside and Lakeside near Newby

Bridge, carried nearly 1.3 million people in 2006—a total that will not surprise anyone who has observed the crowded shores at these three places. Windermere Lake Cruises is also the most popular paid-for attraction in the entire north-west region of England—and the seventh most popular in Britain. Second and third on the list of Cumbrian attractions are Rheged, the visitor centre just off the M6 at Penrith, and Carlisle's Tullie House Museum and Art Gallery. Popular free attractions include the visitor centres and parks run by the Forestry Commission at Grizedale and Whinlatter.

These figures are collated by Cumbria Tourism and require some care, since the list includes only places that publish their visitor figures and excludes many attractions that have no way of calculating their visitors. Some visitor numbers are estimates.

No.	Attraction	Visitors in 2006
1	Windermere Lake Cruises	1,267,066
2	Rheged	463,708
3	Tullie House Museum and Art Gallery, Carlisle	270,766
4	Grizedale Forest Park	250,000
5	Ullswater Steamers	187,656
6	Whinlatter Forest Park	180,985
7	Carlisle Castle	149,762
8	Ravenglass and Eskdale Railway	118,517
9	Lake District Visitor Centre, Brockhole	91,715
10	Cumberland Pencil Museum, Keswick	83,400
11	Muncaster Castle	82,639
12	The Dock Museum, Barrow	79,415
13	The Homes of Football, Ambleside	68,000
14	Dove Cottage, Grasmere	66,094
15	Sizergh Castle and Garden, Kendal	65,062
16	Hill Top, Sawrey	64,584
17	The Teapottery, Allerdale	62,854
18	Northern Lights Gallery, Keswick	60,000
19	Wetheriggs County Pottery, Penrith	50,000
20	Lake District Coast Aquarium, Maryport	47,464

LITERARY LAKELANDERS – ALFRED WAINWRIGHT

Although poets like William Wordsworth are generally the most celebrated of the region's many authors, no writer has chronicled the Lake District as intimately or extensively as Alfred Wainwright. His

books of exquisite sketches and expert commentary on the fells have
no equal, either in the Lake District or anywhere else.

Born in Blackburn in 1907, Wainwright excelled at school but left at
13 to work in the council offices, progressing to become an
accountant. He didn't travel north to the Lake District until he was 23,
but was immediately enchanted by the open spaces, majestic fells and
the contrast to the industrial bleakness of Blackburn. He came back
often, but it wasn't until he found a job in the treasurer's office in
Kendal in 1941 that he was able to settle in the area.

From then on, Wainwright spent all his spare time out on the fells,
and for his own pleasure started producing pen and ink drawings of the
mountains he had climbed. At the age of 45, and after poring over
Ordnance Survey maps to divide the Lake District into seven areas, he
resolved to climb their 214 fells, keeping a record of his routes, the
summits and the views. He set himself a 13-year schedule to climb all
214, and he intended to do it for pleasure, with little idea of writing a
book. But as his notes piled up, he decided to approach a local printer,
who offered to produce the first volume of his *Pictorial Guides to the
Lakeland Fells–The Eastern Fells*—at his own expense and be repaid
when sales began to take off. With the help of a Kendal librarian, Henry
Marshall, local bookshops were persuaded to stock the book, interest
rose, and Wainwright turned his attention to the next book in his series.

After walking all weekend, Wainwright would write up his notes
at home the following week, adding sketches based on photographs
he had taken. Each book was entirely handwritten page by page,
immaculately formatted and presented ready for the printer's press.
If he made a mistake on a page, he tore it up and started again.
Astonishingly, Wainwright completed all his travels to and from his
walks on public transport and without the aid of a car. He claimed
never to have missed a bus home throughout his walking. And all seven
Pictorial Guides were all written while he held down a full-time job as
borough treasurer at Kendal.

Each guide took a couple of years to write, and the seventh and final
title—*The Western Fells*—was finished right on schedule in 1965. By
this time, the job of publishing and selling the books had been taken
over by Wainwright's local newspaper, the *Westmorland Gazette*, and
the series had picked up such a huge following that Wainwright—a
solitary man who enjoyed only his own company while walking—was
sometimes forced to dodge behind boulders to avoid pursuing fans
on the fells.

After completing the *Pictorial Guides*, Wainwright produced new
books about the peripheries of the Lake District and other areas, and
also compiled books of drawings and memoirs. He participated rather
reluctantly in a TV series, and created the Coast to Coast walk from St
Bees in Cumbria to Robin Hood's Bay in Yorkshire, now one of the most

popular long-distance trails in Britain. But although a small fortune of royalties poured in, he never wrote any of his books for money, instead donating a large proportion of it to Cumbrian animal charities. After his death in 1991, Wainwright's ashes were scattered on his instructions on Haystacks, his favourite mountain.

More than fifty years after the first *Pictorial Guide* was published, Wainwright's books are as popular as they ever have been. They have had several publishers over the years, but are now available in original and updated editions from Frances Lincoln. The Wainwright Society was formed in 2002 to celebrate his work and help preserve the things he promoted through his books.

THE LAKE DISTRICT'S TALLEST TREE

A silver fir near Aira Force in Ullswater is thought to be the tallest tree in Cumbria, rising to some 50m (164 feet). It is some distance shorter than the largest in Britain though—a record shared by three Douglas firs in Powys in Wales and Argyll and Inverness in Scotland, which each measure around 63m (205 feet). Measurements of notable trees are kept by the Tree Register.

SMUGGLING IN THE LAKE DISTRICT

Cumbria's coastlines and inland routes across the fells have made it a prime centre for smugglers over the centuries. With sporadic patrols and plenty of remote paths and hiding places, the transport of illicit goods to and from the naval ports could be a lucrative business.

One of the most infamous Lake District smugglers was Moses Rigg, a quarryman at the Honister mines who produced moonshine whisky in his spare time from hideaways in the surrounding fells. He smuggled it out from the quarry concealed in pony-drawn consignments of slate— possibly slipping in some pilfered graphite, too—for sale at Wasdale Head without the inconvenience of paying excise. The remains of one of the huts used for distilling the liquor were found on Gable Crag, making it probably the highest building ever constructed in England. He gives his name to Moses Trod, the route from Honister to Wasdale Head that is still followed by walkers.

Other smugglers include Lanty Slee, a notorious 19th century moonshiner and smuggler who worked from caves in Langdale and took his illicit whisky over the Wrynose and Hardknott Passes to the coast. Several of his old stills and storage places have been unearthed in the Langdale fells, so well hidden that there could well be more still waiting to be discovered. Slee spent much of his time dodging his pursuers from the customs office in the fells, but because his customers included plenty of people in authority, he usually managed to stay several steps ahead of his captors.

The coastal town of Whitehaven has been an important hub for smuggling over the years, and its proximity to the Isle of Man, where duty was much lower than on the mainland, gave smugglers the chance to transport goods across the Irish Sea. A Whitehaven museum, the Rum Story, has an exhibition on smuggling; it is open daily all year round.

LAKE DISTRICT POEMS – 'A THOUGHT SUGGESTED BY A VIEW OF SADDLEBACK' BY SAMUEL TAYLOR COLERIDGE

On stern Blencathra's perilous height
The winds are tyrannous and strong;
And flashing forth unsteady light
From stern Blencathra's skiey height,
As loud the torrents throng!
Beneath the moon, in gentle weather
They blend the earth and sky together.
But oh! The sky and all its forms how quiet!
The things that seek the earth, how full of noise and riot!

CUMBRIA'S CONSTITUENCIES

The county of Cumbria returns six Members of Parliament to the House of Commons. The constituencies and the MPs elected to serve them in the 2005 General Election are:

Barrow-in-Furness – John Hutton, Labour
Carlisle – Eric Martlew, Labour
Copeland – Jamie Reed, Labour
Penrith and the Border – David MacLean, Conservative
Westmorland and Lonsdale – Tim Farron, Liberal Democrat
Workington – Tony Cunningham, Labour

HADRIAN'S WALL IN CUMBRIA

Cumbria's only World Heritage Site is Hadrian's Wall, which enters the county north-west of Carlisle and ends at Bowness-on-Solway on the western coast.

The wall was built by the Romans to defend against tribal raids from the north, following a visit by the emperor Hadrian in AD122. It took around a decade for Roman legions to construct it, using local limestone and, where none was available, turf. It was 95 Roman miles or 78 modern miles (125km) long, and mostly around three metres wide and six metres high. The wall was equipped with milecastles every Roman mile, each holding Roman soldiers and observation points, and there were also full-size forts along the wall, the remains of which can be seen at several locations. Neighbouring Northumberland has the bulk of the Roman sites of interest, though it is worth following the wall to its end at Bowness, where there are fine views out over the Solway estuary. There are good excavated remains of a milecastle near Maryport, which is also home to the Senhouse Roman Museum.

It is a tribute to the Romans' skills that many stretches of the wall are still very well preserved, and it is possible to walk on top of it for short distances. Hadrian's Wall was designated a UNESCO World Heritage Site in 1987, and it has also inspired a National Trail, the Hadrian's Wall Path, that runs close to the wall for about 85 miles from coast to coast and is used by around 200,000 walkers each year.

CUMBRIA'S COUNTY TOWNS

Before the creation of modern-day Cumbria in 1974 from Cumberland, Westmorland and parts of Lancashire, the county towns of its constituent counties were:

Cumberland – Carlisle
Westmorland – Appleby
Lancashire – Lancaster

Carlisle continues to serve as the county town or administrative headquarters of Cumbria.

TEN LAKE DISTRICT MEMORIALS

There are memorials and monuments dotted around the fells and towns of the Lake District. Here are ten of the most interesting.

Air Crash Memorial, Great Carrs. A simple cross and cairn sit alongside the wreckage of a wartime Canadian Air Force plane that crashed on the fellside in thick mist in 1944, killing its eight crew.

Dixon Memorial, Helvellyn. One of several memorials on the fell summit, this was installed in 1858 to commemorate Robert Dixon, who slipped off Striding Edge while following a foxhounds trail.

Hoad Monument, Ulverston. Visible well before you arrive in the town, this 100-feet folly tower is a memorial to the explorer John Barrow, and is a copy of the Eddystone Lighthouse in Devon.

King Charles II Monument, Crosby Ravensworth Fell. This monument, also known as Black Dub, marks the spot where Charles II rested with his army on the return from his coronation in Scotland in 1651.

King Edward VII Memorial, Grange Fell. This fell, with magnificent views across Derwent Water, was purchased by the sister of King Edward VII on his death in 1910, and given to the National Trust. The memorial stone calls it 'a sanctuary of rest and peace.'

National Trust Memorial, Brandelhow Wood. Brandelhow, on the western side of Derwent Water, was the first property purchased by the National Trust in 1902, and a stone slab commemorates the acquisition.

Ruskin Memorial, Derwent Water. A tall slate memorial close to the lake on Friars Crag, erected soon after John Ruskin's death in 1900.

Wainwright Memorial, Buttermere. A tablet in St James' Church is located within sight of Haystacks, Alfred Wainwright's favourite fell.

War Memorial, Great Gable. The Fell and Rock Climbing Club of the Lake District purchased land on and around Great Gable in 1923, and gave it to the National Trust to commemorate the 20 members who died in the First World War. A tablet fixed to the summit rocks remembers their sacrifice.

Wordsworth Memorial, Cockermouth. A bronze bust of the poet stands opposite Wordsworth's birthplace in the town. It was unveiled in 1970, on the bicentenary of his birth, by his great-great-grandson.

MOUNTAIN RESCUE IN THE LAKE DISTRICT

Until the Lake District's first mountain rescue team was set up in the 1940s, responsibility for the recovery of people injured on the mountains tended to fall on local people. It still does, but Cumbria's network of teams now means that walkers and climbers can rely on expert, co-ordinated assistance 24 hours a day, 365 days a year. Many thousands of people have had cause to be very grateful for the teams since.

There are now 13 individual teams across the region, brought together under an umbrella organisation, the Lake District Search and Mountain Rescue Association (LDSAMRA). Their 500 or so members all devote their time and skills free of charge, and are all trained in every aspect of mountain rescue. The nature of the work means that a good proportion of their call-outs occur in the worst of conditions—in foul weather, freezing temperatures and the small hours of the night.

LDSAMRA maintains records of every call-out attended by its teams. Between 1991 and 2006, it logged 5,754 incidents—an average of almost exactly one a day. In 2006 alone, LDSAMRA's mountain rescue teams attended 396 incidents involving 493 people, of whom 333 were male and 160 female. 28 people died—13 from natural causes, 8 from non-mountain incidents and 7 from mountain accidents—while 202 were injured and 263 people without injuries were attended and assisted. 93 incidents required the call-out of a Royal Air Force or Royal Navy helicopter.

Mountain rescue teams spent 24,335 man-hours attending the incidents in 2006—the equivalent of nearly three years in action. That figure was LDSAMRA's highest on record, reflecting both some large-scale searches in the year and the increased numbers of people visiting the Lake District. Greater use of mobile phones has also prompted more people to call for assistance if they become lost—though this has also meant that plenty of call-outs each year are for spurious reasons. The busiest team in the Lake District is usually the Langdale and Ambleside group, which attends as many as 100 call-outs a year.

The Lake District's teams all rely on donations to continue their valuable work, and much of their funding comes from grateful recipients of their help on the fells in years gone by. There have been occasional calls for mountain rescue teams to be publicly funded and staffed on a paid, full-time basis, effectively becoming an extra emergency service—but mountain rescue teams counter that it would be impossible to match their current high standards of service or intimate knowledge of the fells.

Anyone wishing to find out more about the mountain rescue teams' work or donate to their funds can do so at www.ldsamra.org.uk.

WAINWRIGHT'S DEDICATIONS

Each of Alfred Wainwright's seven *Pictorial Guides to the Lakeland Fells* carries a dedication. As befits a man who walked the fells determinedly alone, the dedications are not to individuals but to groups of people and animals—and parts of himself.

Book 1 - 'The Men of the Ordnance Survey'
Book 2 - 'The Men who Built the Stone Walls'
Book 3 - 'The Dogs of Lakeland'
Book 4 - 'The Sheep of Lakeland'
Book 5 - 'The Solitary Wanderers on the Fells'
Book 6 - 'My Right Leg and My Left Leg'
Book 7 - 'All Who Have Helped Me'

FELL-RUNNING

For the hardiest breed of Lake District fell-lovers, walking up and down the steep mountains isn't enough of a challenge—so they run instead.

Although fell-racing is far from unique to the Lake District, most runners agree that this is its spiritual home in the UK. It is a unique sport, requiring all the athleticism of track running but much more besides. Ascents up the fells are hard enough—lung-busting, knee-trembling tests of stamina that can reduce fit runners to a breathless standstill in moments—but it is the descents that usually separate the winners from the rest of the field. Most runners try to pick their way down the fellside without falling or turning an ankle on the uneven ground, but the very best runners descend in virtual freefall, skipping from rock to rock in a blur and trusting to their bodies' instincts to get them down safely. Watching a race from the foot of a mountain reveals the extraordinary speed and skill of the runners; turn away for a moment as they leave the top, and they will be halfway down when you look back.

Fell-runners also need excellent navigational skills and knowledge of the fells to pick their way along the course. It is sometimes the people who know the fells best rather than the fastest runners who win races—and they must be able to cope with the exposure and extremes of temperature that go hand in hand with the races. It is no surprise that fell-running's heroes through the ages have included plenty of Lake District natives, able to navigate their way through the summit mists that slow down other runners.

The Lake District's first fell races date back to the early 19th century, when men of the villages would run up and down nearby fells as part of their communities' annual sports days or other celebrations. Though sponsorship and prize money has improved over the years, most runners still compete for the love of the mountains rather than the glory, and few are known outside of the sport—even though their feats of endurance rival anything achieved on the track. For most, the chance to get out into the Lake District fells is a greater draw than the competition itself. It is a celebration of the landscape as much as a sport.

The Fell Runners Association oversees hundreds of events across the country every year, ranging from short, sharp races of fifteen minutes or so to long-distance runs across several ranges. The majority take place in the spring or summer, but fell-running aficionados often prefer the winter runs, when freezing temperatures and driving rain provide—as if they were needed—extra challenges. Wasdale, Ennerdale and Borrowdale are among the places in the Lake District with celebrated annual races, while shows that incorporate races into their programme include Grasmere. The 'Guides' Race'—from the Grasmere showground to the top of a fell some 300m (985 feet) up and back—was first held in 1852, and has become one of the highlights of the fell-running calendar.

For more on fell-running, see *Feet in the Clouds* by Richard Askwith (Aurum Press). It has an excellent account of the history of the sport, profiles of many of its ferociously fit and hardy legends, and theories on what makes people want to run up and down mountains in the wind and rain for fun.

HOW TO BUILD A CAIRN

Cairns are part of the scenery on the Lake District's fells. Used variously as memorials, to mark summits and, increasingly, to mark routes up or across the fells, they can be useful landmarks for the walker and vital aids to navigation in poor weather. Many walkers follow the tradition of adding stones to cairns as they pass them, and some are now very large indeed. The number is rising so fast in some places that the Lake District National Park Authority is concerned that the transfer of stone from footpaths is contributing to erosion along some popular routes.

The majority of cairns are loose piles of stones, but occasionally much neater assemblies can be found. Here's how the professional dry stone wallers or dykers build their cairns.

Find the right position. Cairns need a firm base, which should be easy to find on rocky hilltops.

Get your stones. Good cairns need good materials. They also need more stones than it appears, since not all of them will be suitable.

Assemble your base. Plot a circular outline for the base. The outer base ring of the cairn needs the largest stones, with the widest ends of them to the outside. The middle of the base—or 'heart' of the cairn—is filled with smaller stones or other debris.

Build upwards. Add stones slowly, walking around the cairn to inspect progress and trying to keep each layer as flat and tight as possible.

Top it off. As the layers become tighter, use smaller or triangular stones on the layers. The final top stone should be larger.

THE FOUNDING FATHER OF LAKE DISTRICT ROCK CLIMBING

The undisputed father of British rock climbing is Walter Parry Haskett Smith. After studying at Eton and Oxford University and excelling at athletics, Haskett Smith first visited the Lake District in the early 1880s with student friends. But instead of merely walking in the fells, Haskett Smith wanted to find new ascents over the rocks that departed from the well-trodden paths followed by tourists. Although some adventurous types had scrambled up the fells rather than walked, it was the first time anyone had sought out routes that took them up and over the rocks rather than safely around them.

Haskett Smith embarked on several expeditions on subsequent visits, but the birth of rock climbing as an activity in its own right is usually dated to the moment in June 1886 when he left his white handkerchief fluttering in the breeze on top of the Napes Needle off Great Gable. At the time only a handful of people had even seen the needle, let alone climbed it or even ascertained if it was safe—but Haskett Smith ascended it alone and without the vast range of protective equipment that climbers carry today.

Haskett Smith wrote about his final ascent in the *Fell and Rock Climbing Club Journal*. 'Gently and cautiously transferring my weight, I reached up with my right hand and at last was able to feel the edge and prove it to be, not smooth and rounded as it might have been, but a flat and satisfactory grip. My first thought on reaching the top was one of regret that my friends should have missed by a few hours such a day's climbing, my next one was of wonder whether getting down again would not prove far more awkward than getting up!'

On the 50th anniversary of his climb, Haskett Smith, by now 74, was led up Napes Needle again. As he was perched at the top once more, one of the crowd below called out to him to tell them a story. 'There is no other story,' he replied, with great presence of mind. 'This is the top storey!' Napes Needle is now ascended hundreds of times each year, and remains the most famous rock climb in the Lake District.

LAKE DISTRICT POEMS – FROM 'A DESCRIPTIVE POEM' BY JOHN DALTON

And last, to fix our wandering eyes,
Thy roofs, O Keswick, brighter rise
The lake and lofty hills between,
Where Giant Skiddaw shuts the scene.
Supreme of mountains, Skiddaw, hail!
To whom all Britain sinks a vale!
Lo, his imperial brow I see,
From foul usurping vapours free!
'Twere glorious now his side to climb,
Boldly to scale his top sublime,
And thence—My Muse, these flights forbear,
Nor with wild raptures tire the fair.

TONY ROGERS' FAVOURITE LAKE DISTRICT WALKS

Tony Rogers is footpath secretary and mountain leader of the Lake District area branch of the Ramblers Association, Britain's biggest walking charity and an active supporter of walkers and their rights. Here are his ten best walks in the Lake District, with the emphasis on high-level routes.

Blencathra via Hall's Fell from Threlkeld. The best walk in the northern Lake District.

The Buttermere Fells from Buttermere. The best walk in the north-western Lake District.

The Coledale Horseshoe from Braithwaite. A really good horseshoe with over 4,000 feet of ascent.

Dow Crag and Coniston Old Man from Coniston. The best walk in the Coniston Fells, and visiting the highest point in real Lancashire.

The Fairfield Horseshoe from Ambleside. Another really good horseshoe.

Green Gable, Great Gable, Brandreth and Grey Knotts from Borrowdale. A classic walk to the most shapely mountain in the Lake District.

Harter Fell and High Street. A good walk in the far eastern Lake District.

Helvellyn and the Dodds to Clough Head. A good high level A-to-B walk, keeping above 2,000 feet for several miles.

Helvellyn via Striding Edge and Swirrell Edge from Glenriding. The finest ridges in England.

Scafell and Scafell Pike from Wasdale Head. Taking in the highest point in England.

JOHN KEATS ON THE LAKE DISTRICT

'What astonishes me more than anything is … the intellect, the countenance of such places. The space, the magnitude of mountains and waterfalls are well imagined before one sees them; but this countenance or intellectual tone must surpass every imagination and defy any remembrance.'

LETTER

LAKE DISTRICT FOOD – CUMBERLAND SAUSAGES

Cumberland sausages have been a speciality of the Lake District for five centuries or more. They have a distinctive shape, texture and taste, formed in long, rope-like coils that are cut to size by butchers, and made from coarsely chopped pork with little filler.

There is uncertainty about the origin of the sausages, though some think they were first created for or by the large number of German miners who came to the Lake District in the 16th century, to remind them of home. Cumberland sausages are highly seasoned and often quite herby and spicy, something that probably dates from the time when the area was a gateway for the import of new and exotic spices such as black pepper and nutmeg via the port of Whitehaven. The name is taken from the Cumberland pig, a breed that died out in the 1960s.

The sausages have been proudly made by Lake District butchers to traditional recipes that are up to a century old, but, encouraged by public demand, more mass-market producers have recently started to offer their own versions. Traditional producers are so concerned by what they see as devaluation of the product that they want Cumberland sausages to receive endorsement from the European Union's Protected Geographical Indication scheme. This would establish rules for the ingredients and origin of anything wishing to be labelled as Cumberland sausage, and has been awarded in the past to products like Parma ham and Stilton cheese. The Cumberland Sausage Association was set up in 2005 to campaign for standards in production and to promote the product in the Lake District and beyond.

A recipe for Cumberland sausages

Preparing your own sausages can be time-consuming when there are plenty of Cumbrian butchers with great recipes—but making them yourself at least means that you know exactly what's gone into them. For proper Cumberland sausages you will also need sausage casings and a stuffing machine to fill them, though this is not essential—the sausage mixture can be cooked as patties or wrapped by hand into parcels in caul fat, available from most butchers. Adjust the quantities of herbs and spices according to taste.

400g pork shoulder
400g belly pork
50g stale white breadcrumbs
2 teaspoons of salt
1 teaspoon of ground black pepper
Several gratings of fresh nutmeg and mace
Pinches of dried sage and cayenne pepper

Either chop the meat or mince it coarsely. Add the other ingredients and combine thoroughly with your hands. Add to the casings and coil it up, or shape into patties. Leave the sausage to rest for at least an hour. Cook slowly in a frying pan, or in a medium oven for 30 to 40 minutes, turning once. Serve with mashed potato and onion gravy. Cumberland sausages are also good in casseroles or toad in the hole.

THE STAR RESTAURANTS

The recent surge in interest in good food and drink across the Lake District means that Cumbria now has four restaurants with a prestigious one-star rating from international assessor Michelin. They are:

L'Enclume, Cartmel, near Grange-over-Sands. Tel 015395 36362 or online at www.lenclume.co.uk.

Gilpin Lodge, Windermere. Tel 015394 88818 or online at www.gilpinlodge.co.uk.

Holbeck Ghyll Country House Hotel, Windermere. Tel 015394 32375 or online at www.holbeck-ghyll.co.uk.

Sharrow Bay Country House Hotel, Ullswater. Tel 017684 86301 or online at www.sharrowbay.co.uk.

HOW TO VIEW THE LAKES, GEORGIAN STYLE

Everyone has their favourite viewing spot in the Lake District, but visitors in the 18th and 19th centuries didn't have much choice in their vantage points.

Many visitors came to the area clutching copies of Thomas West's 1778 book *Guide to the Lakes in Cumberland, Westmorland and Lancashire*. The book was particularly strong on viewpoints, listing various 'stations' from which West declared that the landscape would be seen to its best advantage. The views were chosen for their formal qualities, and tourists were given detailed instructions about how they were to be interpreted.

Facilities for tourists sprung up around these stations, and some, such as Claife Station near Windermere, still remain. They provided sheltered seating areas and some had coloured glass to recreate the light and atmosphere outside and further enhance the view from inside. Orange windows exaggerated autumnal scenes, for instance, while yellow tints added further lustre to summer views. These stations quickly became very fashionable places for tourists to visit.

As was the custom at the time, tourists would stand at these and other viewpoints with their backs to the view and see it framed by a Claude-glass—a hand-held, tinted, convex mirror that framed the landscape into a picturesque vision. The mirror was named after Claude Lorrain, a Baroque French artist who used it in his work, and it is still used by landscape painters today—though not by many tourists.

TEN CUMBRIAN CHURCHES

Cumbria has plenty of lovely churches; here are ten of the best.

Carlisle Cathedral. Red sandstone cathedral founded by Henry I in 1122 and caught in the middle of Border warfare for hundreds of years afterwards. Fine windows and painted ceilings.

Cartmel Priory. Built by Augustinian canons in the late 12th century, and stripped but not destroyed during the Dissolution. The nearby priory gatehouse is looked after by the National Trust.

St James' Church, Whitehaven. Notable 18th century church with striking Italian sculpture and art. Pevsner said it had the finest Georgian church interior in England.

St John's Church, Keswick. Pink sandstone church designed in the 19th century by Anthony Salvin. Lovely stained glass, and the churchyard contains the grave of Hugh Walpole.

St Kentigern's Church, Crosthwaite, Keswick. Originally built in the 12th century, though the present church dates from the 16th and was restored in the 19th by George Gilbert Scott. The church has memorials to Robert Southey and Canon Hardwicke Rawnsley, both of whom are buried here.

Lanercost Priory Church. The original priory was built in 1220 on the orders of Henry II, but battered by Border warfare and dissolved by Henry VIII, though it still serves as a parish church. The priory ruins are looked after by English Heritage.

St Mary's Church, Wreay. Built in the 1840s under the simple but striking design of Sara Losh, based on a Roman basilica and full of ornaments and carvings.

St Michael and All Angels, Hawkshead. Picturesque church and graveyard perched above the village of Hawkshead. Built around 1500, the bell tower is the oldest surviving part.

St Olaf's, Wasdale. One of the smallest churches in England, with a roof built from a Viking longship. The churchyard contains graves of climbers who died on the surrounding fells.

St Oswald's, Grasmere. Pretty church alongside the River Rothay, with a 13th century nave and fine stained glass. Mostly visited for William Wordsworth's grave in the churchyard.

STAYING OVERNIGHT IN THE LAKE DISTRICT

A 2001 survey by the Lake District National Park Authority revealed the types of accommodation chosen by visitors staying in the Lake District. About a third of visitors stayed in serviced accommodation while a quarter rented a self-catering cottage—and only 8 per cent of visitors were hardy enough to camp.

Type of accommodation	Visitors choosing
Self-catering cottage	.28%
Hotel or guesthouse	.20%
Bed and breakfast	.14%
Static caravan	.8%
Tent	.8%
Home of friend or relative	.7%
Touring caravan	.6%
Youth hostel	.4%
Other / no answer	.4%

SCAFELL PIKE AND THE THREE PEAKS CHALLENGE

Scafell Pike forms one-third of a popular fellwalkers' challenge: to climb the highest mountains in England, Scotland and Wales in a 24-hour period. Although it is the highest mountain in both the Lake District and England, Scafell Pike at 978m is actually some way shorter than both Snowdon in Wales (1,085m) and Ben Nevis in Scotland (1,344m).

Most people begin the three peaks challenge at Ben Nevis in the late afternoon during the summer months, descending from it around nightfall. Then it's a six-hour drive through the night down to the Lake District, where walkers can climb Scafell Pike by breakfast time. From here it's about five hours on to the foot of Snowdon, where walkers have to get up and down by the time they started at Ben Nevis the day before.

Completing the challenge obviously requires a good level of fitness and decent navigational skills, as well as the help of a support team and in particular someone to drive between the mountains. The Scafell Pike leg of the route can often be the most difficult of the three climbs, since it follows the climb of Ben Nevis and a fitful night's sleep on the road. Participants also have to rely on the roads being relatively clear if they are to get round within 24 hours, and plenty of attempts have been scuppered by traffic jams somewhere between the mountains.

The challenge has been completed in as little as 15 hours, though this involved running up and down the peaks and, presumably, some lively driving in between. Some purists have preferred to notch up the peaks without the use of motorized transport, by running or cycling between them in relay. Because all three are fairly close to the coastline, there is also an annual yacht race around the peaks, involving 389 miles of sailing, 18 miles of cycling and 72 miles of running. The three peaks challenge has sometimes been extended to four or even five mountains by adding Slieve Donard in Northern Ireland (849m) and Carrauntoohill in the Republic of Ireland (1,039m), though it needs the help of helicopters to complete these in 24 hours.

Thousands of people now attempt the challenge each year, many of them in organised groups and raising sponsorship money for charity. Its popularity has led to some criticisms of the challenge and the way it generates large crowds in the villages around Scafell Pike in particular at anti-social hours. Walkers are sometimes badly prepared for the exertions of the challenge, putting a strain on the resources of mountain rescue teams.

THE COUNTRYSIDE CODE

There are five main points of the Countryside Code, which was drawn up by the Countryside Agency—now Natural England—to help members of the public respect, protect and enjoy their natural surroundings.

Be safe - plan ahead and follow any signs
Leave gates and property as you find them
Protect plants and animals and take your litter home
Keep dogs under close control
Consider other people.

HERMITS OF THE LAKE DISTRICT

The peaceful solitude of the fells and valleys has made the Lake District a popular spot for hermits over the centuries. Many of these have been devoutly religious recluses such as Saint Herbert, who went to live on an island on Derwent Water after bringing Christianity to the area in the seventh century. Remains of his cell can still be seen on St Herbert's Island on the lake.

More recent hermits have fled to the Lake District simply to enjoy the quiet life. One of the most famous is Millican Dalton, who was born near Alston but worked in London as an insurance clerk until he was 30. Fed up with the office life, he quit his job to become a professional mountain guider and camper, tramping around England and camping out wherever he wished, often in the Lake District. He later settled into a cave on Castle Crag and his lean, weather-beaten, bearded figure became well known around Keswick. Dubbing himself the 'Professor of Adventure', he taught people how to rock climb, camp, sail and forage, usually charging nothing for his services, and was by all accounts an excellent and patient instructor.

A vegetarian and teetotaler, Dalton was almost entirely self-sufficient, making his own clothes and finding his food in the wild. His only vices were cigarettes, which he smoked constantly, and strong coffee, which he bought weekly to brew in his cave. He lived a perfectly content life on Castle Crag, making it comfortable with a soft bed of bracken and leaves, and has become something of a hero to people who want to follow him in escaping city life for the Lake District. He died in 1947 at the age of 79, his open-air life clearly having done him no harm. Dalton's cave and some of his carvings can still be found on Castle Crag.

Other hermits include George Smith, who built himself a hut on the Skiddaw range of fells in the 1860s. The 'Hermit of Skiddaw' lived in a wigwam style tent made from branches and reeds on a sheltered part of the slopes, slept on a bed of leaves, and wore only a shirt and trousers, which he washed in becks. He made small amounts of money from painting but unlike Dalton had a drinking habit that got him into trouble on several occasions. Persecution from local youths led him to quit his mountain home for Keswick, and later Scotland, where he is thought to have died in a mental hospital.

LAKE DISTRICT POEMS – 'WRITTEN ON THE BANKS OF WASTWATER DURING A CALM' BY JOHN WILSON

Is this the lake, the cradle of the storms,
Where silence never tames the mountain-roar,
Where poets fear their self-created forms,
Or, sunk in trance severe, their God adore?
Is this the lake for ever dark and loud,
With wave and tempest, cataract and cloud?

Wondrous, O Nature, is thy sovereign power,
That gives to horror hours of peaceful mirth;
For here might beauty build her summer bower!
Lo! Where yon rainbow spans the smiling earth,
And clothed in glory, through a silent shower
The mighty Sun comes forth, a god-like birth;
While, 'neath his loving eye the gentle Lake
Lies like a sleeping child too blest to wake!

PULLING FACES

Cumbria is home to the prestigious World Gurning Championships, which each year celebrate the ugliest contortions of the human face.

The competition is held at the Egremont Crab Fair, first staged by royal charter as far back as 1267. The fair has run on the third Saturday of September virtually every year since then, and celebrates the crab apple rather than the crustacean. Modern-day events include traditional Lakeland sports such as hound trailing, wrestling and fell-running—somewhat more civilized than the cock fighting and bull baiting that were popular in years gone by. Those events were finally banned in the 19th century, but the gurning competition continues to thrive. There are separate contests for juniors and women, while the men's competition serves as the climax to the fair.

Competitors take it in turns to pull faces, framed by a horse collar or 'braffin' around their heads. Gurns must be natural, unaided by hands or artificial aids—though contestants who wear dentures are allowed to enhance their performance by removing them. Noises are permitted, and add to the terrifying effect. Contestants are assessed by a panel of judges, marked on the extent to which their features are changed and on the overall hideousness of the gurn.

Heroes of gurning include Gordon Mattinson, champion ten times between 1967 and 1977. He has a talented family: his son, Tommy Mattinson, won six straight titles between 2001 and 2006 and has eight in all. Other legends include Gordon Blacklock, Wyndham 'Taffy' Thomas and the aptly-named Ron Looney, winners on four, five and eight occasions respectively. Gurners now come to Egremont from all over the world to compete, but all winners so far have been home-grown, which perhaps says something for the talents of the local area.

THE YEAR IN WEATHER

Barry Colam of the Cumbria House guesthouse in Keswick keeps a weather station which records temperature and rainfall every day of the year. These were his monthly findings in 2006—when the temperature ranged from a chilly -7 degrees Celsius to a sweltering 36, and Cumbria House got enough rainfall to submerge a person of average height.

	Max /°C	Min/°C	Rain/mm	Max wind/mph
January	14	-2	100.6	40
February	12	-5	74.9	39
March	14	-7	132.1	32
April	19	-3	72.6	41
May	28	2	120.1	36
June	29	6	61.7	40
July	36	7	65	25
August	24	8	114.8	30
September	28	6	149.4	35
October	21	2	201.7	49
November	13	-1	264.2	44
December	11	6	337.3	54
Year	**36**	**-7**	**1,694.4**	**54**

LITERARY LAKELANDERS – DOROTHY WORDSWORTH

Although she lived and wrote in the shadow of her brother, Dorothy Wordsworth was a literary force in her own right—and just as devoted to the Lake District as William.

Dorothy was born in Cockermouth in 1771, and the early death of her parents meant she and her siblings were sent to live with relatives. She was rarely apart from William after they were reunited, and settled with him at Dove Cottage in Grasmere in 1799. William subsequently married her best friend, Mary Hutchinson. Dorothy was a good poet and kept diaries, but she had little interest in advancing her writing career and was instead happy to support William in his writing, living with him most of her life and acting as both secretary and inspiration to him. Many of his poems were prompted by Lake District walks together, or by things that Dorothy had seen alone and told him about.

Dorothy's work was never published in her lifetime—nor intended to be—and it was only in the 1930s when Beatrix Potter bought the Wordsworths' old home of Dove Cottage that her old diaries were discovered. They were published in 1933 as *The Grasmere Journals*, and have been popular ever since as a vivid snapshot of life in the Lake District in the early 19th century. They are also a wonderful documentation of the lives of the poets of the time—of Robert Southey, Samuel Taylor Coleridge and Walter Scott as well as William—and mix the humdrum business of everyday life with glimpses of the poets' characters and stimulations. The journals prompted a fresh evaluation of Dorothy as a writer, and more of her work was subsequently published. Introducing the first edition of her journals, Ernest de Selincourt called Dorothy 'the most distinguished of English writers who never wrote a line for the general public.'

Dorothy battled against declining physical and mental health for the last 25 years of her life, and died at Rydal in 1855. She is buried alongside William in St Oswald's Churchyard in Grasmere. The nearby Dove Cottage and its attached museum contain much about the Lake District life of Dorothy as well as William.

THE NATIONAL TRUST'S PROPERTIES

The National Trust owns around a quarter of the land in the Lake District National Park, including whole valleys, towns and fell ranges and dozens of lakes and tarns. The Cumbrian properties listed in its 2007 handbook are:

Acorn Bank Garden and Watermill

Gondola steam yacht

Temple Sowerby

Coniston Water

Grasmere and Great Langdale

Beatrix Potter Gallery, Hawkshead

Hawkshead and Claife

Borrowdale

Hill Top, Near Sawrey

Force Crag Mine, near Braithwaite

Sizergh Castle, near Kendal

Buttermere and Ennerdale

Stagshaw Garden, Ambleside

Cartmel Priory Gatehouse

Townend, Troutbeck

Coniston and Tarn Hows

Ullswater and Aira Force

Dalton Castle

Wasdale, Eskdale and Duddon

Derwent Island House

Windermere and Troutbeck

Fell Foot Park, Newby Bridge

Wordsworth House Cockermouth

TEN LOST RAILWAYS

Though Cumbria still has several active and scenic railway lines, plenty more have been abandoned and closed over the years. Some fell out of use because of a decline in the industries that they were set up to serve, while others were cut after the Beeching Report, the landmark review of the rail service that cut swathes through Britain's passenger network in the 1960s. Remains of some lines and the stations they served can still be seen, while others have been nicely converted into walking or cycling trails. Here are ten of the county's most significant and fondly remembered railway companies.

Carlisle and Port Carlisle Railway and Dock Company. Built along an old canal and by the Solway Firth to carry goods from the port to the city of Carlisle. Shut in 1932.

Carlisle and Silloth Bay Railway. Founded in 1855 to link north Cumbria to the port of Silloth. The final section closed in 1969.

Cleator & Workington Junction Railway. Founded in 1876 to link the west Cumbrian towns of Whitehaven, Workington and Cleator Moor. Mostly used by the area's coal and iron works. The last sections of it closed in the 1980s.

The Cockermouth, Keswick and Penrith Railway. Traversed the Lake District from east to west, linking Keswick and Penrith to the coastal towns via the shores of Bassenthwaite Lake. The last section of the route, from Penrith to Keswick, closed in 1972, but there is now a campaign to re-open it.

The Eden Valley Railway Company. Built in 1856 to link Kirkby Stephen and Clifton, just south of Penrith. Closed in 1989, though a trust is now protecting the line for possible future use.

The Furness Railway. Established in 1846 to connect towns along the Furness peninsula, from Ulverston to Whitehaven. Branch lines closed in the 1960s, though the main route continues to be used.

Maryport and Carlisle Railway. The Aspatria to Aikbank Junction loop of this line was set up to transport coal in the 1860s, but finally closed in the 1950s. The rest of the line is still used by Northern Rail.

The South Durham and Lancashire Union Railway. Linked Cumbrian towns including Kirkby Stephen with neighbouring counties of Durham and Yorkshire. Closed in 1962.

The Waverley Line. Famous old route linking Edinburgh and Scotland with Carlisle and England, closed following the Beeching Report. In 2006, the Scottish Executive voted to reopen some sections of it.

Whitehaven, Cleator and Egremont Railway. Built around the iron and steel industries, this served a network of towns along the west coast. Parts are now a cycle route.

WORDSWORTH ON... CLIMBING MOUNTAINS

'It is not likely that a mountain will be ascended without
disappointment, if a wide range of prospect be the object,
unless either the summit be reached before sunrise, or
the visitant remain there until the time of sunset, and
afterwards. The precipitous sides of the mountain, and the
neighbouring summits, may be seen with effect under any
atmosphere which allows them to be seen at all; but he *is*
the most fortunate adventurer, who chances to be involved
in vapours which open and let in an extent of country partially,
or, dispersing suddenly, reveal the whole region from centre
to circumference.'

FROM *GUIDE TO THE LAKES* BY WILLIAM WORDSWORTH

RUSHBEARING

One of the Lake District's oldest summer traditions, rushbearing dates from the times when churches had only mud floors covered with rushes, which were changed once a year amid great ceremony. The changeover would prompt a general sprucing up, with men and children fetching the rushes and women decorating the church with flowers, before communities celebrated afterwards with food and sports. The sweet smelling rushes would also help to freshen the air—since bodies were often buried within the church as well as around it—and keep the church warm.

When churches' mud floors were replaced by paving through the 19th century, the rushbearing celebrations began to die out in most areas, but some Cumbrian churches continue to honour the tradition in the summer. Village children carry the rushes and flowers to the church, accompanied by clergy and bands playing traditional music, before laying them around inside. The rushbearing events and services usually take place close to the saints' day of the particular church. One of the churches, St Mary's in Ambleside, has a mural depicting the ceremony. The dates of Cumbria's five surviving Rushbearing Days are:

St Columba's Church, Warcop
29th June (St Peter's Day)

St Mary's Church, Ambleside
First Saturday in July

St Theobald's Church, Great Musgrave
First Saturday in July

St Oswald's Church, Grasmere
Third Saturday in July

St Mary and St Michael's Church, Urswick
Sunday closest to 29th September (St Michael's Day)

LAKE DISTRICT FISH

The lakes of the Lake District are home to several rare species of fish, some of them 'glacial relics' from the last Ice Age that are now endangered because of rising temperatures or the introduction of new species. They are:

Arctic charr. Usually found in deep, cold waters much further north, this member of the Salmonidae family survives in eight lakes including Wastwater, Windermere and Coniston Water.

Schelly. Rare whitefish that is almost unique to the Lake District, and found in Ullswater, Haweswater and Brothers Water. It has been the subject of special protection laws from the Environment Agency, and there are plans to introduce it to some tarns.

Vendace. One of the rarest and most endangered species of freshwater fish, because its traditional gravel-based spawning grounds are being silted up. Now found only in Derwent Water and Bassenthwaite Lake, although there is a project to create new populations in high tarns.

Other more common fish include **brown trout**, which are found in clean waters across the Lake District, and **Atlantic salmon**, numbers of which have declined a little recently.

HOW TO BUILD A DRY STONE WALL

Dry stone walls contribute a great deal to the distinctive character of the Lake District landscape—but few visitors are aware of the skill and graft that go into building them.

As the name suggests, they are walls that contain no mortar or cement but that are held together by the weight of each stone in them. Some of the walls in the Lake District date back to medieval times, though most are from the 18th or 19th centuries, built to indicate boundaries to common land or to enclose livestock. Building them is a great craft and backbreaking labour: each stone has to be fitted like a piece in a jigsaw, and a single metre of wall requires around a tonne of stone. A badly constructed wall will often collapse after a few years, but a well-built one can last centuries with little maintenance— far longer than cemented walls or fences. The achievements of dry stone wallers building in remote areas, on steep slopes and often in dreadful weather, are extraordinary. Their walls have helped to shape the Lake District, and have also provided important habitats for its wildlife.

While some dry stone walls remain in perfect condition despite being buffeted by rain, snow and high winds for hundreds of years, many others are now falling into disrepair. A survey by the Countryside Agency in 1996 found that 49 per cent of England's walls were either in remnants, derelict or in early stages of dereliction. A further 38 per cent had signs of potential deterioration, leaving only 13 per cent in sound or excellent condition, and the total is likely to have deteriorated since the time of the survey. Landowners often find it easier and cheaper to allow walls to disintegrate or replace them with wire fences than to rebuild them. Organisations such as the Dry Stone Walling Association and the National Trust are helping to maintain stretches of walls, but the size of the job is enormous. The number of professional wallers in the Lake District has fallen over the last few decades, but those that remain are mostly very skilled and in high demand.

Wallers choose their materials carefully. There is plenty of stone in the Lake District, but only a small proportion of it is suitable for building. Techniques vary across the country and even across different valleys in the Lake District, but most wallers begin by digging a trench several feet wide, into which large 'footing' stones are tightly fitted. Onto these, rows of large, flattish stones are laid, with 'hearting'— smaller chock stones or gravel—filling the gaps in between. Walls are sometimes built as parallel, double rows with occasional cross-stones spanning both to bond them together.

The wall is assembled layer by layer, with each stone resting on at least two others below and the width gradually tapering towards the top, usually four or five feet high. Dry stone walls work because the outer weight of the stones supports the inner core, so stones must fit together snugly and not slip. At the top comes a row of upright 'cams' or 'coping' stones, laid perpendicular to the others below them. These are usually the most attractive stones, giving the wall a nice finish but also making it more difficult for sheep to climb over. The leeward side of walls can also provide shelter for livestock in high winds or drifting snow.

The appearance of dry stone walls varies according to the available stone, which reflects the geology of its region. The volcanic rocks of the central Lake District make for very thick, durable walls, while huge supplies of slate in some areas in the north and south result in thinner, angular walls. Limestone and sandstone areas also produce very distinctive walls. Most walls must also be built to allow or restrict the passage of people or animals through them. Squeeze or step stiles are common, and 'hogg holes' allow young sheep to pass through while keeping older ones out. 'Smoots' are small holes in the base of a wall to let animals like badgers pass through rather than encouraging them to dig underneath. Features like these, and the effort that goes into building a good wall, add to their character and increase the affection in which they are held.

A YEAR IN LAKELAND SHEEP FARMING

Oct-Nov	Tups (males) put in with ewes (females) on the low land
Dec	Ewes returned to the fells until lambing time
Mar-Apr	Ewes brought down for lambing
May	Lambs get flock marks. Ewes with single lambs return to the fells
July	All sheep clipped
Sep	Lambs weaned from their mothers Sheep dipped, ewes returned to fells
Oct	Wether lambs (castrated males) sold or fattened for sale
Nov	Gimmer lambs (young females) sent to winter on lowland fells

SEAN MCMAHON'S FAVOURITE
LAKE DISTRICT FELLS

Sean McMahon runs Striding Edge, an online photographic diary of his walks in the Lake District. It is a record of how, since 2003, he has walked all 214 'Wainwrights'—the fells mentioned in Alfred Wainwright's *Pictorial Guide to the Lakeland Fells*. The site is an enclyclopaedic guide to walking in the Lake District, with pages dedicated to each fell and its views. Striding Edge can be found at www.stridingedge.net.

Few walkers today have seen so many Lake District fells from so many different directions. 'It's so hard to pick my top ten favourite fells as they are all special to me,' says Sean. 'To give a definitive list would require me to visit all the fells in all weathers and from all angles; something I haven't achieved to date—but I am working on it! Here's my top ten in no particular order.'

Pillar/Steeple. A bit of cheat really because there are two fells here, but normally one is visited with the other. Pillar is rugged and feels remote—a real fell walkers' fell. There are no easy ways up and no short cuts to it. Steeple is an airy pinnacle overlooking Ennerdale with standing-room only.

Bow Fell. A lovely peak with a shape recognisable from everywhere in the Lake District.

Stickle Pike. This diminutive fell overlooks remote Dunnerdale and is Lakeland in miniature, offering rocky scrambles, gentle grass slopes and a tarn nestling below the summit. A great reminder of family walks for me.

Scafell. I prefer this one to its higher and busier neighbour, Scafell Pike. Combining the walk along Upper Eskdale to Great Moss with Lord's Rake and the West Wall Traverse makes one of the finest walks in the Lake District.

Yewbarrow. This rugged fell has the shape of an upturned boat and the summit ridge can only be reached by a scramble. The views to Wast Water and the Scafells are simply superb.

Blencathra. Lots of fells within a fell and many ways to climb to the summit, Sharp Edge being the most exciting and rewarding.

Coniston Old Man. The fell I have visited the most, I think, and one I still love the views from.

Helvellyn. A deservedly popular fell. Ascent can be via the gentler slopes on its western side, but much better is to climb via Striding Edge and Swirral Edge on the eastern side.

Wetherlam. Perhaps less well known and less glamorous than some in this list, but a walk up it by Steel Edge and down by Wetherlam Edge makes a brilliant medium-distance walk with great views to the central fells.

Grasmoor. The finest of the north-western fells, with a distinctive shape and marvellous views over Buttermere.

RED SQUIRRELS

Cumbria is home to 90 per cent of England's red squirrels, but its population is under threat from the advancement north of grey rivals. The red population have been increasingly out-competed for food since greys were introduced to the UK a century or so ago, and are also endangered by the parapox virus spread by the greys. Red squirrels are now outnumbered by greys by about 70 to 1, and there are thought to be fewer than 1,000 left in Cumbria. A 'Save Our Squirrels' campaign is run by the Friends of the Red Squirrel, which organises woodland refuges in Cumbria and elsewhere and campaigns to raise awareness of the problem. See www.redsquirrel.org.uk.

LAKE DISTRICT FOOD – TATIE POT

The Tatie Pot is a classic farmers' and shepherds' dish that has been cooked in Cumbria for centuries. It is hearty and tasty, and a good use of the Lake District's famous and distinctive Herdwick lamb or mutton. More vegetables and herbs can be added to this recipe, but this is a simple, classic version.

800g neck of Herdwick lamb or mutton
200g black pudding
700g potatoes
2 large onions
6 medium carrots
600ml stock
Salt
Ground black pepper
Butter

Peel and slice the potatoes into rounds about half a centimetre thick. Peel and thickly slice the onions. Peel and roughly chop the carrots. Trim the fat from the meat and cut into pieces. Slice the black pudding.

Grease a deep casserole dish with butter. Arrange an overlapping layer of potatoes on the bottom. Scatter onions, meat, black pudding and carrots on top, and season well with salt and pepper. Add a further layer of potatoes and more onions, meat, black pudding, carrots and seasoning on top. Finish with a neatly arranged layer of potatoes, season well and pour over the stock. Dot with butter.

Place in a low oven (gas mark 3) for three to four hours, or even longer at a lower temperature if you have time. Turn the heat up towards the end to brown the potatoes. Serve with pickled red cabbage and bread.

TOURISM IN NUMBERS

15,540,000	estimated visitors to Cumbria in 2005
28,580,000	estimated number of days spent by visitors
1,129,300,000	estimated pounds spent by tourists
210,000	estimated number of overseas visitors. Australians are the most common visitors, followed by Americans, Germans, Canadians and Japanese
25,525	jobs supported by tourism in Cumbria
6.1	percentage increase in visitor numbers since 2000 the average days spent on a visit, excluding day-trippers
112,055	number of beds available in serviced and non-serviced accommodation in Cumbria (61,338 of them within the Lake District National Park)
18,815	camping, caravan and touring units or pitches in Cumbria (8,446 in the National Park)
17,582	rooms available in serviced accommodation in Cumbria (8,057 in the National Park)
6,404	houses, cottages, flats and chalets available for hire in Cumbria (4,184 in the National Park)
48	percentage of visitors to the National Park who cite walking as the purpose of their visit
5	percentage of visitors who cite 'fresh air' as the purpose

A BEATRIX POTTER TRAIL

Beatrix Potter may well be the biggest single crowd-puller in the Lake District. Here are ten places closely associated with her life and stories.

Wray Castle, near Ambleside. Where Potter stayed on her first holiday visit to the Lake District in 1882 and was inspired to write. Now privately owned, although the gardens are open to the public.

Lindeth Howe, Bowness. Potter wrote many of her early books during stays here, and later bought the property. It is now a smart country house hotel and restaurant. Tel 015394 45759 or online at www.lindeth-howe.co.uk.

Lingholm and **Fawe Park**, near Derwent Water. More holiday homes for the Potter family. A vegetable garden and red squirrels near here inspired aspects of the tales of *Peter Rabbit* and *Squirrel Nutkin* respectively. Not now open to the public, though both can be glimpsed from nearby footpaths.

Troutbeck Park Farm, near Troutbeck. Large sheep farm bought by Potter in 1923. She ran it herself with a shepherd, Tom Storey, and built up a flock of Herdwick sheep. The farm was among her bequests to the National Trust.

Hill Top Farm, Near Sawrey. The 17th century house bought by Potter with royalties from her books, and where many stories are set. Bequeathed to the National Trust and now the principal stop for Potter tourists. Tel 015394 36269 or online at www.nationaltrust.org.uk.

Tower Bank Arms, Near Sawrey. Picture-postcard Lakeland pub close to Hill Top, featured in *The Tale of Jemima Puddle-Duck*. A popular place to stay for Potter fans. Tel 015394 36334 or online at www.towerbankarms.co.uk.

Castle Cottage, Near Sawrey. Farm where Potter—by now Beatrix Heelis—lived from 1913 until her death in 1943. Not now open to the public.

Beatrix Potter Gallery, Hawkshead. Exhibition of Potter's original illustrations and a display about her life. Hawkshead itself was the setting for *The Tale of Johnny Town-Mouse*. Tel 015394 36355 or online at www.nationaltrust.org.uk.

The Armitt, Ambleside. Museum to which Potter bequeathed her collection of fungi, moss and microscopic drawings. Tel 015394 31212 or online at www.armitt.com.

The World of Beatrix Potter, Bowness. Hugely popular children's attraction that brings Potter's characters to life. Tel 015394 88444 or online at www.hop-skip-jump.com.

LAKE DISTRICT POEMS – UNTITLED BY EDMUND CASSON

All day I have climb'd by slate and ling.
Now by the low becks' murmuring
I walk in humble quietude;
Till I turn and see the mountain's brood,
Long backs, wild manes, against the sky,
And their steaming flanks: and I triumph, 'I
Have laid on your sides my pride's fierce rods:
I have tamed and bitted you, steeds of the gods.'

THE STEEPEST CLIMB

There are plenty of hard uphill slogs in the Lake District, and paths up the fells often seem to be at absurd gradients. But the steepest sustained climb is generally reckoned to be the backbreaking ascent from Wasdale Head to the summit of Kirk Fell. On a footpath just over a mile (1.7km) long, walkers climb 2,336 feet or 712m. That's a gradient of 42% or 1 in 2.4. Looked at from Wasdale Head, the path up appears to be almost vertical, and the contour lines on an Ordnance Survey map are so close as to be almost on top of one another. Wainwright called it 'a relentless and unremitting treadmill, a turf-clutching crawl, not a walk.' This is a path to come down rather than up.

TEN UNUSUAL MUSEUMS

The Lake District has dozens of museums battling it out for visitors' time and money, including a handful of quirky attractions. Here are ten museums you might not be expecting to find in the Lake District—and though they might seem a little esoteric, they are all worth a visit.

Cars of the Stars, Keswick. Want to see the car used in Chitty Chitty Bang Bang or driven by James Bond in Goldeneye? Of course you do. Tel 017687 73757 or online at www.carsofthestars.com.

The Cumberland Pencil Museum, Keswick. The Lake District's history of graphite mining makes it the perfect place to find out about the history of pencil making. Includes a display of what was at one time the world's biggest pencil, at 25 feet and 446kg. Tel 017687 73626 or online at www.pencils.co.uk.

Honister Slate Mine, Honister Pass, Borrowdale. Runs underground tours of what was once one of Lakeland's most important industries. Tel 017687 77230 or online at www.honister-slate-mine.co.uk.

Lakeland Motor Museum, Holker Hall, Cark-in-Cartmel (but due to move to Backbarrow in late 2007). 30,000 motoring exhibits, and includes the Campbell Legend Bluebird Exhibition about Donald Campbell's world speed record attempts. Tel 015395 58509 or online at www.lakelandmotormuseum.co.uk.

Laurel and Hardy Museum, Ulverston. Stan Laurel was born in Ulverston, and this museum grew out of one man's affection for the comic duo. Tel 01229 582292 or online at www.laurel-and-hardy-museum.co.uk.

Museum of Lakeland Life, Kendal. The history and heritage of the Lake District. Tel 015397 22464 or online at www.lakelandmuseum.org.uk.

The Rum Story, Whitehaven. Traces the old rum trading route from the Caribbean to England's north-west coast. Tel 01946 592933 or online at www.rumstory.co.uk.

Sellafield Visitor Centre, Sellafield. A nuclear power station might not seem the obvious place for a family day out, but its emphasis on making science fun makes it popular with children. Tel 01946 727027 or online at www.go-experimental.com.

Stott Park Bobbin Mill, Finsthwaite, near Newby Bridge. Everything you ever wanted to know about bobbins, in a mill that once fed Lancashire's spinning and weaving industries. Looked after by English Heritage. Tel: 015395 31087 or online at www.english-heritage.org.uk.

Windermere Steamboat Museum, Windermere. The heritage of the Lake District on water—a steam enthusiasts' dream. Tel 015394 45565 or online at www.steamboat.co.uk.

WILD WEATHER

Some of the more memorable weather events in the Lake District over the years.

1683 Windermere freezes over for three months, the longest period ever.

1898 Windermere rises nearly two metres above its normal level due to flooding.

1934 The temperature in Ambleside reaches 32C.

1940 The temperature in Ambleside drops to -21C and 30cm of ice forms over Derwent Water.

1953 Langdale gets 16cm of rain in less than 24 hours.

1954 Sprinkling Tarn in Borrowdale gets more than 21 feet of rain in the year—the most ever recorded anywhere in the country.

1984 High fells receive up to 60cm of snow.

1995 A drought leaves Haweswater reservoir nearly 90 per cent empty and makes the drowned village of Mardale visible.

2005 Prolonged stormy rain leaves Carlisle flooded and prompts large-scale evacuation.

ARE THERE ANY LAKES IN THE LAKE DISTRICT?

This is one of the questions asked of tourist information staff at Visit Britain's London office in 2006. Staff there also had to keep straight faces to questions including 'Is Wales closed during the winter?', 'Are the churches in England open at Christmas?' and 'What time does the midnight train leave?'.

Odd questions reported by Tourist Information Centres in the Lake District include 'Where are the Beatrix Potteries?' and 'What time does the Isle of Man ferry sail from Windermere?'. One visitor to Hawkshead asked where Anne Hathaway's cottage was to be found, while another asked for directions to the bagpipe maker. On being told there wasn't one, he replied: 'I am in Skye, aren't I?'.

THE ISLANDS OF THE LAKES

Part of the beauty and appeal of the Lake District's lakes are the tiny islands dotted around many of them. Eight of the 18 areas of water usually defined as lakes have islands, sharing 43 between them. Windermere has the most with 20, and the largest island of all, Belle Isle, which stretches just over 1 km from top to bottom. Many are called Holm or Holme, the words for islet derived from the Old Norse *holmr*. The islands of the Lake District are:

Coniston Water
Fir Island
Peel Island

Crummock Water
Holme Islands
Iron Stone
Scale Island
Woodhouse Islands

Derwent Water
Derwent Isle
Lingholm Islands
Lord's Island
Otter Island
Otterbield Island
Rampsholme Island
St Herbert's Island
Scarf Stones

Haweswater
Wood Howe

Rydal Water
Heron Island
Little Isle

Thirlmere
Deergarth How Island
Hawes How Island

Ullswater
Cherry Holm
Lingy Holm
Norfolk Island
Wall Holm

Windermere
Belle Isle
Blake Holme
Chicken Rock
Crag Holme
Crow Holme
Curlew Crag
Grass Holme
Green Tuft Island
Hartley Wife
Hen Holme
Hen Rock
Lady Holme
Lilies of the Valley
Ling Holme
Maiden Holme
Ramp Holme
Rough Holme
Seamew Crag
Silver Holme
Thompson's Holme

LITERARY LAKELANDERS – THOMAS DE QUINCEY

Thomas de Quincey is not so closely associated with the Lake District as William Wordsworth or Samuel Taylor Coleridge, but much of his work was influenced by the time he spent there.

De Quincey was born in Manchester in 1785 and was a weak, shy child who spent much of his time alone in his imaginary worlds. He was lined up for a scholarship to Oxford University, but eloped from his education and spent some of his teenage years walking around the country and eluding his family. When he eventually did get to Oxford he began to take opium, to which he was addicted for most of his life, and left without finishing his studies.

After meeting his literary heroes Wordsworth and Coleridge in 1807, de Quincey moved to the Lake District and lived for ten years at Dove Cottage, Wordsworth's former home in Grasmere. Unlike many of his contemporaries, he had to write out of necessity, and contributed pieces to periodicals as well as producing his own books. He was also one of the early editors of the local newspaper, the *Westmorland Gazette*. His most famous work was *Confessions of an English Opium-Eater*, which caused a sensation at the time and became a major influence on later writers, and he also wrote colourfully about Wordsworth, Coleridge and Robert Southey in *Recollections of the Lakes and the Lake Poets*.

De Quincey fell out with Wordsworth, partly because he was somewhat indiscreet about his hero in his writings, and he moved away from the Lakes to Edinburgh in 1826. He continued to write prolifically, but spent much of the rest of his life in some hardship and running from his creditors. He was convicted for debts several times, and was wracked by opium addiction, family tragedy and internal turmoil. He died in Edinburgh in 1859. De Quincey's home at Dove Cottage is now one of the Lake District's most popular tourist attractions, though it is for the connections with Wordsworth that it is usually visited.

BRITAIN'S STEEPEST ROADS

The Lake District lays claim to the steepest road in Britain. Hardknott Pass, connecting the eastern and western halves of the National Park, has an overall gradient of 1 in 3 (33%) and rises to 1 in 2.5 (40%) in places. The Kirkstone, Honister and Wrynose Passes all have gradients of 1 in 4 (25%) in places.

SKI-ING IN THE LAKE DISTRICT

Not many visitors come to the Lake District to ski—but a good number of enthusiasts find that the area often has some of the best conditions for the sport in Britain.

The Lake District Ski Club was founded in 1936 after excellent terrain for the sport was found around Raise on the Helvellyn range of mountains. The club's founding members built a basic tow rope to get skiers up the slopes, but this has since been developed into a modern, 400m button lift. When ski-ing is possible, the lift runs every weekend from late November to early April, and the height of 2,700 feet means the snow record is good—though it also means skiers have a fair walk up to the slopes. The club operates on a totally voluntary basis, with members maintaining the lift and small club hut.

Yad Moss near Alston in north Cumbria, meanwhile, has some wide slopes and the longest ski lift in England, maintained by the Carlisle Ski Club. Cross-country ski-ing is also popular in some of the valleys—if only because it's sometimes the only way to get around after heavy snowfalls.

CUMBRIA'S FOOD HEROES

Rick Stein's *Food Heroes* TV series and books uncover the best small food producers and retailers in the UK. Here are the 34 selections that are based in Cumbria.

The 1657 Chocolate House, Kendal. Chocolate heaven.

Barwise Aberdeen Angus, Appleby. Top-quality, traditionally-reared Angus beef.

Bessy Beck Trout Farm, Kirkby Stephen. Low-intensity trout rearing.

Border County Foods, Crosby-on-Eden. Rare breed pork products.

Bromley Green Farm, Ormside. Home-produced beef and lamb.

Broughton Village Bakery. Speciality breads, with on-site café.

Cartmel Village Shop. Home of the world-famous sticky toffee pudding.

Country Fare, Kirkby Stephen. Home-made cakes and treats.

Cowmire Hall Damson Gin, Crosthwaite. Made from Lyth Valley damsons.

Cream of Cumbria. Blackford. Produces wonderful butter and some Cumbrian specialities.

Demels, Ulverston. Multi-award winning Sri Lankan chutneys and pickles.

Farmer Sharp, Lindal-in-Furness. Co-operative of 27 Herdwick lamb farmers.

Greystone House, Stainton. Farm shop.

Hallsford Butchery, Hethersgill. Traditional breeds from family-run farm.

Hawkshead Trout Farm. Organic fish producer, also offers private fishing.

Hazelmere Café and Bakery, Grange-over-Sands. The Tea Guild's top tea place.

Howbarrow Organic Farm, Cartmel. Farm shop with more than 600 organic lines.

Kitridding Farm, Kirkby Lonsdale. Swaledale lamb and home-made sausages.

Mansergh Hall Farm, Kirkby Lonsdale. Organic family farm.

Moody Bakers Workers Co-op, Alston. Workers' co-operative and organic specialist.

Nether Hall Farm, Kirkby Lonsdale. Produces Lune Valley meat.

The Old Smokehouse, Brougham. Renowned smokers of local fish and meat.

Organic Pudding Company, Cartmel. Side business of Howbarrow Organic Farm.

Richard Woodall, Waberthwaite. Dry cured pork specialist.

Savin Hill Farm, Lyth Valley. Rare breed pork and beef.

Sillfield Farm Products, Endmoor. Products from free-range rare breeds.

Slacks of Cumbria, Orton. Bacon and sausage specialist.

Staff of Life, Kendal. Artisan baker.

Stoneyhead Hall Farm, Orton. Traditionally-reared pork.

Strawberry Bank Liqueurs, Crosthwaite. Damson gin and beers from the Lyth valley.

Thornby Moor Dairy, Thursby. Cows, goats and ewes' milk cheeses.

The Village Bakery, Melmerby. Organic baker, restaurant and shop.

The Watermill, Little Salkeld. Organic flour miller in a restored watermill.

Whiteholme Organic Farm, Roweltown. Organic farm, butchery and shop.

THE WELL-TRODDEN PATHS

The Lake District National Park has 1,880 miles (3,010 km) of public footpaths, bridleways or other rights of way. That distance is equivalent to a return trip from John O'Groats to Land's End at the top and bottom of Britain, with a hundred miles or so left over for detours along the way. Other permissive paths and open-access areas add to the total. Cumbria-wide, there are 3,406 miles (5,450 km) of public footpaths and 4,650 miles (7,441 km) of public rights of way in all. Across England and Wales, there are around 140,000 miles (224,000 km) of rights of way.

The Lake District National Park Authority is responsible for the upkeep of all rights of way, except urban rights of way in Ambleside, Windermere and Keswick. It works to maintain these paths with partners including the National Trust, which has four full-time footpath gangs to work on some of the most badly eroded paths. Despite their efforts, heavy use means that around 90 paths in the Lake District are seriously eroded, according to a joint survey by several organisations.

PETER WILDE'S FAVOURITE WILDLIFE ATTRACTIONS...

Peter Wilde runs www.cumbria-wildlife.org.uk, a website dedicated to the abundance of wildlife to be found in Cumbria. This is Peter's personal selection of the species and habitats that draw people to the Lake District from all over Britain and beyond.

Alpine catchfly. This is the Lake District's most famous rare flower, growing in just one place on the north-west fells. Fortunately it has natural protection from sheep and unscrupulous humans, as you would probably need pitons and ropes to be able to see it on the crags!

Bogs. Cumbria's coastal plains have some of the best examples of 'raised' bogs in the world. These bogs have a higher water level in the middle than on the outside because the sphagnum moss defies gravity and soaks up the water. Many rare insects, flowers and insect-eating flowers are found here.

Cliffs. St. Bees Head has a stretch of sandstone cliff that is home in the summer to the unforgettable sight and smell of thousands of nesting seabirds. The odd Peregrine falcon may turn up in search of a meal, while keen birders will be looking for the few puffins and the rare black guillemots that nest here.

Dark-red helleborine. This tall delicate orchid is only found on limestone rocks around the head of Morecambe Bay and in north-west Scotland, so fans of orchids from the south make the long journey in July to photograph it. If they stopped long enough, they might be surprised to learn that there are about 30 species of orchid to be seen in the county.

Hay meadows. There are still a few traditional hay meadows in the Lake District, where the rich tapestry of colours created by plants such as Meadow Cranesbill, Ragged Robin and Ox-eye Daisy can be seen, instead of the monotonous greens and yellows of modern agriculture. Visitors can also enjoy the same species on a smaller scale in many of our protected roadside verges.

Mountain ringlet butterfly. This brown and orange butterfly lives just below the tops on many of the Lake District mountains, and is otherwise found only in Scotland. Strangely for a species that chooses such a hostile environment it only flies in sunshine, much to the annoyance of the many butterfly enthusiasts who travel long distances to see it in June and July, only to find the fells in cloud or worse!

Natterjack toad. The sand dune systems on the Cumbrian coast hold around two-thirds of all the Natterjack toads in Britain. In early spring residents and visitors listen to the mating calls as hundreds of these yellow-striped toads gather in the early evening.

Ospreys. Ospreys have nested in the Bassenthwaite area since 2001, and attract around half a million visitors between March and August to special viewing sites.

Red squirrels. Still widespread in Cumbria, but increasingly scarce in the south, this charming mammal is a delight to watch. It is now protected in several refuges, one of which doubles as a holiday park in the Whinfell Forest, where thousands of visitors each week can watch it close up.

Wild daffodils. The genuine and original native species has been synonymous with the Lake District in spring ever since Wordsworth penned his homage to the flowers on the banks of Ullswater. In fact there are many other places with displays that are just as good, especially in open woodland in the southern half of the county.

... AND HIS HIDDEN WILDLIFE GEMS

Peter Wilde's choice of attractive Lakeland species that are hard to find but well worth the effort.

Butterfly orchid. This superb orchid can be found in open woodland, old meadows and even on railway embankments throughout Cumbria, but it is always very local and never abundant. Although the flowers are white they have a luminous glow to attract moths at dusk.

Eidur ducks. More at home in Iceland, this heavyweight duck has taken a liking to the mussels of Morecambe Bay. A raft of up to 2,000 birds floating out with the ebbing tide, covering the waters almost as far as the eye can see, is an unforgettable sight. The black and white male has a beautiful pale green nape patch in the breeding season and its 'ah-ooo' call carries over long distances—for me, it's one of the most endearing sounds in nature.

Elephant Hawkmoth. Cumbria has several of the large hawkmoths. A July night-time garden search of honeysuckle might produce a sighting of the lovely olive-green and pink Elephant Hawkmoth. Its caterpillar resembles an elephant's trunk and can be found on Rosebay Willowherb.

Guelder Rose. This gorgeous shrub, a member of the honeysuckle family, grows wild in dampish spots in the county but is not native. It is often planted in the verges of new stretches of road and bypasses. The showy flat white flower heads of June turn into red translucent berries that are attractive to birds, and in autumn the stunning leaf colours of red, yellow and purple make it a real gem in our countryside.

Kingfisher. For an area noted for its water, the central Lake District has surprisingly few kingfishers. The Bassenthwaite area is one possibility, but for a chance of seeing the amazing spectacle of a diving and fishing bird the rivers and canals of the outer regions of Cumbria are much better.

Ladybirds. The familiar orange-red ladybird of our gardens is just one of over 20 species found in Cumbria. While walking in less well-cultivated places in summer there is always the chance of an unexpected meeting with one of these colourful and attractive beetles. They come in several base colours—red, yellow, orange, brown, and black. Spots or blotches can be in black, red, cream and white, with the number of spots varying from two to 24.

Marsh Fritillary butterfly. Once common, this gorgeous butterfly has suffered a catastrophic decline in the Lakes as wet areas have been drained for pasture. The last colony was recently saved from extinction by removing eggs and breeding them in captivity under licence. In 2007, around 30,000 caterpillars were released back at three sites—hopefully the start of a resurgence of the species.

Southern Hawker dragonfly. This large dragonfly has turquoise and black bands with noticeable bright blue bands at the tail. It is the most inquisitive of dragonflies, often approaching a shoulder or arm and hopping from side to side as it assesses the situation.

Weasels. This little mustelid can regularly be seen in daylight hours throughout the county. I love their agility and speed as they chase each other around, and a real treat is to see a family party of six or more moving in line, nose to tail. If it's got a black tip to the tail then it's the larger stoat.

Wood Warbler. This summer visitor to the oak woods that are so typical of the upper valleys of central Lakeland is best located by its trilling call—like a spinning coin gradually settling. Watching this delightful species as it sings its heart out is difficult, as its yellow, white and green plumage makes it hard to spot against leaves in dappled sunlight!

More information on all of Peter's choices and other wildlife across the county can be found at his encyclopedic website, www.cumbria-wildlife.org.uk.

THE LEGEND OF LONG MEG AND HER DAUGHTERS

Cumbria has around 60 stone circles—more than a quarter of England's total. The largest and most celebrated is Long Meg and her Daughters at Little Salkeld, near Penrith in the Eden Valley.

Also known as Maughanby Circle, the Daughters measures 90 to 100 metres across, making it the third largest in England and the largest in the north of the country. It has about 50 stones, though there may once have been more than 70. Long Meg is a three-metre high sandstone monolith close by. The circle dates from the Bronze Age, though the name is thought to have been derived from the legend of a 17th century witch who was turned to stone by a wizard for dancing with her coven on the Sabbath. One local theory suggests that anyone who can count the stones in the circle twice and get the same number will release Long Meg from the wizard's spell.

William Wordsworth visited the stone circle in 1833. As with most things he saw, he was moved to poetry, later writing the following:

> A weight of awe, not easy to be borne,
> Fell suddenly upon my Spirit – cast
> From the dread bosom of the unknown past,
> When first I saw that family forlorn.

A DIARY OF LAKE DISTRICT SHOWS

Agricultural, horticultural and sporting shows are an important part of spring and summer in the Lake District. Many have been running for centuries—in the case of the Egremont Crab Fair, since 1267—and are a proud and popular aspect of Cumbria's heritage.

The biggest shows of the season are those of the old counties of Westmorland and Cumberland at Kendal and Carlisle respectively, but most Lakeland communities of reasonable size will have an event close by at some stage during the summer. The busiest month is August, when good weather and the school holidays can help to pull in thousands of visitors and bring gridlock to the otherwise quiet lanes around the showgrounds.

Many of the shows have their roots in farmers' meets, where shepherds displayed their best animals and competed at building dry stone walls, shearing sheep or carving crooks. Those traditions still continue at many shows, and sheepdog trials also remain important dates in farmers' diaries. Some enduringly popular shows such as Grasmere and Ambleside focus on traditional Cumbrian sports such as wrestling and fell-running, and others on horticultural activities, with competitions for largest vegetables or prettiest flower displays. While other shows have developed more modern traditions, the traditions of decades or even centuries ago are still paramount. Entry for the public is usually only a few pounds, and the shows offer a great flavour of life in the fells and valleys. Though most of these shows have been running on the same days for years, it's always worth checking that details haven't changed before you plan a visit.

May
Bank Holiday Sunday and Monday: Carlisle and Borders flower show
Whit Weekend: Coniston Water Festival
Last Friday to Sunday: the Great Garden Show, Holker

June

First Thursday to second Wednesday: Appleby Horse Fair
Third Sunday: Brough Hound and Terrier Show
Last Sunday: Endmoor Country Fair; Ullswater Country Fair, Patterdale

July

First Sunday: Westmorland Horticultural Show, Kendal; Langdale Gala
Second Saturday and Sunday: Appleby Annual Carnival and Sports
Third Saturday: Cumberland County Show, Carlisle; Cleator Moor Sports
Fourth Saturday: Penrith Agricultural Show; Cockermouth Agricultural Show
Second last Sunday: Coniston Country Fair
Last Thursday: Ambleside Sports; North Lonsdale Show, Ulverston

August

First Wednesday: Cartmel Agricultural Show
First Thursday: Lake District Sheepdog Trials, Staveley
First Friday to Sunday: Lowther Horse Driving Trials and Country Fair
First Saturday: Beetham Sports
Second Tuesday: Lunesdale Agricultural Show, Kirkby Lonsdale
Second Thursday: Appleby Agricultural Show; Rydal Sheepdog Trials
Second Friday to Sunday: Lowther Driving Trials and Country Show
Second Saturday: Dalston Show
Third Tuesday: Hawkshead Agricultural Show
Third Wednesday: Gosforth Agricultural Show; Threlkeld Sheepdog Trials
Third Thursday: Brough Agricultural Show
Third Saturday: Ravenstonedale Agricultural Show; Skelton Agricultural Show
Third Sunday: Langdale Country Fair; Lakeland Country Fair, Torver
Bank Holiday Sunday: Grasmere Sports and Show; Esthwaite Sheepdog Trials; Kentmere Sheepdog Trials
Bank Holiday Monday: Keswick Show; Dentdale Gala; Muncaster Fair and Sheepdog Trials
Last Wednesday: Ennerdale and Kinniside Show
Last Thursday: Burton, Milnthorpe and Carnforth Show; Crosby Ravensworth Show

September

First Saturday: Alston Show; Lowick and District Agricultural Show
Second Thursday: Westmorland County Show, Crooklands
Third Thursday: Loweswater and Brackenthwaite Agricultural Show
Third Saturday: Egremont Crab Fair
Third Sunday: Borrowdale Shepherds' Meet and Show
Last Saturday: Eskdale Show, Boot

October
First Saturday: Cockermouth Sheepdog Trials
Second Saturday: Wasdale Head Shepherds' Meet and Show
Fourth Saturday: Buttermere Shepherds' Meet and Show

November
First Saturday: Walna Scar Shepherds' Meet and Show
Second Saturday: Stoneside Shepherds' Meet and Show, Ulpha

THE CLINTONS IN THE LAKE DISTRICT

Former US president Bill Clinton proposed to his wife Hillary on the shores of Ennerdale Water in the western Lake District during a holiday in 1973. The romantic location didn't have quite the desired effect, as Hillary turned him down. She later relented though, and the Clintons married two years later in the US.

LAKE DISTRICT POEMS – 'YEARNING FOR THE LAKES' BY JOHN RUSKIN (WRITTEN AGED 14)

I weary for the fountain foaming,
For shady holm and hill,
My mind is on the mountain roaming,
My spirit's voice is still.

I weary for the woodland brook
That wanders through the vale,
I weary for the heights that look
Adown upon the dale.

The crags are lone on Coniston
And Glaramara's dell,
And dreary on the mighty one
The cloud enwreathed Sca-fell.

Oh, what although the crags are stern,
Their mighty peaks that sever,
Fresh flies the breeze on mountain fern
And free on mountain heather.

I long to tread the mountain head
Above the valley swelling,
I long to feel the breezes sped
From grey and gaunt Helvellyn.

There is a thrill of strange delight
That passes quivering o'er me,
When blue hills rise upon the sight
Like summer clouds before me.

WEATHER ADVICE FOR THE FELLWALKER

Weather lore has plenty of proverbs to help walkers predict what kind
of a day they have in store. Since many of them seem to have no basis
in science and indeed contradict one another, and since the Lake
District often seems to possess its own micro-climate, they should be
treated with a great deal of caution! The last two of these ten proverbs
are perhaps most appropriate to the Lake District walker.

Rain before seven, fine for eleven,
Evening red and morning grey, two sure signs of one fine day.

When grass is dry at morning light,
Look for rain before the night.

The sudden storm lasts not three hours,
The sharper the blast the sooner 'tis past.

The farther the sight, the nearer the rain.

Sun sets on Friday clear as bell,
Rain on Monday sure as hell.

A ring around the sun or moon,
Means that rain will come real soon.

Red sky at night is a shepherd's delight,
Red sky at night, shepherds take warning.

The sharper the blast, the sooner it's past.

He that is weather wise, is seldom other wise

Whether the weather be hot
Or whether the weather be not
We'll weather the weather whatever the weather
Whether we like it or not!

LAKE DISTRICT FOOD – SARAH NELSON'S GRASMERE GINGERBREAD

If the fells and poetry are the sights and sounds that define the Lake District, then the smell that best evokes it for many is that of Sarah Nelson's famous Grasmere gingerbread.

Nelson, born in Bowness in 1815, came from a poor family but worked hard to become an accomplished cook. When she moved into a Grasmere cottage—formerly a tiny school run by the village church—she started selling her gingerbread to passing travellers, and it quickly developed a reputation as the best around. When she died in 1904, the shop passed to her great-niece, and it has baked and sold gingerbread continuously since. Though output has increased dramatically and new machinery and products introduced, much of the small cottage looks much the same as when Nelson lived there.

The shop bakes its gingerbread fresh every day, and approaching visitors are likely to smell it well before they see it. The gingerbread is thin, flat and closer in texture and appearance to a biscuit than to a bread or cake, with a buttery, warmly spiced flavour, at once crunchy and chewy. It can be eaten on its own or served with a scoop of vanilla ice cream, slices of melon, a crisp pear or plenty of other fruits. It's a good accompaniment to creamy cheeses such as brie and makes a good topping mix for crumbles or base for a cheesecake when broken into crumbs.

A recipe for gingerbread

Sarah Nelson's recipe is a closely-guarded secret, locked securely away in the NatWest bank safe in Ambleside. Nothing beats the real thing, but this is a fair approximation.

250g plain flour
150g butter
150g soft brown sugar
2 teaspoons ground ginger
Half teaspoon bicarbonate of soda
1 tablespoon golden syrup

Melt the butter with the syrup. Combine the other ingredients and bind together well with the melted butter and syrup. Spread the mixture thinly in a large tin lined with baking parchment and greased. Bake in a low to moderate oven (gas mark 4) for 30 minutes. Mark into pieces with a knife, and sprinkle over a little more mixed brown sugar and ground ginger. Leave to cool. The gingerbread will keep for a few days.

TEN ROMAN REMAINS

Evidence of four centuries of industrious work by the Romans can be found all over Cumbria. Here are ten of the most interesting reminders of their presence.

Ambleside Fort. Sited at the head of Windermere near Ambleside on the important Cumbrian trade routes, this fort has well-preserved foundations. Known to the Romans as Galava.

Birdoswald Fort. One of the best-preserved Roman forts on Hadrian's Wall, just inside Cumbria near Brampton. Looked after by English Heritage, which also runs a visitor centre.

Bowness Fort. Sited at the far western end of Hadrian's Wall, this was the second biggest fort along its stretch and known as Maia—larger.

Brougham Fort. Remains of this fort, known as Brocavum, can be found just south of Penrith. The site also has remains of the castle built nearby, and there is a display of Roman objects found in excavations.

Hadrian's Wall. The most important Roman monument in Britain as well as Cumbria, and the most vivid reminder of the empire's power. Enters the county near Carlisle and ends at Bowness-on-Solway.

Hardknott Fort. The most spectacularly located Roman fort, perched in the fells above the old pass connecting Ambleside and Ravenglass. The walls and parade ground are well preserved. Known to the Romans as Mediobogdum—'the fort in the middle of the bend'.

High Street. Old Roman road connecting forts in the north and south of the Lake District. Now a spectacular ridge route over the fells for walkers, passing over the fell of the same name.

Maryport Fort. A heavily excavated fort, now more notable for the nearby Senhouse museum which includes one of the biggest collections of Roman objects in the country.

Papcastle Fort. Located near Cockermouth and known as Carvetiorum. Discovered when a local resident dug up remains, and excavated by Channel 4's Time Team in 1999.

Ravenglass Fort. Most of the Glannaventa fort is now gone, but the bath house is one of the biggest surviving Roman buildings in the country. Ravenglass was an important naval base for the Romans.

AN 18TH CENTURY LAKE DISTRICT DINNER

Joseph Budworth's *A Fortnight's Ramble to the Lakes*, first published in 1792, was one of the earliest Lake District tour memoirs. In it, Budworth recalls 'as good and well-dressed a dinner as a man could wish' at Grasmere, and notes its contents—obtained for ten pence a head.

Roast pike, stuffed
Boiled fowl
Veal-cutlets
Ham
Beans and bacon
Cabbage
Pease and potatoes
Anchovy sauce
Parsley and butter
Plain butter
Butter and cheese
Wheat bread and oat cake
Preserved gooseberries and cream

A WILLIAM WORDSWORTH TRAIL

Ten locations in Cumbria closely associated with the Lake District's most famous poet.

Wordsworth House, Cockermouth. Where William was born on 7th April 1770. Tel 01900 820884 or online at www.wordsworthhouse.org.uk.

Market Square, Penrith. Wordsworth spent much unhappy time in childhood at his grandparents' home here. The house is now an outfitters, Arnisons.

The Old Grammar School, Hawkshead. Where Wordsworth was educated from 1779 to 1787, now home to a small museum. Overlooking it is the church he attended. Tel 015394 36735.

Ann Tyson's Cottage, Hawkshead. Where Wordsworth stayed while at school. Now a private residence.

Dove Cottage, Grasmere. Wordsworth's home between 1799 and 1808, and a place where he was at his most productive. Now the principal Lake District shrine to Wordsworth. Tel 015394 35544 or online at www.wordsworth.org.uk.

Gowbarrow Park, Ullswater. Where, in 1802, Wordsworth saw the daffodils that prompted his most famous poem, 'I Wandered Lonely as a Cloud'.

Allan Bank, Grasmere. Wordsworth moved here with his wife and three children in 1808. It is now a private house and not open to the public.

The Old Rectory, Grasmere. Family home for a short while from 1810. Two of Wordsworth's children died during the time here.

Rydal Mount, near Ambleside. Family home from 1813 to 1859. The nearby churchyard contains Dora's Field, dedicated by Wordsworth to his daughter. Tel 015394 33002 or online at www.rydalmount.co.uk.

St Oswald's Church, Grasmere. Wordsworth's final resting place.

WHERE THE OLD COUNTIES MEET

The three old counties of Cumbria—Cumberland, Westmorland and parts of Lancashire—used to meet at a point in the heart of the Lake District along the Wrynose Pass. The spot was marked by three stones inscribed W, C and L and, later, by a pillar known as the Three Shire Stone. It was first erected in 1860 but had to be repaired after it was smashed in a car accident in 1997.

LITERARY LAKELANDERS – SUSANNA BLAMIRE

Susanna Blamire is perhaps the best known and respected of poets writing in the Cumberland dialect, and one of the most important female writers of her time.

Born in 1747 into a good Cumberland family, Blamire's parents died when she was young, and she was raised by an aunt at Stockdalewath, south of Carlisle. She wrote poetry from an early age and was also an accomplished musician, soon becoming known variously as the 'Muse of Cumberland' and the 'Poet of Friendship'. Her poetry was firmly in the oral tradition, written to be sung and performed rather than read from a book. She wrote largely for the pleasure of her family and friends, and her work was only occasionally distributed in manuscript or songbook form. Much of it is thought not to have survived on paper, and what remains was not collected in a book until 1842, nearly 50 years after her death.

Blamire's poems are rooted in Cumberland, celebrating country life and its people and places. She had an excellent eye and ear for local stories, incidents and characters, and her poems are humorous, lively and affectionate snapshots of 18th century life. After living for several years in Scotland, Blamire wrote extensively in the Scottish dialect too; she was a contemporary of Robert Burns, though there is no evidence that they knew one another's work. But as well as being a composer of local ballads, Blamire was also a sophisticated lyrical poet whose accomplished work in standard English helped to usher in the Romantic era of verse.

Though she was little known in her lifetime south of Cumbria, Blamire's reputation has grown over the years, and her poems are now available in several editions. Her stock has also risen as Cumbria seeks to celebrate and preserve its distinctive dialect—and there are few better exponents of it than Blamire.

THE 214 TOPS

214 is a magic number for many Lake District walkers. It is the number of peaks over 1,000 feet that are recorded, sketched and described by Alfred Wainwright in his classic seven-volume *Pictorial Guides to the Lakeland Fells*. Wainwright, of course, climbed them all during his research, many of them several times over. Because walkers by nature relish a good challenge and a list of peaks to bag, emulating Wainwright's feat has become a popular obsession.

Climbing to the top of all 214 fells is the achievement of a lifetime for many, while others set themselves a year or even a summer to complete the set. The Wainwright Society now holds a register of walkers who have walked all 214, and in 2005 it organised a mass climb by its members of all the fells to celebrate the 50th anniversary of the publication of the first of the *Pictorial Guides*. For good measure, it added 56 more tops that featured in Wainwright's guide to the outlying fells.

The 214 peaks challenge has also been embraced by fell runners. One of the legends of the sport, Wasdale farmer Joss Naylor, holds the record for the fastest round of the Wainwright fells, notched up in a scarcely believable six days, 23 hours and 11 minutes from first summit to last. He tells the story of his lunatic achievement in a pamphlet, *Joss Naylor MBE Was Here*, which is now out of print but well worth scouring second-hand bookshops for. It is just one of Naylor's numerous records, made even more extraordinary by the fact that he ran the 214 fells at the age of 50, as a novel way of celebrating his milestone birthday.

A no less remarkable round of the 214 Wainwrights was completed by Jordan Ross in October 2006 when he reached the top of Castle Crag. Plenty of people have completed a full set quicker than the five years it took Jordan, but no one has done it at a younger age—he was just nine years and seven months when he reached the magic number, and still in the cub scouts. His first fell was Cat Bells aged four years and three months, and his favourite one Blencathra. Earlier in 2006, Ellen Regan, aged nine years and ten months, completed all 214 peaks when she climbed Scafell Pike—but her challenge clearly spurred on her even younger rival.

In alphabetical order, Wainwright's 214 peaks are:

Allen Crags, Angletarn Pikes, Ard Crags, Armboth Fell, Arnison Crag, Arthur's Pike

Bakestall, Bannerdale Crags, Barf, Barrow, Base Brown, Beda Fell, Binsey, Birkhouse Moor, Birks, Black Crag, Blake Fell, Blea Rigg, Bleaberry Fell, Blencathra, Bonscale Pike, Bowfell, Bowscale Fell, Brae Fell, Brandreth, Branstree, Brim Fell, Brock Crags, Broom Fell, Buckbarrow, Burnbank Fell

Calf Crag, Carl Side, Carrock Fell, Castle Crag, Cat Bells, Catstye Cam, Caudale Moor, Causey Pike, Caw Fell, Clough Head, Cold Pike, Coniston Old Man, Crag Fell, Crinkle Crags

Dale Head, Dodd, Dollywagon Pike, Dove Crag, Dow Crag

Eagle Crag, Eel Frag, Esk Pike

Fairfield, Fellbarrow, Fleetwith Pike, Froswick

Gavel Fell, Gibson Knott, Glaramara, Glenridding Dodd, Gowbarrow Fell, Grange Fell, Grasmoor, Gray Crag, Graystones, Great Borne, Great Calva, Great Carrs, Great Cockup, Great Crag, Great Dodd,

Great End, Great Gable, Great Mell Fell, Great Rigg, Great Scafell, Green Crag, Green Gable, Grey Crag, Grey Friar, Grey Knotts, Grike, Grisedale Pike

Hallin Fell, Hard Knott, Harrison Stickle, Hart Crag, Hart Side, Harter Fell (Eskdale), Harter Fell (Mardale), Hartsop Above How, Hartsop Dodd, Haycock, Haystacks, Helm Crag, Helvellyn, Hen Comb, Heron Pike, High Crag, High Hartsop Dodd, High Pike (Caldbeck), High Pike (Scandale), High Raise (Langdale), High Raise (Martindale), High Rigg, High Seat, High Spy, High Stile, High Street, High Tove, Hindscarth, Holme Fell, Hopegill Head

Ill Bell, Illgill Head

Kentmere Pike, Kidsty Pike, Kirk Fell, Knott, Knott Rigg, The Knott

Lank Rigg, Latrigg, Ling Fell, Lingmell, Lingmoor Fell, Little Hart Crag, Little Mell Fell, Loadpot Hill, Loft Crag, Long Side, Longlands Fell, Lonscale Fell, Lord's Seat, Loughrigg Fell, Low Fell, Low Pike

Maiden Moor, Mardale Ill Bell, Meal Fell, Mellbreak, Middle Dodd, Middle Fell, Mungrisdale Common

Nab Scar, The Nab, Nethermost Pike

Outerside

Pavey Ark, Pike O'Blisco, Pike O'Stickle, Pillar, Place Fell

Raise, Rampsgill Head, Rannerdale Knotts, Raven Crag, Red Pike (Buttermere), Red Pike (Wasdale), Red Screes, Rest Dodd, Robinson, Rossett Pike, Rosthwaite Fell

Sail, St Sunday Crag, Sale Fell, Sallows, Scafell, Scafell Pike, Scar Crags, Scoat Fell, Seat Sandal, Seatallan, Seathwaite Fell, Selside Pike, Sergeant Man, Sergeant's Crag, Sheffield Pike, Shipman Knotts, Silver How, Skiddaw, Skiddaw Little Man, Slight Side, Sour Howes, Souther Fell, Starling Dodd, Steel Fell, Steel Knotts, Steeple, Stone Arthur, Stybarrow Dodd, Swirl How

Tarn Crag (Easdale), Tarn Crag (Longsleddale), Thornthwaite Crag, Thunacar Knott, Troutbeck Tongue

Ullock Pike, Ullscarf

Walla Crag, Wandope, Wansfell, Watson's Dodd, Wether Hill, Wetherlam, Whin Rigg, Whinlatter, White Side, Whiteless Pike, Whiteside

Yewbarrow, Yoke

ENGLAND'S HIGHEST RACE TRACK

The eastern Lake District fell of High Street, named after the Roman road that ran over it, was home in the 18th and 19th centuries to annual summer fairs and shepherds' meets. The celebrations would include wrestling and games, and the long flat summit also made it very suitable for some raucous racing of horses. At 828m or 2,720 feet, it is undoubtedly the highest racing venue in the country.

The tradition of fairs and racing died out around the 1830s, but the summit of High Street is still known and marked on Ordnance Survey maps as Racecourse Hill, and fell ponies are occasionally grazed there. Modern-day race courses in Cumbria can now be found at Carlisle and Cartmel, where summer meets bring thousands of spectators flooding in to the picturesque village.

PASSES IN THE LAKE DISTRICT

The Lake District has more than 30 passes through the fells, but only a handful are accessible by road. The highest of them is the Kirkstone Pass, but on foot Mickledore, connecting Scafell and Scafell Pike, has nearly twice its altitude at 2,760 feet or 840m.

These are the road passes reaching 1,000 feet in height. (Other passes including the Newlands Pass and the Pass of the Dunmail Raise do not quite reach this altitude.)

Kirkstone Pass. Links Ullswater and Patterdale to Windermere and Ambleside and reaches a height of around 1,480 feet (450m). The pass has been cut off by the snow for weeks on end in the past.

Honister Pass. Connecting Seatoller and Buttermere, the pass was constructed in 1934 and is subject to some ferocious winds at times. Rises up to 1,100 feet (330m).

Wrynose Pass and Hardknott Pass. Link Eskdale and Little Langdale via some tortuous bends, meeting in the middle at Cockley Beck. Each reaches 1,300 feet (390m).

Whinlatter Pass. Links Keswick to Cockermouth via Whinlatter Forest. Reaches a height of 1,000 feet (305m).

LAKE DISTRICT POEMS – 'ON BLACK COMBE' BY BRANWELL BRONTË

Far off, and half revealed, 'mid shade and light,
Black Combe half smiles, half frowns; his mighty form
Scarce bending into peace, more formed to fight
A thousand years of struggles with a storm
Than bask one hour subdued by sunshine warm
To bright and breezeless rest; yet even his height
Towers not o'er this world's sympathies; he smiles –
While many a human heart to pleasure's wiles
Can bear to bend, and still forget to rise –
As though he, huge and heath-clad on our sight
Again rejoices in his stormy skies.
Man loses vigour in unstable joys.
Thus tempests find Black Combe invincible,
While we are lost, who should know life so well.

LAKELAND BOOKS OF THE YEAR

The Lake District has as rich a literary heritage as any county in England, and since 1984 books on the area have had their own award. The Lakeland Book of the Year prize was set up by writer Hunter Davies, whose 30 or so books include many about the Lake District. The prize has expanded in recent years to take in different categories and new sponsors, but Davies' prize remains the most prestigious. Here are the winners since its inception.

1984   *AA and OS Guide to the Lake District* (AA / Ordnance
        Survey) and
        William Green of Ambleside by Mary Burkett and David
        Sloss (Abbot Hall)
1985   *Fellwalking with Wainwright*
        by Alfred Wainwright and Derry Brabbs (Frances Lincoln)
1986/7 *Lakeland from the Air* by Peter Thornton (Dalesman) and
        Walking with a Camera in Herries' Lakeland
        by Trevor Hayward (Fountain Press)
1988   *The Bondage of Love: A Life of Mrs Samuel Taylor Coleridge*
        by Molly Lefebure (Gollancz)
1989   *Country Diary* by Enid Wilson (Hodder)

1990	*Dream Gardens: A Magical Corner of England* by Vivian Russell (Trafalgar Square)
1991	*The Diaries of Lady Anne Clifford* by Anne Clifford (Sutton)
1992	*Coleridge Walks the Fells* by Alan Hankinson (Flamingo)
1993	*Rocky Rambler's Wild Walks* by Ian Peters (Lake District National Park Authority)
1994	*A Literary Guide to the Lake District* by Grevel Lindop (Sigma Press)
1995	*The Tale of Mrs William Heelis - Beatrix Potter* by John Heelis (Sutton)
1996	*Cumbrian Women Remember: Lake District Life in the Early 1900s* by June Thistlethwaite (Thyme Press)
1997	*An American President's Love Affair with the English Lake District* by Andrew Wilson (Lakeland Press Agency)
1998	*Percy Kelly: A Cumbrian Artist* by Mary Burkett and Valerie Rickerby (Skiddaw Press)
1999	*Sam Bough RSA: The Rivers in Bohemia* by Gil and Pat Hitchon (The Book Guild)
2000	*The Coniston Tigers: 70 Years of Mountain Adventure* by A Harry Griffin (Sigma Press)
2001	*Rex Malden's Whitehaven* by John and Eilean Malden (Try Malden)
2002	*Cumbrian Mining* by Ian Tyler (Blue Rock)
2003	*The Breeding Birds of Cumbria* by Malcolm Stott et al (Cumbria Bird Club)
2004	*Lakeland Life in the 1940s and 50s* ed Martin Varley (Halsgrove)
2005	*The Lake Artists' Society: A Centenary Celebration* by Jane Renouf (Lake Artists' Society)
2006	*The Garden at Levens* by Chris Crowder (Frances Lincoln)

THE MYSTERIOUS CREATURES OF THE LAKE DISTRICT

Most regions of the UK have recorded sightings of mysterious unidentified creatures, but the Lake District seems to attract more than most.

South Cumbrian newspaper the *Westmorland Gazette* has reported around 50 sightings of a large, black, cat-like animal in the last decade, many of them in relatively urban areas of the county including Kendal and Windermere. Spotters claim that they resembled either panthers or pumas, and several blurry photos have been produced to support the sightings. Specialists suggest that small populations of these animals could sustain themselves in countryside such as the Lake District, feeding on wildlife or livestock. The government's Department for Environment, Food and Rural Affairs is a bit more sceptical, saying that it holds no physical evidence of any non-native cats in Cumbria or anywhere else in the UK and suggesting that sightings may have been mistaken for large domestic cats.

Other legendary creatures include the 'Wild Dog of Ennerdale', an animal responsible for savaging hundreds of sheep in the remote valley in 1810. The creature—often called the 'Girt [great] Dog' in the local dialect—evaded capture from pursuing farmers for months in the remote valley, leading some to think it had supernatural powers, before it was finally shot and killed near the River Ehen. It was reported to weigh eight stones, and was displayed in Keswick for some time afterwards. Witnesses claimed variously that it had drunk the blood of its victims and eaten their internal organs, and some of its physical descriptions match the thylacine, a wolf-like marsupial that featured in some travelling circuses of the time.

NATIONAL NATURE RESERVES

Cumbria has 25 sites designated as National Nature Reserves—more than any other county. These sites are nationally important areas of wildlife habitat and receive extra protection to make sure that their wildlife is protected and cultivated. National Nature Reserves are managed by English Nature or its approved bodies and cover every type of vegetation, from cliffs to marshes to woodlands. Cumbria's reserves are:

Bassenthwaite Lake	North Walney
Blelham Bog	Park Wood
Clawthorpe Fell	Roudsea Wood and Mosses
Cliburn Moss	Rusland Moss
Drumburgh Moss	Sandscale Haws
Duddon Mosses	Sandybeck Meadow
Finglandrigg Woods	Smardale Gill
Gowk Bank	South Solway Mosses
Great Ashby Scar	Tarn Moss
Hallsenna Moor	Thornhill Moss and Meadows
High Leys	Walton Moss
Moor House-Upper-Teesdale	Whitbarrow
North Fen	

TEN LAKE DISTRICT ARTISTS

The Lake District has always been as great a lure for artists as for writers. It was a key part of the classic domestic tour of England that rivalled the European Grand Tour that so inspired writers and artists in the 17th, 18th and early 19th centuries, and many painters used the landscapes of the Lakes to perfect their techniques. The dramatic, contrasting scenery has prompted many fine paintings, some of which can be seen in galleries including the Abbot Hall Art Gallery in Kendal, the Tullie House Museum and Art Gallery in Carlisle and the Keswick Museum and Art Gallery. Here are ten artists who either lived in the Lake District or made important visits.

William Bellers (dates uncertain). Artist of what are probably the first Lake District scenes to be published.

George Romney (1734–1802). Born near Dalton-in-Furness and apprenticed in Kendal, Romney was a famous portrait painter of his day and a contemporary of Reynolds and Gainsborough.

William Green (1760–1823). Detailed observer of Lakeland scenes with a studio in Keswick.

JMW Turner (1775–1851). Romantic landscape painter who used several Lake District visits to perfect his techniques.

Thomas Girtin (1775–1802). Watercolour artist and friend of Turner whose Lake District scenes advanced his reputation before his death from consumption aged just 27.

John Constable (1776–1837). Perhaps England's most famous landscape artist, he spent two weeks in the Lake District in 1806.

Alfred Heaton Cooper (1864–1929). Prolific landscape artist who moved to the Lake District to sell his work to tourists. His Grasmere studio still stands and now sells art and painters' equipment.

Kurt Schwitters (1887–1948). German abstract artist and an acknowledged master of collage. After the Second World War he came to live in Ambleside and worked on an installation in Elterwater, funded by the New York Museum of Modern Art. He died in Kendal and was originally buried in Ambleside, though he was later disinterred and reburied in Germany.

Winifred Nicholson (1893–1981). Modern impressionist with a mastery of light who lived near Lanercost for the second half of her life.

William Heaton Cooper (1903–1995). Son of Alfred and one of the best-known painters of the Lakeland fells, he was among the first to use new reproduction techniques to sell prints of his watercolours in large quantities.

WAINWRIGHT'S SIX BEST PLACES

Alfred Wainwright revealed his 'six best places for a fellwalker to be'—
excluding the summits of fells—in the seventh and final volume of his
Pictorial Guides to the Lakeland Fells.

Striding Edge on Helvellyn
The first col of Lord's Rake on Scafell
Mickledore on Scafell
Sharp Edge on Blencathra
The South Traverse of Great Gable
The Shamrock Traverse on Pillar

HOW TO WORK OUT THE WIND CHILL ON THE FELLS

Winds on the Lake District fells can make the temperature seem
much lower than the forecast suggests it ought to be. This is the wind
chill—the temperature that is felt on exposed skin rather than the air
measurement. Lots of different methods have been used to measure
and index wind chill, but the Met Office in the UK currently uses a
Canadian algorithm based on up-to-date research. The formula is:

Wind Chill = 35.74 + 0.6215T – 35.75(V0.16)+ 0.4275(V0.16)
Where T is the air temperature in degrees Fahrenheit and
V is the wind speed in miles per hour

This table shows the wind chill according to the air temperature and
wind. With an air temperature of 30°F and wind of 40mph, for instance,
the wind chill is 13°F. Frostbite can set in in less than 30 minutes if the
wind chill falls beneath -18°F (-28°C).

Wind/mph

Air temp/°F	10	20	30	40	50	60
50 (10°C)	46	44	42	41	40	39
40 (4)	34	30	38	27	26	25
30 (-1)	21	17	15	13	12	10
20 (-7)	9	4	1	-1	-3	-4

SHEEPDOG TRIALS

Sheepdogs are as much a part of the Lake District landscape as the Herdwicks they work with, and Cumbria is one of the UK's heartlands for trials of them.

The intricacies of sheepdog trials can seem baffling to the uninitiated, but the skills of the dogs are clear for all to see. Essentially, sheepdogs—usually Border Collies in the Lake District—have to move sheep around a field via fences, gates and enclosures, as directed by their shepherds. Dogs are usually sent to retrieve up to six sheep about a quarter of a mile away, and must return them to their pen via a series of obstacles. These can include separating some sheep from the herd, following a straight line across the field, or loading sheep on to a vehicle, all the time directed and cajoled by their handler. They must also drive sheep away from their handler—something that is usually against dogs' instincts and so a good test of their abilities.

The speed with which the course is completed is sometimes important, but more crucial are the obedience of the dogs and the accuracy with which they follow the course. Judges award and deduct points for different elements of the course, with the highest aggregate score winning. Trials can often be quite competitive, and were featured on the BBC's *One Man and His Dog* show for nearly 15 years until the late 1990s, since when the show has been occasionally revived.

Trials have been popular for centuries, and are thought to have started in the Borders between England and Scotland. The first recorded trial is usually accepted to have been held in Wales in 1873, but records of events in the Lake District began soon afterwards, and they have since been a showcase for the skills of the dogs, their handlers and breeders in the region. The International Sheepdog Society was formed in 1906 and organises international and continental European trials as well as four national trials in England, Scotland, Wales and Northern Ireland. Trials in the Lake District are a part of many of the region's annual agricultural and sporting shows, and there are dedicated trials at Caldbeck, Keswick, Ings, Patterdale, Rydal, Staveley and Winderemere among other places.

Sheepdog lingo

Away drive Herding sheep away from the handler rather than towards him.

Bring The act of returning sheep towards the handler or pen.

Cast A dog's outward run to retrieve the sheep.

Cross drive Moving the sheep in a straight line in front of the handler.

Eye-dog A dog that can control sheep by its head movement alone.

Lift The act of retrieving the sheep. A *double lift* involves the retrieval of two separate groups of sheep.

Penning Herding the sheep into a pen or enclosure.

Shedding Separating some marked sheep from the group.

Singling Separating one sheep from the group.

Timed out Unable to complete the course in the allotted time.

… and some sheepdog commands

Away Go anti-clockwise around the sheep.

Balance Position so that the sheep move towards the handler.

Come by Go clockwise around the sheep.

Come or **here** Move towards the handler.

Easy Slow down.

Get back Retreat to give the sheep more room.

Stand Stop and remain on feet.

That'll do Stop and return.

There Stop and wait for instructions.

Walk up Move towards the sheep.

STAYING SAFE ON THE FELLS

Some mountain advice from the rescue teams.

Plan and prepare. Check the weather forecast, consider the experience and ability of anyone walking with you, and learn first aid.

Take suitable footwear and clothing. Boots should have a treaded sole and clothing should be warm, windproof and waterproof. Take spare warm clothing as it is always colder on the tops of the fells.

Pack food and drink. Take energy restorers like chocolate or Kendal mint cake, and make sure you have reserves for emergencies.

Look after your party. Take special care of the weakest walkers. If you're walking on your own, let people know your route and expected time of return.

Get the right equipment. A map, compass, watch, whistle and torch are all essential.

Beware of the dangers. Look out for precipices, steep slopes, icy or wet paths, unstable boulders and streams in spate.

Keep alert. Watch for weather changes, signs of exhaustion and the time—darkness can fall quickly.

Don't be too proud. Turn back if you have any concerns about what's ahead.

THE BORDER WARS

Cumbria has been a battleground for the English and the Scots over the centuries, and strife between the two has been a major influence on the county's history.

Ownership of Cumbria switched frequently from English hands to Scottish during the late Middle Ages, and periods of peace only occasionally interrupted centuries of warfare until the union of the crowns at the end of the 16th century, by which time the wars had wreaked devastation across the Border region, to monasteries, castles, churches and towns as well as upon the rural people. The savagery of the royal-led forces on both sides was brutal.

But the violence of the armies was at least matched by that of rival clans or alliances of families on both sides of the Borders, who fought one another in feuds that often lasted centuries. The Border 'Reivers' would raid rivals' livestock or other possessions, and the remote, rugged nature of the territory meant it was virtually impossible to police. Reivers were loyal to their families rather than their kings, making the violence virtually indiscriminate and the area lawless. Raids were most common in the winter, when the long nights provided cover of darkness and animals were at their fattest after a summer feeding. Wealthier Cumbrian families caught up in the warfare built pele towers and bastles to protect themselves—many examples of them can still be seen across the county—but poorer people had no such defences.

The surnames of some of the Border Reivers are still common in Cumbria today. The conflicts also inspired a genre of Border Ballads— atmospheric stories from the wars that were sung unaccompanied and that are still proudly performed in some places today. The Reivers also give their name to a popular cycle route that traces the battlegrounds of the 15th and 16th centuries across the Border region. The Reivers Cycle Route stretches 171 miles from Tynemouth on the east coast to Whitehaven on the west.

SOME VICTORIAN CURIOSITIES ON DISPLAY AT THE KESWICK MUSEUM

'The musical stones', a 14-foot long, one-tonne xylophone
made from slate, played for Queen Victoria in 1848
A naturally mummified 500 year-old cat
A four-metre scale model of the Lake District
Robert Southey's clogs
Napoleon's teacup
The skin of a giant cobra
Victorian roller blades
John Peel's rocking chair
A spoon made from the leg bone of a sheep
A man trap

Keswick Museum and Art Gallery is located in the town's Fitz Park and
is open from April to October. Admission is free. The museum also has
interesting collections relating to the history of the Lake District and
its industries, plus collections of work by William Wordsworth, Robert
Southey and Hugh Walpole.

TEN GARDENS

Cumbria is home to dozens of majestic gardens, both private and
public; here are ten of the best. Check opening times when planning a
visit, as many are open only for part of the year.

Acorn Bank, near Penrith. National Trust sheltered garden with more
than 250 varieties of herbs and some old English fruits. Tel 017683
61893 or online at www.nationaltrust.org.uk.

Brantwood, Coniston. Garden by the fells and Coniston Water laid out
by John Ruskin in the 1870s. Extensive displays of bulbs and ferns. Tel
015394 41396 or online at www.brantwood.org.uk.

Dalemain, near Penrith. Tranquil garden with lovely rose walk, part of
a Georgian estate close to Ullswater. Tel 017684 86450 or online at
www.dalemain.com.

Graythwaite Hall, near Windermere. Mix of formal and informal
gardens with rhododendrums and azaleas, designed by renowned
landscape architect Thomas Mawson. Tel 015395 31273 or online at
www.graythwaitehall.co.uk.

Holehird, near Troutbeck Bridge. Ten acres of gardens above Windermere, voluntarily maintained by the Lakeland Horticultural Society. Voted one of the nation's favourite gardens by BBC TV's *Gardener's World* viewers. Tel 015394 46008 or online at www.hole-hirdgardens.org.uk.

Holker Hall, near Cark-in-Cartmel. Woodland and formal Victorian gardens over 25 acres. Stages a garden festival each June. Tel 015395 58328 or online at www.holker-hall.co.uk.

Levens Hall, near Kendal. Formal Elizabethan gardens with world-renowned topiary, 15,000 plants and plenty of walks.Tel 015395 60321 or online at www.levenshall.co.uk.

Mirehouse, near Keswick. Carefully restored gardens close to Bassenthwaite Lake, with children's play areas and a bee garden. Tel 017687 72287 or online at www.mirehouse.com.

Muncaster Castle, Ravenglass. Ancient woods, trails and Europe's oldest collection of rhododendrums, set beneath Scafell Pike.Tel 01229 717614 or online at www.muncaster.co.uk.

Sizergh Castle, Kendal. Lakes, limestone rock garden and views over the fells and Morecambe Bay, set in the sprawling estate of a fine medieval house.Tel 015395 60070 or online at www.nationaltrust.org.uk.

HELVELLYN'S MEMORIALS

Walkers climbing Helvellyn are often alarmed by the number of memorials along the way. There are three monuments—two commemorating men who died on the fell, and one honouring a couple who got off it safely.

The **Dixon Memorial** along Striding Edge remembers Robert Dixon of Patterdale, who died there in 1858 while following the Patterdale Foxhounds.

The **Aeroplane Stone** close to the summit shelter honours the first ever landing of an aircraft on a British mountain in 1926. The plane landed on the top at 80mph, stopping 30 yards short of the edge. The two-man crew rested on the summit for a while before taking off again.

The **Gough Memorial Stone** on the summit ridge honours Charles Gough, who fell to his death in 1805 while trying to cross from Patterdale to Wythburn. His dog remained with the body until it was found three months later, an act of loyalty that inspired poets including William Wordsworth and Sir Walter Scott.

MARTIN CAMPBELL'S FAVOURITE WATERFALLS

Martin Campbell is a professional photographer and waterfall enthusiast who has combined his passions in an e-book, *42 Lakeland Waterfalls*. He has established a brave tradition of 'head dipping' in waterfalls during and after his walks across the Lake District, and has become an expert on the best falls in the area. His book was the result of a commission for the Waterhead Hotel in Ambleside, which now carries his waterfall photographs in each of its rooms. His website at www.lakedistrict-images.com has more examples of his work and details of how to obtain his photographs. Here are his ten favourite waterfalls in the Lake District.

The Cascades, Aira Beck, Ullswater
(Ordnance Survey grid reference NY 400212)

Most people visit Aira Force but miss the stunning set of falls and cascades above this iconic waterfall. They are best walked in the autumn sunshine. Take one bank on the way up and return on the other to make a great round trip.

Dob Gill, Thirlmere (NY 314137)

Probably the most picturesque of the Lakeland falls, best visited on a sunny day. The falls cascade down dark black rocks, under a canopy of trees. There are dark pools and beautiful ribbon cascades, set off by shaded trees and elegant ferns. You have to leave the normal path to find it, so follow your ears.

Dungeon Ghyll, Great Langdale (NY 291067)

Dungeon Ghyll falls into an enclosed green pool. How close you can get to it depends on the conditions, as a huge boulder straddles the ravine. In dry conditions you can reach the base of the falls, but take care. You will get wet, but it's worth the effort!

Esk Gorge Falls, Eskdale (NY 228036)

The river Esk, its falls and emerald green pools get better and better as you walk further in, ending at the stunning Esk Gorge Falls. Save this walk for a sunny day—it's one of the best in the Lakes.

Fisher Place Gill, Thirlmere (NY 323182)

This impressive waterfall has three main sections. It's worth climbing to the top falls, particularly when in full spate. The middle part falls into a circular plunge pool and the viewing platform is quite exposed, so take care. Picnic in the sunshine under the trees by the river, just above the aqueduct.

Lingcove Beck, Eskdale (NY 228038)

These falls can be visited when exploring Esk Gorge. The main upper fall strikes a large black rock before flowing into its pool, while the lower falls empty into a stunning emerald green basin.

Measand Beck, Haweswater (NY 486155)

Collectively known as the Forces, this small but beautiful area is well worth visiting on a sunny day. Explore the pools, falls and cascades, and bring a picnic.

Scale Force, Buttermere (NY 151172)

Lakeland's longest vertical drop is located inside a sheer, moss-covered fissure. Easy viewing can be had upstream of the bridge. After dropping 35m vertically, the lower section falls a further 2m, elegantly cascading into a pool, then flowing under the bridge into Crummock Water.

Sour Milk Gill, Seathwaite (NY 226123)

Amongst trees, the 12m lower section is very impressive. The middle section has numerous falls and cascades, mostly visible from the road. You can stay close to this fall while climbing and scrambling a considerable height to the top.

Stickle Ghyll, Great Langdale (NY 291070)

It's a great walk to Stickle Tarn, but make sure you get up close and personal with the lower sections of Stickle Ghyll. The falls are pretty and you can do some gorge walking early on, while the upper falls are more serious and larger. It's a river with great character that has the added bonus of a cracking pub at the bottom.

THE LAKE DISTRICT'S HIGHEST PUB

The highest public house in the Lake District is the Kirkstone Pass Inn at 1,480 feet (450m). It is perched at the top of the Kirkstone Pass linking Ullswater and Windermere, and has in the past been cut off for days or even weeks on end by snow. The pub is the third highest in England, behind the Tan Hill Inn in North Yorkshire (1,730 feet or 530m) and the Cat and Fiddle Inn in Cheshire (1,690 feet or 515m).

LITERARY LAKELANDERS – HARRIET MARTINEAU

Harriet Martineau is probably the Lake District's second most celebrated female author after Beatrix Potter, and was renowned in her day as a journalist, philosopher, economist and feminist.

Martineau was born in Norwich in 1802 and took up writing after the death of her father and the loss of the family's income. She first found success in the early 1830s with an accessible series of stories on politics and economics for the ordinary reader, and moved to London where she became part of the literary circle of the time. After a trip to America that inspired more journalism and novels and began her lifelong support of the abolition of slavery, she became poorly while travelling in Europe and returned home, though she refused a Civil List pension because she thought it would compromise her writing. She remained unmarried and independent for the whole of her life.

Having spent several years recovering from her illness, Martineau moved to the Lake District for its quiet and serenity in 1845, building herself a home, 'The Knoll', at Ambleside. She continued to write prolifically, turning her attention in particular to religion and a rejection of the strict Unitarian faith of her upbringing. She advanced women's rights in employment and education, and petitioned parliament for the entitlement to vote.

Martineau died from bronchitis in 1876 at her Ambleside home, which is now privately owned. Her work has been somewhat neglected since her death, but she was a substantial intellectual and influential force in 19th century sociology and feminism. In a typically modest obituary of herself, compiled rather prematurely 20 years before her death, she wrote: 'Her original power was nothing more than was due to earnestness and intellectual clearness within a certain range. With small imaginative and suggestive powers, and therefore nothing approaching genius, she could see clearly what she did see, and give a clear expression to what she had to say. In short, she could popularize, while she could neither discover nor invent.'

TO SPEED OR NOT TO SPEED?

The introduction of speed limits on boats using Windermere has prompted one of the most heated debates in the Lake District. Water sports enthusiasts including water-skiers and powerboat users have been among the users of the lake for decades, but protesters claimed their noise and speed ruined the tranquility of the lake and spoiled it for sailors, canoeists and anglers. After a long public inquiry and a five-year moratorium to give businesses time to adapt to the changes, a byelaw limiting lake users to a speed of 10mph came into force in 2005. It was immediately flouted by some skiers despite threats from the Lake District National Park Authority and its partners to enforce it with prosecutions.

Skiers and powerboat users have mounted a vigorous campaign against the limit ever since. Similar restrictions on other lakes over the years had left Windermere as the last area open to high-speed water-skiers, and opponents argue that the move risks turning the Lake District into a museum. They claim that boats of all speeds can share the lake happily, and point to research from the Cumbria Tourist Board that suggests the limit has cost the Lake District's tourism industry £7m a year as water-skiers and power boaters go elsewhere for their sport. Supporters of the new limit, including the Friends of the Lake District, counter that it has restored the lake to its traditional use and made rowing, canoeing and windsurfing much safer.

HOUND TRAILING

The sport of hound trailing is not unique to the Lake District, but this is certainly its heartland and one of the area's most enduring and evocative pastimes.

Though its origins are uncertain, it is likely that hound trailing in the Lake District dates back at least two hundred years. The sport itself is simple. A trail is set by dragging cloths drenched in an aniseed- and paraffin-flavoured mixture across the fells and fields for the hounds to follow. Courses are usually eight to ten miles long, or shorter for puppies, and cover a wide variety of terrains. Most are set so that the winning hounds return in around 30 minutes.

Hound trailing meets make for a unique and striking sight in the valleys of the Lake District. Owners congregate before the start to chat about the course, weather conditions and the favourites running that day. Lean hounds, bred for speed and stamina, are let loose from their transporters and warmed up for the races. Bookmakers chalk odds on their boards—betting on the outcome of races is a popular pastime, and the bookies' stalls do steady business among owners and knowledgeable spectators. As the hounds are let loose, those watching reach for their binoculars to follow progress. Once they're out of sight, there is nothing to do but wait for the hounds' return. As the leaders eventually come into view, often leaping field fences or walls in spectacular fashion as they do so, owners roar their hounds' names, whistle at screeching volume or bang bowls of favourite foods to lure them over the finishing line.

Hound trailing in the Lake District is run by the Hound Trailing Association, which celebrated its centenary in 2006 and has close to 1,000 members. The association registers all hounds and trainers, and organises the hundreds of trails that are run during each season between April and October. Hound trails are also set at most of the Lake District's popular annual agricultural shows or sports days.

The sport is highly organised. Prize money isn't large, but competition is always fierce and there are long-running rivalries between trainers. As well as running in individual races, hounds compete for overall championships, awarded for the most wins in the season. Unlike in many other sports involving animals, the trail hounds—relatives of the foxhound—seem to genuinely enjoy it.

Like most sports, hound trailing has had its moments of controversy. Owners strive for competitive advantage, and the substantial bets that are often placed on races have encouraged some unscrupulous practices. Dogs have been known to be swapped halfway round the course, or obstructed by rival owners. The practice of flogging—taking hounds on a practice run of the course beforehand so that they remember the obstacles and short cuts come race day—is particularly frowned on by the HTA, which publishes strict rules and administers heavy penalties. Though rival entertainments mean that interest in hound trailing has fallen away slightly, there is still plenty of enthusiasm for it around the Lake District to make sure that its proud tradition continues.

Hound trailing lingo

Blanket finish A group finish that makes it difficult to tell who has won.

Clipping The cutting of a coat to make a hound sleeker and faster.

Cutting Taking a short cut.

Flogging Banned practice of taking hounds on a reconnaissance run of a course before a race.

Hot trail or **cold trail** A course that is either easy to follow because the scent is strong, or difficult to follow because it is faint.

Hound catchers People who lure hounds the final yards to the finish line.

Maiden A hound that has yet to win a major trail.

Ringer A fresh hound substituted for a tired one partway round a trail. Banned, obviously.

Scouts Race officials along the course who check that dogs are following the right route.

Slip The release of hounds from their leads at the start of a race.

Trailer The person or persons setting a trail.

Yellow card As in football, a warning, given for the obstruction of other hounds or various other offences. Four yellow cards can cause a hound's registration to be cancelled.

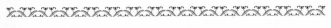

WORDSWORTH ON... THE WEATHER

'The rain here comes down heartily, and is frequently succeeded by clear, bright weather, when every brook is vocal, and every torrent sonorous; brooks and torrents which are never muddy, even in the heaviest floods, except, after a drought, they happen to be defiled for a short time by waters that have swept along dusty roads, or have broken out into ploughed fields. Days of unsettled weather, with partial showers, are very frequent; but the showers, darkening, or brightening, as they fly from hill to hill, are not less grateful to the eye than finely interwoven passages of gay and sad music are touching to the ear. Vapours exhaling from the lakes and meadows after sunrise, in a hot season, or, in moist weather, brooding upon the heights, or descending towards the valleys with inaudible motion, give a visionary character to everything around them.'

FROM *GUIDE TO THE LAKES* BY WILLIAM WORDSWORTH

MINE'S A PINT: CUMBRIA'S BREWERIES

The Lake District has undergone something of a brewing revolution in the last few years—although for somewhere that is blessed with so much water, it is perhaps only right that this part of the country should have so many brewers.

Cumbria's longest-running brewery is Jennings of Cockermouth, which has been using Lakeland water in its beers since it was founded in 1828. Jennings was bought by the giant Wolverhampton and Dudley Breweries in 2005, ending its proud independence but prompting fresh investment in the Cockermouth site. Back in the late 1970s, the poor economics of the industry and a decline in tastes for real ale had left Jennings as the only independent brewery in the county, but a revival of interest and a change in tax laws to offer incentives to microbreweries have since prompted many new companies to set up. Cumbria now boasts more than 20 breweries, giving thirsty walkers plenty of ales to choose from after a day on the fells. Some, such as Jennings, Coniston and Hawkshead, have branched into bottled beers that can now be found in supermarkets across the country, and several offer visitor centres and tours for anyone interested in finding out more about the brewing process. Others have grown out of pubs where the beers can be sampled in their best condition, and more are springing up every year. Cumbria's breweries are:

Abraham Thompson Brewery, Barrow. Tiny home-based brewery. Tel 07708 191 437.

Barngates Brewery, Ambleside. A brewery attached to the popular Drunken Duck Inn. Tel 015394 36575 or online at www.drunkenduckinn.co.uk.

Beckstones Brewery, Millom. Housed in a converted dairy. Tel 07761 605782.

Bitter End Brewery, Cockermouth. Brewery situated behind Cockermouth's pub of the same name. Tel 01900 828993 or online at www.bitterend.co.uk.

Coniston Brewery, Coniston. Multi-award winner, mostly for its Bluebird Bitter. Tel 015394 41133 or online at www.conistonbrewery.co.uk.

Cumbrian Legendary Ales, Hawkshead. Names its beers after famous Cumbrian characters. Tel 015394 36436 or online at www.cumbrianlegendaryales.com.

Dent Brewery, Dent. Uses local spring water for its beers. Tel 01539 625326 or online at www.dentbrewery.co.uk.

Derwent Brewery, Silloth. Best-known for its Carlisle State Bitter. Tel 016973 31522.

Foxfield Brewery, Broughton-in-Furness. Attached to Foxfield's Prince of Wales pub. Tel 01229 716238 or online at www.princeofwalesfoxfield.co.uk.

Geltsdale Brewery, Brampton. Newly opened brewery with
beers named after local landmarks, run by a former archaeologist.
Tel 016977 41541 or online at www.geltsdalebrewery.com.

Great Gable Brewing Company, Wasdale Head. Based
at the Wasdale Head Inn, one of the most popular pubs for
Lake District walkers. Tel 019467 26229 or online at
www.greatgablebrewing.com.

Hardknott Brewery, Eskdale. The brewery of the Woolpack Inn
in the Eskdale Valley. Tel 019467 23230 or online at
www.woolpack.co.uk.

Hawkshead Brewery, Hawkshead. Fast-growing brewery,
now with a second site and visitors' centre in Staveley.
Tel 015394 36111 or online at www.hawksheadbrewery.co.uk.

Hesket Newmarket Brewery, Hesket Newmarket.
Run by a co-operative of villagers, like the Old Crown Inn
to which it is attached. Tel 016974 78068 or online at
www.hesketbrewery.co.uk.

Jennings Brewery, Cockermouth. Cumbria's biggest
brewer since 1828. Tel 0845 1297 185 or online at
www.jenningsbrewery.co.uk.

Keswick Brewery, Keswick. New microbrewery on an old
brewing site. Tel 017687 80700.

Loweswater Brewery, Loweswater. Brewery of the Kirkstile Inn,
where beers were first brewed as far back as the 19th century.
Tel 01900 85219 or www.kirkstile.com.

Tirril Brewery, Brougham Hall. Founded at the Queen's Head
in Tirril but moved to a larger site when demand rose.
Tel 017688 63219 or online at www.tirrilbrewery.co.uk.

Ulverston Brewing Company, Ulverston. Brews such as Another
Fine Mess are named after Stan Laurel, Ulverston's most famous son.
Tel 01229 584280.

Watermill Brewing Company, Ings. The brewery of Ings'
Watermill Inn, a long-time mecca for real ale fans.
Tel 015398 21309 or online at www.watermillinn.co.uk.

Yates Brewery, Wigton. Set up in 1986, this is Cumbria's
oldest micro-brewery. Tel: 016973 21081 or online at
www.yatesbrewery.co.uk.

THE DROWNED VILLAGES

The lake of Haweswater was a third of its present size until it was artificially expanded in the 1930s by the local waterworks corporation. The aim was to create a reservoir that would provide more water for Manchester, but the government's decision to allow the expansion caused controversy, since it meant that several lakeside villages in the pretty Mardale valley would have to be flooded. The settlements of Measand and Mardale Green were thriving farming communities in the 19th century, producing large quantities of butter in particular.

The building of a 470m dam—at the time one of the most technically advanced ever to be built—raised the water level and joined together what were previously two separate lakes. By 1941, the water had risen enough to submerge several farms, cottages, a church and a 17th century pub, the Dun Bull Inn, most of which had been largely dismantled in advance. A school was taken apart and rebuilt elsewhere, and a new hotel, the Haweswater Hotel, built to replace the Dun Bull. It is now the only building in the valley.

In long, dry summers when the water level falls, some remains of Mardale such as its dry stone walls and bridges often reappear. This happened most notably in 1976 and 1984, when thousands of people flocked to Haweswater to see the outline of the lost villages. Remains also appeared in 1989, 1995 and 2003. The flooding of the Mardale valley is also the subject of a novel by Lake District author Sarah Hall, *Haweswater* (Faber), which won a Commonwealth Writers' Prize in 2003.

LAKE DISTRICT POEMS – 'SKATING ON DERWENT WATER' BY HARDWICKE RAWNSLEY

In fairyland we revelled all the day,
Clear glass of gold lay Derwentwater's flood,
Far Glaramara mailed in silver stood,
And Skiddaw bright for ivory inlay
Shone purple clad with royalest array
To see our kingly sport. How leapt the blood!
As on from sunny bay to shadowy wood
We flashed above the mirrors steely grey.

But when the sun o'er Newlands sank to rest,
Enchantment in the valley seemed to grow.
There, while the snows were flushed on fell and moor
Loud rang the skates upon a lilac floor,
And burning upward thro' the lake's dark breast
Fire gleamed with unimaginable glow.

CUMBRIA INDUSTRIES – LEAD

Lead has been mined sporadically in the Lake District since at least Roman times, but it wasn't until the 1820s that it was retrieved in a concerted way. The Greenside Mining Company was formed in 1822 and mined more than two million tons of lead around Ullswater before it exhausted the ore supplies in the 1960s. The North Pennines area around Alston was also important mining territory. Here, a Quaker-led mining company built the industrial village of Nenthead around the mines, providing welfare for its workers and their families that made conditions there a lot better than other mines in northern England—although the work was still tough and dangerous. Over the centuries, lead miners flocked to the Lake District from Europe to work the rich seams.

Nenthead's mines closed in the 1960s, but they have since been restored by the North Pennines Heritage Trust into one of the largest accessible mines in the UK. The Nenthead Mines Heritage Centre is now open daily from April to October, and is a good place to find out more about the lead industry and its influence on Cumbria. It also runs tours of restored mines. The Lake District's last working lead mine, at Force Crag in the Coledale Valley, was abandoned in 1990, and is now looked after by English Heritage and the National Trust.

LAKE DISTRICT PROPERTY GIVEN TO THE NATIONAL TRUST BY BEATRIX POTTER

The National Trust is one of the biggest landowners in the Lake District, and it owes much of its presence to the generosity of Beatrix Potter. As royalties from her books poured in, Potter bought land and property across the area, and by the 1940s had acquired dozens of farms and cottages and surrounding land.

Most of the property was bequeathed to the National Trust in 1944 under the terms of Potter's will, though she had also sold some at cost in 1930. In all, the National Trust picked up nearly 7,000 acres of land and property, as well as the farms' flocks of Herdwick sheep. More property, not listed here, was either purchased by the National Trust with money given by Potter, or bequeathed by her husband, William Heelis, on his death three years after his wife.

Sold to the National Trust at cost in 1930
High Tilberthwaite Farm
Land on Holme Fell
Holme Ground Farm
Low Hallgarth Farm and two cottages
Low Tilberthwaite Cottages
Tarn Hows, including Rose Castle Cottage
Yew Tree Farm, Coniston, with part of High Yewdale Farm

Bequeathed under will in 1944—farms and houses
Bank End, Sawrey (two cottages)
Belmount, Hawkshead
Black Beck Lodge and Cottage, Hawkshead
Bridge End Farm, Little Langdale
Brow Cottage, Little Langdale
Busk Farm, Little Langdale
Castle Farm and The Castle, Sawrey
Currier House, Sawrey
Dale End Farm, Little Langdale
Far End, Coniston
Hawkshead Fields, Hawkshead (three houses)
High Loanthwaite Farm, Hawkshead
High Oxenfell Farm, Coniston
High Park Farm, Coniston
High Yewdale Farm, Coniston
Hill Top Farm, Sawrey
Low Greengate and Old Post Office, Sawrey (three houses)
Low Loanthwaite Farm, Hawkshead
Low Oxenfell Farm, Coniston
Low Yewdale (three houses)
Penny Hill Farm, Eskdale
Stang End, Coniston
Thimble Hall and The Corner Shop, Hawkshead
Tower Bank House, Sawrey
Troutbeck Park Farm
Waterhead Cottages, Coniston (four houses)

Bequeathed under will in 1944—land
Briery Park and Bullneck Grassings, Troutbeck
Broad Moss and Ruffle Hows, Tilberthwaite

Crag Wood, Colthouse
The Croft, Sawrey
Two closes at Ees Parrock, Sawrey
Elm Craggs, Troutbeck
Great Intake, Tilberthwaite
Ill Step and Bank End, Troutbeck
Ings Meadow, Troutbeck
Knipe Fold Intake, Hawkshead
Little Close, Troutbeck
Three closes in Little Langdale
Little Stoney Beck and an unnamed wood, Troutbeck
Marshall Bank, Park Moss, and Holme Gill Syke, Troutbeck
Closes at Skelwith, part of Low Park
Plus land at or near: Hill Top, Sawrey; Far Sawrey; The Brows, Outgate;
Randy Pike, Outgate; High Park; Elterwater

PLACE NAMES: LONGEST AND SHORTEST

The longest single-word place name in the Lake District is the 16-letter Rowantreethwaite—though it is dwarfed by Britain's longest, Llanfairpwllgwyngyllgogerychwyrndrobwllllantysiliogogogoch, on the island of Anglesey. The shortest name in the Lakes is the admirably succinct Y, a gully that drops from St Sunday Crag down towards Grisedale Beck.

THE LAKE DISTRICT'S OSPREYS
AND GOLDEN EAGLES

The Lake District's unique habitats have been home to some rare birds over the last few years.

In 2001 a pair of ospreys landed on a nest platform near Bassenthwaite Lake and became the first wild ospreys to successfully breed in England for nearly a century. They were encouraged to stay by a purpose-built nest provided by the Forestry Commission, the Lake District National Park Authority and the Royal Society for the Protection of Birds, and have returned each summer since. The ospreys' nests are watched over by volunteer wardens who prevent disturbance and watch for egg thieves, and the nearby lake provides fish for the birds. An open-air viewpoint has been set up at Dodd Wood to allow the public to observe the ospreys each summer, and the Lake District Osprey Project has an exhibition at the Whinlatter Forest Visitor Centre with live video coverage of the nest.

Haweswater, meanwhile, has been home since 1969 to the only regularly nesting pair of golden eagles in England. Scotland still has several hundred pairs, but attracting the birds over the border has been difficult. The golden eagles have been diligently watched over by RSPB volunteers, but there has been no successful breeding for several years and the female is thought to have died in 2004. The younger male bird can still be seen around Haweswater, hoping to attract a mate, and the RSPB's reserve at the southern end of the lake has a viewpoint.

CUMBRIA'S TEN MOST ROMANTIC PLACES

Jenkyn's Crag overlooking Windermere is the best place in the Lake District to propose marriage, according to a list compiled by Cumbria Tourism. The Lake District is often promoted as a romantic destination, and has a thriving weddings industry. Other romantic spots include the Aira Force waterfalls near Ullswater and a vantage point on Catbells. The full top ten is:

1 Jenkyn's Crag, Ambleside
2 Aira Force, Ullswater
3 Catbells and Ashness Bridge, Keswick
4 Whinlatter Forest, near Keswick
5 Tarn Hows, Coniston
6 Loughrigg Tarn, Elterwater
7 Wastwater
8 Gummer's How, near Newby Bridge
9 Talkin Tarn Country Park, near Brampton
10 The Lake District Lovestone at Fell Foot Park, Windermere

LITERARY LAKELANDERS – ROBERT SOUTHEY

Along with William Wordsworth and Samuel Taylor Coleridge, Robert Southey was one-third of what have become known as the Lake Poets.

Born in 1774, Southey was expelled from Westminster School for protesting about flogging. He met Coleridge for the first time in 1794, the year he published his first collection of poems. After marrying the sister of Coleridge's wife, he moved to Keswick in 1803 to live at Greta Hall with Coleridge and his family. He soon received a pension from the government to fund his writing, and was appointed poet laureate in 1813. He held the position until his death, when he was succeeded by Wordsworth.

Southey was an industrious writer of essays, biographies, letters and reviews as well as verse. His most famous work includes *Letters from England*, an account of a tour of the country in 1808, and *The Inchcape Rock*, a poem about a reef off the east coast of Scotland. Like Wordsworth, Southey was originally a supporter of the French Revolution but became more conservative in his politics as he grew older and closer to the establishment. This earned him derision from other, more radical writers, and Byron's epic poem *Don Juan* is satirically and scornfully dedicated to him.

Thomas de Quincey contrasted Southey with Wordsworth in his *Recollections of the Lakes and Lake Poets*. 'Wordsworth lived in the open air; Southey in his library, which Coleridge used to call his wife.' That library had accumulated 14,000 books by the time Southey died in 1843. He is buried in the churchyard of St Kentigern's in Crosthwaite, Keswick, which contains a sculpture in his memory and an inscription by Wordsworth.

THE LAKES AND THEIR MEANINGS

Bassenthwaite Lake Lake by Bastun's clearing or meadow. Bastun may have been a Viking leader, or a nickname.

Brothers Water Likely to have been named in tribute to two brothers who drowned in the lake in the 18th century. It may also be a derivation of the Old Norse for broad water.

Buttermere The lake by the grazing pastures, which obviously had a good reputation for dairy products.

Coniston Water Coniston derives from *cyning tun*, meaning king and settlement.

Crummock Water Crummock means the crooked one, probably referring to a river.

Derwent Water Named after the River Derwent that flows through it. Derwent is probably derived from the Old English *derwa* meaning oak; the river with oak trees.

Elter Water The swans' lake. Swans still winter on this lake.

Ennerdale Water The valley in which it lies is called after a Viking chieftain, named Anund or something similar.

Esthwaite Water The lake by the ash-tree clearing, or water by the eastern clearing.

Grasmere The grassy lake.

Haweswater Hafr's lake. Hafr was probably a Viking name.

Loweswater The leafy lake. From the Old Norse *laufsaer* meaning leaves.

Rydal Water Takes its name from nearby Rydal, meaning the valley of the rye.

Thirlmere The lake with a gap or narrowing, from the Old English *thyrel* for gap. The lake had a narrow middle section until it was dammed to form a reservoir.

Ullswater The lake of Ulf or Ulfr, both common Old Norse names.

Wast Water An interesting tautology. Wast is derived from Wasdale, which means the valley of the lake.

Wet Sleddale Takes its name from the valley of Wet Sleddale, meaning the wet valley.

Windermere The lake of Vinand, an Old Norse name.

NAISMITH'S RULE

Want to estimate how long a walk in the Lake District fells will take you? A popular way of working it out is to use Naismith's Rule, devised by Scottish mountaineer William Naismith in the 1890s.

Allow 1 hour for every 3 miles (5 km), plus 1 hour
for every 2,000 feet (600m) of ascent.

Because they either climbed faster in the 19th century or didn't stop to enjoy the views and have lunch, Naismith's Rule usually produces a rather optimistic estimate for all but the liveliest of walkers. As a result, several corrections have been made over the years, adding a quarter, third or even half to the Rule's estimate to get a more realistic idea of how long a walk will take. More specific corrections have been made to accommodate poor weather, rough terrain, fatigue or the size of your rucksack.

TEN RUINED CASTLES

Cumbria's history as a military area means there are plenty of abandoned castles around the county. Here are ten interesting ones that are open to the public.

Bew Castle, Bewcastle. After the original fort on this Borders site was destroyed in the 12th century, a new castle was built in the 14th century, but abandoned soon afterwards when Scots raiders took its occupants prisoner. The ruins are accessed via Demesne Farm, which gives permission to view.

Brough Castle. Built around the 12th century, destroyed by fire in the 16th and restored by the Clifford family in the 17th. The ruins of the gatehouse, keep and tower are well-preserved. Looked after by English Heritage.

Brougham Castle, near Penrith. Built as a fortification against the Scots in the 13th century on the site of a Roman fort, and later used as a home. In the care of English Heritage.

Egremont Castle. Built in the 12th century and ruined in the 16th. The gatehouse and some walls are in good condition. The ruins are on public land.

Kendal Castle. 12th century castle of Kendal barons, perched on a hill above the town. Most of the walls survive in good condition. The ruins are on public land.

Kirkoswald Castle, near Penrith. Destroyed by Robert the Bruce, rebuilt in the 15th century but then plundered, a tower is all that remains. It can be seen from nearby footpaths but not explored.

Lowther Castle, near Pooley Bridge. Though there have been buildings on the site since the 13th century, the present castle was built in the early 1800s for the Earls of Lonsdale, but abandoned in the 1940s. The atmospheric shell of the castle stands on well-maintained estates.

Pendragon Castle, near Kirkby Stephen. Reputedly founded by Uther Pendragon, the father of King Arthur. Rebuilt in the 14th century and again in the 17th, the ruin of a tower is all that remains. It is on private land with access permitted. Another ruin, Lammerside Castle, is nearby.

Penrith Castle. A 14th century defence against Scottish raiders, its walls and layout are still fairly intact. Looked after by English Heritage.

Piel Castle. Fortification guarding against pirates and raiders on Piel Island, off Barrow-in-Furness. Run by English Heritage, its keep, baileys and towers are still in place.

THE WELL-DRESSED GHOST OF THE FELLS

There have been plenty of stories of ghosts in the Lake District, but one of the most unusual and enduring is that of a man walking the fells. A succession of walkers claim to have seen the apparition of an immaculately dressed city gent, complete with bowler hat, umbrella and brief case, and wearing smartly polished black town shoes that are clean and dry even in the worst conditions. He was first spotted striding across the fells in the 1930s, and has since been observed on Green Gable, Helvellyn, Scafell Pike and High Street among others. The mystery appeared to have been solved a few years ago when a fellwalker recalled a colleague who did actually walk the fells for many years in a suit and town shoes—although not even this man carried a briefcase and umbrella.

FOOT-AND-MOUTH IN THE LAKE DISTRICT

The outbreak of foot-and-mouth disease in 2001 caused the Lake District immense economic, environmental and social trauma, and its dramatic impact is still keenly felt.

Of the 2,000 or so outbreaks of the disease in Britain between mid-February and late-September that year, close to half were in Cumbria. The disease spread like wildfire around the county, and at its peak in mid-March nearly 150 new cases were being identified each week. As the Army moved in to help contain the spread of the disease and organise the slaughter of infected animals, farmers saw their livestock and income wiped out virtually overnight. The sight of pyres and mass burials across Cumbria was particularly distressing, and the slaughter could not be confined to farms that had been infected with foot-and-mouth disease; nearly 2,000 more farm holdings were also subject to partial or total slaughter of livestock.

The devastating impact on farming was matched by the effect on tourism. As restrictions on access to the farms and fells were imposed to stem the spread of the disease, visitors to the area plummeted. The Foot-and-Mouth Disease Inquiry later estimated that that the loss to agriculture was worth some £130m, while £200m was lost to the tourism economy. Foot-and-mouth cut 4 per cent off the GDP of Cumbria in 2001.

Farmers in Cumbria were furious at the slow and haphazard handling of the spread of foot-and-mouth. 'We found that on the ground there had been confusion, disorder and delay,' the Inquiry later reported. 'We found widespread dissatisfaction with the "system" and with many operational aspects of the disease control and clean-up measures.' Money eventually reached farms that had been subject to slaughter, and the income from this actually outstripped farmers' losses, according to the Inquiry—but foot-and-mouth nevertheless forced many farmers out of business and caused immense distress among those that survived.

Some positives came out of the crisis. Government assistance for affected farms and businesses did help to tide many over the outbreak, and the disease prompted farms to diversify into other activities such as bed and breakfast, farm shops and farmers' markets. This, together with the lessons learned from the spread of the disease, should mean that any future outbreak of foot-and-mouth will have less impact—but 2001 will be remembered with a shudder by Cumbrians for years to come.

Foot-and-mouth disease—the impact in numbers

2,026	total outbreaks of foot-and-mouth disease in Britain in 2001
893	number of outbreaks in Cumbria
45	percentage of farm holdings that were subject to partial or total slaughter of livestock
1,087,000	estimated number of sheep slaughtered in Cumbria
215,000	cattle slaughtered
39,000	pigs slaughtered
1,000	goats, deer and other animals slaughtered
466,312	number of carcasses in Britain's biggest mass-burial site at Watchtree near Great Orton
315	amount in millions of pounds of Cumbria's average annual livestock income before 2001
185	amount in millions of Cumbria's livestock income in 2001

SIR WALTER SCOTT AND THE WORDSWORTHS' PORRIDGE

William and Dorothy Wordsworth received many notable visitors at their Dove Cottage home in Grasmere, but they were not renowned for their lavish hospitality. When Sir Walter Scott stayed with them, he reported that he was fed three meagre meals a day, 'two of which were porridge'. William thought that plain living enabled purer, clearer thinking, but Scott soon became hungry and fed up. He later admitted that he would climb out of his bedroom window after mealtimes and creep over to the nearby Swan Inn for a more substantial feed. The inn is now the Swan Hotel in Grasmere.

LAKE DISTRICT FOOD – MORECAMBE BAY SHRIMPS AND COCKLES

Stretching along the coast in Lancashire as well as Cumbria, Morecambe Bay is 120 square miles of open sands and Britain's second largest bay after the Wash. Cockles and shrimps have been farmed here for centuries, and are still an important industry along the Lake District peninsulas.

Shrimps are caught in nets trawled across the sands and shallow water that were originally drawn by hand, then by horses and now by tractors. Once the nets have been emptied, the brown shrimps are boiled alive on the sands, then taken to nearby factories or homes to be peeled, washed, packed or potted. The fiddly and laborious job of peeling used to be done by hand, but the arrival of machines in factories means it is now a dying art.

Cockling is an even more labour-intensive job. Buried a centimetre or two beneath the sand and exposed once the tide goes out, cockles are sucked to the surface using a 'jumbo'—essentially a plank of wood that softens the sand—and then raked out. It is back-breaking work, often done with the wind and rain hammering across the sands. Stocks are tightly controlled, and the cockling beds are sometimes closed if they have been over-farmed.

Shrimps and cockles have a small market in Lancashire and Cumbria, but a large proportion of sales are to Europe, where appreciation of them is far greater and they are used more creatively in cooking. Demand is such that cockles in particular can fetch good prices, making the job of farming them potentially lucrative. But collecting shrimps and cockles is dangerous work as well as hard: tractors can sink in the boggy sands, and tides can race in across Morecambe Bay at the speed of a galloping horse. In 2004, 23 Chinese immigrant workers drowned when they were overtaken by water while cockling in Morecambe Bay, and there are concerns that inexperienced people are still at risk working there.

A recipe for potted shrimps
250g cooked Morecambe Bay shrimps
150g butter
Good pinches of salt, cayenne pepper and nutmeg

Gently melt the butter. Stir in the shrimps and coat well. Add the salt, cayenne pepper and nutmeg and simmer for five minutes, stirring often. Tip the mixture into pots and spoon a little more melted butter over the top to seal. Leave to cool and set. Serve warmed with brown bread or toast. Potted shrimps are also good sautéed with a few other ingredients or tossed into pasta.

A WALKER'S GUIDE TO THE BEAUFORT WIND SCALE

Although Beaufort's Wind Force Scale was designed primarily for seafarers, it has been adapted for use on land too—and since walkers in the Lake District frequently come up against a gust or two, it's worthwhile knowing what forecasters mean when they refer to it. Walking usually becomes challenging above 5 on the scale.

Force	mph	Effect
0	0	*Calm* – smoke rises vertically
1	1-3	*Light* – smoke moves in wind
2	4-7	*Light breeze* – wind felt on exposed skin
3	8-12	*Gentle breeze* – leaves and small twigs move
4	13-18	*Moderate breeze* – paper blows about
5	19-24	*Fresh breeze* – small trees sway
6	25-31	*Strong breeze* – using an umbrella becomes difficult
7	32-38	*Moderate breeze* – hard to walk into
8	39-46	*Gale* – walking is very difficult
9	47-54	*Strong gale* – loose tiles blown away
10	55-63	*Storm* – trees uprooted
11	64-75	*Violent storm* – widespread damage
12	76+	*Hurricane* – devastation

KEEP ON TRUCKING

Eddie Stobart can claim with some justification to be Cumbria's biggest-ever export and one of its best-known names.

Stobart was the founder of a road haulage empire that grew out of an agricultural contracting business based in Hesket Newmarket. His trucking operation grew during the 1970s and 1980s and, from an original single depot in Carlisle, the company now has a fleet of 800 trucks, 27 depots across the UK and Europe, and an annual turnover of around £140 million. After a few years of declining sales, Eddie Stobart sold the company to his younger brother William in 2003, and it is now the largest independent haulage firm in the UK, with plans to move into rail and air distribution. Its headquarters remain in Carlisle.

During the 1980s and 1990s, Eddie Stobart and his company developed an extraordinary cult following. The trucks' distinctive livery and Stobart's habit of naming each of his lorries after his favourite women—Twiggy, Tammy (Wynette) and Dolly (Parton), among many others—prompted a legion of truckspotters to try to collect sightings of them all. The bizarre following grew into an official fan club selling Eddie Stobart merchandise and running tours of the depots. The peak of the company's fame came with the opening of a merchandise shop in Carlisle and an entry into the pop charts with the Wurzels' 'I Wanna Be an Eddie Stobart Driver', released to mark the 25th anniversary of Eddie Stobart Ltd. The fan club is still going strong with thousands of members around the world, and its popular services include tips on sighting the vehicles and a league table of top spotters. The full story of the success of Stobart and his company is told in an excellent biography by Hunter Davies, *The Story of Eddie Stobart* (HarperCollins).

THE LAKE DISTRICT ON THE BIG SCREEN...

Its spectacular scenery has made the Lake District a popular location for film shoots. Here are some of the results.

Miss Potter (2006). The Beatrix Potter biopic starring Renee Zellwegger was filmed in various Lake District locations. Yew Tree Farm at Coniston became Hill Top for the film.

28 Days Later (2002). Danny Boyle's futuristic horror film about the last survivors of an incurable virus filmed its final scenes around Ennerdale Water.

Killing Me Softly (2002). Scenes of the drama starring Joseph Fiennes and Heather Graham were shot at Matterdale Church and Tarn Hows.

Tomorrow La Scala! (2002). Comedy about an opera company in a maximum security prison, partly shot at Haverigg Prison near Millom with inmates as extras.

Pandaemonium (2000). Drama about the Wordsworths and Coleridge, partly set in the Lakes.

Alien Blood (1999). Weird, poorly-reviewed alien thriller that used the Kirkstone Pass, Lake Windermere and the Rusland valley among other locations.

Without a Clue (1988). Sherlock Holmes comedy with Ben Kingsley and Michael Caine, partly set around Windermere.

The Rainbow (1989). Ken Russell's version of DH Lawrence's classic novel was shot in Borrowdale and Keswick.

Withnail and I (1986). A cult classic following two friends who come on holiday to the Lake District 'by mistake'. Much of it was shot around Penrith and Shap.

The French Lieutenant's Woman (1980). The final scenes of the adaptation of John Fowles' book were shot around Windermere.

Tommy (1975). Parts of Ken Russell's star-studded film were shot around Derwent Water.

Swallows and Amazons (1974). Coniston Water was the appropriate location for the film version of Arthur Ransome's classic.

Brief Encounter (1945). Carnforth Station, where the film's most famous scene was shot, is actually just over the border into Lancashire, but Cumbria likes to call it its own. Fans of the film still flock there.

... AND THE SMALL SCREEN

Some TV programmes shot around Cumbria.

Ted and Alice (2002). Odd but engaging BBC comedy about an alien meeting a woman who runs a Lake District B&B, starring Dawn French and Stephen Tompkinson.

Nature Boy (1999). Barrow-in-Furness and surrounding towns provided the backdrop for this gritty BBC drama.

Oliver Twist (1999). The ITV adaptation was filmed in the picturesque Eden market town of Alston, which also provided many of the extras.

Wives and Daughters (1999). The BBC filmed much of Elizabeth Gaskell's novel at Levens Hall near Kendal.

The Lakes (1998). The two series of this dark BBC drama received around 150 complaints from the public. It was filmed around Patterdale and Glenridding.

Neville's Island (1998). ITV comedy drama about a group of men trapped on an island on Derwent Water, starring Martin Clunes and Timothy Spall.

Jane Eyre (1997). The Dalemain house and gardens near Pooley Bridge and Naworth Castle at Brampton lent themselves to this TV series.

The Tenant of Wildfell Hall (1996). Outdoor scenes for the TV adaptation of Anne Brontë's novel were filmed around Appleby.

A Time to Dance (1992). TV adaptation of Melvyn Bragg's novel, shot around Wigton and Carlisle.

The Monocled Mutineer (1986). BBC drama based on the true story of the leader of a World War One mutiny who is captured in the Lake District.

Postman Pat (1981 onwards). The Greendale location of the popular children's cartoon series is fictional, but creator John Cunliffe's people and places were inspired by the Longsleddale valley.

LAKE DISTRICT POEMS – FROM 'THE PRELUDE, BOOK IV' BY WILLIAM WORDSWORTH

Those walks, well worthy to be prized and loved—
Regretted!—that word, too, was on my tongue,
But they were richly laden with all good,
And cannot be remembered but with thanks
And gratitude, and perfect joy of heart—
Those walks did now, like a returning spring,
Come back on me again. When first I made
Once more the circuit of our little lake,
If ever happiness hath lodged with man,
That day consummate happiness was mine,
Wide-spreading, steady, calm, contemplative.
The sun was set, or setting, when I left
Our cottage door, and evening soon brought on
A sober hour, not winning or serene,
For cold and raw the air was, and untuned:
But as a face we love is sweetest then
When sorrow damps it, or, whatever look
It chance to wear, is sweetest if the heart
Have fulness in itself; even so with me
It fared that evening. Gently did my soul

Put off her veil, and, self-transmuted, stood
Naked, as in the presence of her God.
As on I walked, a comfort seemed to touch
A heart that had not been disconsolate,
Strength came where weakness was not known to be,
At least not felt; and restoration came,
Like an intruder, knocking at the door
Of unacknowledged weariness.

PENCILS AT THE READY

The Lake District is the home of pencils, which have provided the area with an important industry for centuries.

Borrowdale shepherds are credited with the first discovery of graphite in the 16th century—something achieved by accident when they looked under tree roots after a storm had felled it. After first thinking it was coal but finding that it would not burn, they discovered it was very effective for marking sheep. When its value was realised, the mines were soon taken over by England's rulers and their output transported to London, where graphite was mostly used to make cannonballs.

Splinters of graphite were later wrapped in sheepskin to make the use of them easier, but a pair of Italians then had the idea of fitting them into a wooden groove—thereby creating the world's first pencil. The industry of producing Cumberland graphite pencils for artists grew up in and around Keswick in the 19th century, and became a skilful process. The Cumberland Pencil Company factory was set up in the 1830s, and continues to operate in Keswick today, though its graphite is now imported. The factory's site is also home to the Cumberland Pencil Museum, open seven days a week all year round.

LITERARY LAKELANDERS – JOHN RUSKIN

Like many people made famous from their work in the Lake District, John Ruskin was what Cumbrians call an 'offcomer'. Born in London in 1819, he made his first visit there aged five, and a memorial to him by Derwent Water records that this was the first event in life that he could remember. It certainly had a lasting effect on Ruskin and his family, who went back to the Lake District many times on holiday.

Aged a precocious 11, Ruskin wrote a 2,000 line poem about one of his visits, and he returned to the Lakes throughout his life and work.

As with many eminent Victorians, Ruskin was busy in numerous fields, establishing himself as an artist, poet, critic, geologist, conservationist and social philanthropist among other things. He worked to preserve countryside in the Lake District and elsewhere, and campaigned for free education and public libraries. Although he had known the Lake District very well since that first visit, it wasn't until the age of 52 that he established himself there, when he bought Brantwood near Coniston. He quickly expanded the property and estate into his vision of a perfect home, filled with art, books and other artefacts from his travels.

Ruskin died at Brantwood in 1900. The house is now a memorial to him, preserved close to how he left it and with much of his work and collections on display. It is open to the public all year round. Coniston also has an interesting Ruskin Museum, open from March to November.

LUCY'S FAVOURITE LAKE DISTRICT FOODS

Lucy Nicholson runs Lucy's of Ambleside, a small empire of delicatessen, restaurant, café, wine bar, cookery school and outside catering services. Her main shop and restaurant can be found on Church Street in Ambleside, or online at www.lucysofambleside.co.uk. She has been a passionate supporter and champion of local food and producers since her first business opened in 1989. Here are her ten favourite foods from the Lake District, with some tips on how to make the most of them.

Charr. A landlocked species from the Ice Ages, and the Lakes' fish of fishes. Like a cross between salmon and trout with the best of both, it has a soft pink flesh and a glorious rainbow skin and is deliciously sweet to eat—ideal for the barbecue. Its season lasts from April to October.

Cheeses. Once upon a time France had no rival—but move over brie and make way for Cumberland Farmhouse! There are so many Cumbrian cheeses to choose from now that it's hard to pick a favourite, but the earthily smoked versions are perfect with some damson pickle and a glass of local ale.

Cumberland mustard. From the high hills at Alston, this mustard is tops. Perfect with cold meats and cheeses, but wonderful stirred into a macaroni cheese or combined with the juices of a steak to make a creamy, peppery sauce. Try the horseradish mustard stirred into crème fraîche, to accompany Windermere charr fillets—fantastic.

Cumberland sausage. It has to be Richard Woodall's... but then I also love the combination of Cumberland sausage with apricot from Saddleback... and Peter Gott makes a pretty mean one too. Whatever you choose, make sure it's Cumberland!

Cumbrian frutta cotta. Made by a lovely lady called Lizzie Smith in Penrith, this is a fabulous combination of prunes, apricots and figs, steeped in rum with a hint of cinnamon and star anise and vanilla. Perfect over ice cream. She also makes a savoury version that is great with cheese.

Damsons. Lyth Valley is famous for them, and they have so many uses. They make the famous damson gin, revered by many as not so much a 'mother's ruin' but a 'maiden's making', and are also perfect for desserts, excellent when pickled, or delicious turned into damson cheese. And as a jam they have no rival.

Herdwick lamb. When you see these woolly backs out on the fells, you have no idea that they can taste so good! Herdwicks embody all that the fells mean to me, and have a wonderful aroma of heather and the hills, proving the point that you are what you eat. Try the air-dried version from Farmer Sharp—fabulous as a simple starter together with some Cumberland sauce.

Penrith fudge. This is the best fudge in the world—the simplest of ingredients with a flavour that has no compare. Simple packaging and a great concept.

Sarah Nelson's Grasmere gingerbread. This embodies the traditions, people and all things wonderful about the Lakes. For years I couldn't decide whether it was a biscuit or cake, but I find I appreciate it more and more as years go by.

Sticky toffee pudding. Synonymous with the Lake District, this celebrates the proper British pudding and is known throughout the land. I like Lucy's version best—but then I would. It needs lashings of English Lakes ice cream to really appreciate the hot-cold contrast.

AN UNHAPPY TOURIST

Novelist Daniel Defoe passed through the Lake District in 1724—and wasn't very impressed by what he saw.

'Westmorland [is] a country eminent only for being the wildest, most barren and frightful of any that I have passed over in England, or even in Wales... Nor were these hills high and

formidable only, but they had a kind of unhospitable terror in them. Here were no rich pleasant valleys between them, as among the Alps; no lead mines and veins of rich ore, as in the Peak; no coal pits, as in the hills about Halifax, much less gold, as in the Andes, but all barren and wild, of no use or advantage either to man or beast.'

FROM *A TOUR THROUGH THE WHOLE ISLAND OF GREAT BRITAIN*
BY DANIEL DEFOE

ANIMALS IN LAKE DISTRICT PLACE NAMES

Many of the fells, waters, towns and villages in the Lake District get their names from the animals of the region. Here are some of them.

Bee Holme	Goats Water
Buckbarrow	Great Cockup (woodcock)
Bull Crag	Harter Fell
Calva	Hawkshead
Cat Bells	Heron Crag
Crowmire	High Buzzard Knott
Curlew Crag	High Raven Crag
Dove Crag	Hindscarth
Eagle Crag	Otter Island
Eel Crag	Oxendale
Ewe Crag	Swine Crag
Falcon Crag	Troutbeck
Foxes Tarn	

THE MOST HAUNTED CASTLE IN BRITAIN

Plenty of tourist attractions claim to be haunted by ghosts, but few have quite the reputation of Muncaster Castle. Visitors over the years have often reported sounds of footsteps and children crying, and the most common apparitions include Tom Fool, a court jester; and the Muncaster Boggle, the ghost of Mary Bragg, a young girl murdered at the castle in the 19th century. Hauntings are especially common in the castle's Tapestry Room, where a sudden cold chill is sometimes felt and the door handle turns of its own accord.

The castle doesn't seem too concerned at ridding itself of its ghostly reputation, which brings in thousands of visitors a year. It even runs 'Ghost Sits' in the Tapestry Room, allowing groups of people to stay up all night to watch for ghosts, and hosts visits from paranormal researchers. The castle was home to Britain's first-ever 'Ghost School', a two-day residential course attempting to find rational explanations for the phenomenon and run by a university psychologist.

TEN ARTS FESTIVALS

Cumbria has more than 40 regular arts festivals, putting on some 800 performances, screenings, readings and exhibitions each year. These are the pick of the bunch.

Appleby Jazz Festival, July. Three-day festival covering a broad spectrum of jazz and attracting some top names. See www.applebyjazz.com.

Cockermouth Summer Festival, June and July. Film screenings, music performances, book readings, drama and storytime sessions. See www.cockermouth.org.uk.

Kendal Mountain Festivals, November. Celebrations of mountain films, books, art and photography. The film segment puts on around 250 screenings in six Kendal venues. See www.mountainfilm.co.uk.

Lake District Summer Music, August. A fortnight-long programme of recitals by some top international artists and summer school students at venues across the Lake District. See www.ldsm.org.uk.

Lakeland Festival of Storytelling, Staveley and Ings, September. Three days of professional storytelling, performances and workshops run by renowned storyteller Taffy Thomas. See www.taffythomas.co.uk.

Maryport Blues Festival, July. Nationally renowned gathering of blues musicians, staged in the town's pubs and on the quayside. See www.maryportblues.com.

Potfest in the Park, Hutton-in-the-Forest, July. Showcase of the work of 100 potters and ceramics experts from all over the world. See www.potfest.co.uk.

Sedbergh Festival of Books and Drama, August and September. Book readings, signings, discussions and workshops in England's only official Book Town. See www.sedbergh.org.uk.

Words by the Water, Keswick, March. A ten-day celebration of writing, reading and ideas, hosted by the Theatre by the Lake on the shores of Derwent Water. See www.wayswithwords.co.uk/cumbria.

Wordsworth Trust Arts and Book Festival, Grasmere, January. Annual weekend of lectures and workshops run by the Wordsworth Trust at Dove Cottage. See www.wordsworth.org.uk.

TEKK HOD – WRESTLING IN THE LAKE DISTRICT

Wrestling is an ancient sport played in different forms all over the world, but the Lake District is particularly proud of the Cumberland and Westmorland version of it.

The region's form of wrestling may have been introduced by the Vikings, though the earliest records of it as a competitive sport are from the 17th century. Traditional styles of wrestling are popular in Lancashire, Northumberland and other pockets of the country—but Cumbria is its heartland. A million miles from the showmanship, glitz and mindless violence of American TV wrestling, Cumberland and Westmorland wrestling is essentially unchanged from its early Georgian days. Even the charmingly Victorian costume of embroidered white long-johns, colourful trunks and socks remains in use.

The sport is simple in theory. To begin, wrestlers stand chest to chest and 'tekk hod', each linking his fingers behind the back of his opponent, one arm over the shoulder and the other underneath. Once the referee starts the bout, each wrestler aims to throw his opponent to the floor or break his grasp behind the back. Most contests are the best of three bouts and always take place on grass, in an enclosed playing area.

Behind these simple rules lie a wider variety of tactics and moves. Wrestlers may lift, swing, twist and trip an opponent to force him to the floor, and the best of them are as skilful and nimble on their feet as they are strong. To the onlooker it can seem a very aggressive sport, but Cumbrian wrestlers are keenly aware of their sport's noble traditions, and each bout starts and ends with a handshake. On observing a bout during a visit to the Lake District, Charles Dickens wrote: 'They strip to their drawers and flannel vests, shake hands in a token of amity and then, while exerting every muscle to the utmost, these fine fellows never exhibit a trace of savageness or animosity.'

Wrestling's heyday came in the 19th century, when it was a vital part of Lake District culture and contests pulled five-figure crowds. But they attracted gamblers and bookmakers too, and in 1906 a ruling body, the

Cumberland and Westmorland Wrestling Association, was set up to help purge the sport of a gambling problem that had led to many bouts being fixed or—pardoning the pun—thrown. The association now oversees some 60 wrestling events during the season from April to October, and most of the Lake District's popular summer shows have contests for various age groups and both sexes. After a steady decline in interest due to competing sports and leisure interests, wrestlers hope that their sport is now becoming more popular again among both participants and spectators, perhaps because of a decision to relax the rules on dress to allow youngsters to compete in more modern sports clothes. Its revival is also partly due to a nostalgic desire to preserve it as part of the Lake District's heritage, values and identity, but wrestlers today compete no less vigorously than any of their ancestors.

Wrestling lingo

Back-heel Kicking an opponent's legs away from under him.

Barneying The practice of match-fixing in wrestling.

Chip A move to throw an opponent to the floor.

Dog-fall When two wrestlers land simultaneously and judges cannot decide a winner. The bout then restarts.

Full buttock Pulling an opponent up over the back and to the ground. Usually painfully.

Hank Twisting a leg around an opponent's leg to pull him to the ground.

Hipe or **hype** A lifting throw to the ground from the hip.

Inside-click Hooking between an opponent's legs to throw him to the ground.

LAKE DISTRICT POEMS – FROM 'WEY, NED, MAN!' BY SUSANNA BLAMIRE

This is poetry in the Cumberland dialect, though it is close enough to standard English to be mostly understood. William Wordsworth called it 'the great Cumbrian ballad.'

Wey, Ned, man! Thou luiks sae down-hearted,
Yen wad swear aw thy kindred were dead;
For sixpence, thy Jean and thee's parted—
What then, man, ne'er bodder thy head!

There's lasses enow, I'll uphod te,
And tou may be suin as weel match'd;
Tou knows there's still fish i' the river
As guld as has ever been catch'd.

Nay, Joe! Tou kens nought o' the matter,
Sae let's hae nae mair o' thy jeer;
Auld England's gown's worn till a tatter,
And they'll nit new don her, I fear.
True liberty never can flourish,
Till man in his reets is a king, —
Till we tek a tithe pig frae the bishop,
As he's duin frae us, is the thing.

What, Ned, and is this aw that ails thee?
Mess, lad! Tou deserves maist to hang!
What! Tek a bit lan frae its owner! —
Is this then thy fine *Reets o' Man*?
Tou ploughs, and tou sows, and tou reaps, man,
Tou cums, and tou gangs, where tou will;
Nowther king, lword, nor bishop, dar touch thee,
Sae lang as tou dis fwok nae ill!

CUMBRIA'S RECLAIMED RAILWAYS

While much of Cumbria's old rail network has fallen out of use, the hard work of enthusiasts means that some of the lines have been preserved for passenger use. Faithfully restored steam locomotives run on these lines through some of the area's loveliest scenery. Here are the county's four reclaimed railway companies.

The Ravenglass and Eskdale Railway. This scenic narrow-gauge line runs for seven miles from the west coast to a terminus near the village of Boot. Steam trains run every month of the year, and there is a visitor centre at the Eskdale end. The line was originally opened in the 1870s to transport iron ore to the main train line at Ravenglass, and while a decline in the industry meant it closed in 1913, enthusiasts soon turned it into a private rail company. The line has always been known locally as La'al Ratty, dialect for 'the little narrow way'. Tel 01229 717171 or online at www.ravenglass-railway.co.uk.

The Lakeside and Haverthwaite Railway. Steam engines run along this pretty line from the southern shores of Windermere through the Leven Valley to Haverthwaite near Newby Bridge. Trains run every day from April to October, as well as several times over Christmas. The three miles of track form the last surviving branch line of the Furness Railway, which carried freight and passengers along the peninsula until its closure in the 1960s. Tel 015395 31594 or online at www.lakesiderailway.co.uk.

The South Tynedale Railway. Runs for just over two miles from Alston in Cumbria to Kirkhaugh in neighbouring Northumberland. It follows an old branch line of the Newcastle to Carlisle railway, which was built in the 1850s to serve Alston's lead mines but closed in 1976. Volunteers soon built a new narrow-gauge line along the trackbed, and now run steam locomotives from Good Friday to the end of October. Tel 01434 382828 or online at www.strps.org.uk.

The Eden Valley Railway. The original railway opened in 1862 to carry goods and passengers from Kirkby Stephen to Clifton, just south of Penrith. After use of it declined, the final stretch of the line was closed in 1989. The Eden Valley Railway Society was formed six years later with the aim of restoring parts of the line, and the first section, from Warcop to Appleby, began carrying passengers in 2006. It is now working towards continuing the line on to the original Kirkby Stephen East terminus. Online at www.evr.org.uk.

A DICTIONARY OF LAKE DISTRICT DIALECT

The Cumbrian dialect is among the most distinctive in England, built and changed over centuries. While some dialect words are similar to nearby areas like Scotland and Yorkshire, others are close corruptions of received pronunciation, or influenced by Scandinavian colonists and Celtic languages. Use of the traditional dialect is fading in some areas, but in others it is still widely used and fiercely protected. Vocabulary also varies widely across Cumbria, but everywhere it is spoken it helps to define the special character of the region. Here's a selection of 100 words from the vast dictionary of dialect.

Aald = Old
Abacka = At the back of
Aboot = About
Afore = Before
Ah = I
Any road = Anyway
Areet = Alright

Arl = Old
Aye = Yes
Bairn, bairden or *barn* = Child
Bait = Food
Barie = Good, nice
Bezzel = Beat severely
Blather = Noisy talk

Brass = Money
Britches = Trousers
Bust = Break
Cack = Bad
Chatter watter = Tea
Chess = To chase
Clack = To chat
Claggy or *clarty* = Dirty
Coo = Cow
Crack = Gossip, news, conversation
Cuddy = Cow or donkey
Deek or *deekaboot* = To look or look about
Divent = Don't
Dree = Dreary, tedious
Enoo = Enough
Flaiten = Frightened
Frey = From
Gadge or *gadgee* = Man
Gammerstang = An awkward person
Gan = To go
Gay = Very
Giz = Give us
Glem = A look
Handsturn = Work, occupation
Hoy = To throw
Ill-turn = Injury, wrong
Jigger = A good dancer
Kaylied = Drunk
Kersmas = Christmas
Kirk = Church
Ladgeful = Embarassing
Laik = Play
La'l = Little
Lamp = To hit
Lang = Long
Langsom = Lonely, wearisome
Larn = To learn
Lowp = To leap
Lug = Ear
Maff = To make a mess of
Marra = Mate, friend
Mek = To make

Mizzlin = Misty, drizzly rain
Moy = Mouth
Nah = No
Nash = To dash, run
Nigh on = Nearly
Nix or *nowt* = Nothing
Nobbut = Only
Offcomer = A non-native
Owt = Anything
Owwer = Over
Parney = Water
Pun = Pound sterling
Radge or *radgee* = Crazy
Reet = Right
Rive = To pull
Ross = Horse
Rowky = Foggy
Russler = Wrestler
Scop = To throw
Scower = To look at
Scran = Food
Seck or *sic* = Such
Slape = Slippery
Slatter = To rain heavily
Sling = To depart
Summat = Something
Tek = Take
Telt = Told
Thew = You
Tudder = The other
Twa = Two
Vanaye or *vanear* = Almost
Wam = Warm
Wedder = Weather
Wi or *wid* = With
Wuk = Work
Wulf = To eat fast, hungrily
Yacker = Farm worker
Yam or *yem* = Home
Yan = One
Yat = Gate
Yatter = To talk
Yon = That
Yonder = Over there

CUMBRIA'S PRISONER-OF-WAR CAMPS

The remote, spacious landscape meant that Cumbria had its fair share of prisoner-of-war camps during the Second World War. All of the camps were either dismantled at the end of the war or returned to their original use as accommodation, but some nearby residents still have memories of the sudden influx of Germans and Italians. The eight PoW sites that have been identified in the county are:

Carlisle Camp. An existing military camp repurposed for PoWs.

Beela River Camp. Camp close to Milnthorpe. Locals recall that Italian PoWs appeared very happy to be staying there, and that guards spent more time keeping local girls out than the prisoners in.

Grizedale Hall. Camp Number 1 in the official classification system, and the destination for some of the first German PoWs as well as some of the most important. Located on the edge of the Grizedale Forest, the 30 huts and watchtower around the stately home were demolished after the war. It was known to locals as 'U-Boat Hotel'.

Hornby Hall Camp. Some features of this camp of 25 Nissan huts east of Penrith can still be seen. Hornby Hall is now a country house offering accommodation.

Longtown Camp. The exact site of this camp north of Carlisle has not been identified.

Merry Thought Camp. Intriguingly named, purpose-built camp at Calthwaite in north Cumbria, very close to where the M6 now runs.

Moota Camp. German PoWs built a chapel at this 1,000-man camp near Cockermouth and filled it with some fine artworks, but it was all destroyed after the war. The site now houses a hotel.

Shap Wells Camp. A smart country hotel and spa a few miles south of Shap that was requisitioned as a camp for senior German air and naval officers. Now a hotel again.

THE UNHAPPY CRIER OF CLAIFE

The wooded hill on the western side of Windermere close to Sawrey is reputedly home to the spectral Crier of Claife. Local legend has it that this is the ghost of a medieval monk whose job it was to rescue fallen

women, and who went mad after being rejected by one of them. He
howled his anguish on the Claife Heights, and his ghost is reckoned to
have been seen and heard there ever since.

The ghost's most notable appearance was to an 18th century
Windermere boatman, who returned from the western shore on a
stormy night terrified and struck dumb by what he had seen. He died a
few days later. A monk was asked to exorcise the crier with a bell and
bible, dispatching him to an area now marked on OS maps as *Crier of
Claife*. Strange sounds and sightings are said to continue on the Claife
Heights.

THE 20TH CENTURY IN LOCAL NEWS

The *Westmorland Gazette* has been carrying the news to the southern
half of the Lake District for close to 200 years, and is one of the best
local newspapers in the country. Here are some of the more arresting
of its headlines through the decades of the 20th century.

1998 *Caterpillars Out-graze Sheep*
A plague of caterpillars wreaks havoc on the Howgill Fells, decimating
grassland and leaving sheep searching for alternative grazing land.

1985 *Topless Bathing is NOT for the Lakes*
A 17 year-old woman from Kendal is bound over after diving topless
into Windermere. 'Bathing topless in certain areas of the Mediterranean
and parts of England is accepted,' said the magistrate, 'but it is not
accepted in Windermere.'

1979 *Iced-up Afghan Fellside Rescue*
The Langdale and Ambleside Mountain Rescue Team stretchers a frozen
Afghan hound down from a snowy Green Burn near Grasmere. Its coat
had become so weighted down with ice and snow that it could no
longer walk.

1964 *Mystery of 50 Missing Piglets*
Piglets reared near Brigsteer disappear. Suspects include foxes, dogs,
badgers and a cannibal sow.

1953 *Longer Bed Sheets May Solve Divorce Problem*
The Westmorland Federation of Women's Institutes suggests that
extending the size of bed sheets so that there is more to tuck in at the
sides will lead to happier marriages. A Mrs Wetherell comments: 'To my
surprise, I have been told that many a divorce has been caused by too
short a sheet.'

1945 *18 Nazi Chiefs Detrain at Windermere*

Locals stop to watch German war prisoners at Windermere station on their way to a camp near Hawkshead. 'Many of the crowd were not amused, and there were some caustic comments muttered audibly.'

1935 *Highgate Traffic Jam*

Traffic is slightly slower than usual in Kendal. 'For about ten minutes last Friday there was a traffic jam in Highgate that tried the patience of travellers in a hurry.'

1928 *First Time in Fifty Years: No Woman Charged with Drunkenness in Kendal Last Year*

Kendal's chief constable notes 26 charges of drunkenness in the town's court—all of them for men and none for women, 'which was very gratifying'.

1913 *Sealion Escapes in Kendal*

A travelling showman reports that a sealion has escaped from his van and into the River Kent. It was recaptured down river four days later.

1908 *Americans in the Lake District*

'Americans have begun to invade the Lake District' as 60 arrive for the night in Grasmere. 'Some boast that they are "doing" the Lake District in three days.'

TEN FAMOUS CUMBRIANS

Beyond the people profiled in more detail elsewhere in this book, Cumbria has had plenty of notable sons, daughters and residents through the ages. Here are ten of them.

Catherine Parr (1512–1548). Kendal-born wife of Henry VIII—his sixth, and the only one to survive him.

John Paul Jones (1747–1792). One of the naval heroes of the American revolution, and often regarded as one of the founders of the American navy. He became a mariner in Whitehaven at the age of 12, and joined the Americans in 1775. Three years later he returned to Whitehaven—to wreck much of it in a hit-and-run raid.

Fletcher Christian (1764–1793). Infamous leader of the mutiny on Captain Bligh's Bounty in 1789. Born in Cockermouth, he was killed on Tahiti, though there is a theory that he faked his own death and returned to England.

John Dalton (1766–1844). Born at Eaglesfield near Cockermouth. Chemist, physicist, biologist and the founder of atomic theory.

Fearon Fallows (1789–1831). Cockermouth-born astronomer to King George IV, who also built the Royal Observatory at the Cape of Good Hope in South Africa.

Thomas Henry Ismay (1836–1899). Maryport-born shipping magnate and chairman of the White Star Line during the building and sinking of the Titanic.

Hugh Lowther, Fifth Earl of Lonsdale (1857–1944). Part of the Lowther family, responsible for much of west Cumbria's mining and shipbuilding. Known for a while as 'England's greatest sporting gentleman', first president of the AA and a chairman of Arsenal FC. His Lonsdale name was lent to boxing belts and equipment.

Stan Laurel (1890–1965). The smaller half of the Laurel and Hardy film double act, and Ulverston's most famous son.

Gus Risman (1911–1994). Perhaps Cumbria's most famous sportsman, Risman played rugby league for Workington and Great Britain and was one of only nine original inductees into the sport's hall of fame.

Chris Bonington (1934–). Mountaineer, author and broadcaster, knighted for services to his sport, now living in Hesket Newmarket.

❦❦❦❦❦❦❦❦❦❦❦❦❦❦❦

SAMUEL TAYLOR COLERIDGE, ROCK CLIMBER

Samuel Taylor Coleridge is probably the second best-known of all Lake District poets after William Wordsworth—but few remember him as a pioneer of rock climbing.

Coleridge was a frequent and energetic walker, often covering 30 miles or more in a day. In 1802, he made what the Fell and Rock Climbing Club acknowledges as the first-ever recorded, recreational rock climb in England—and he did it by accident. Walking between Scafell and Scafell Pike, Coleridge encountered Broad Stand, a 30 feet high rockface and now well known by modern rock climbers—and by mountain rescue teams as an accident blackspot. Without quite realising what he was letting himself in for, Coleridge eventually crossed Broad Stand, emerging shaken but triumphant on the other side to continue his walk. The next day, he recorded his experiences in self-effacing style in a letter to Sara Hutchinson.

'The first place I came to, that was not direct Rock, I slipped down, and went on for a while with tolerable ease—but now I came (it was midway down) to a smooth perpendicular rock about 7 feet high—this was nothing—I put my hands on the ledge and dropped down—in a few yards came just such another—I dropped that too, and yet another, seemed not higher? I would not stand for a trifle so I dropped that too—but the stretching of the muscles of my hands and arms, and the jolt of the fall on my feet, put my whole limbs in a tremble, and I paused, and looking down, saw that I had little else to encounter but a succession of these little precipices—it was in truth a path that in a very hard rain is, no doubt, the channel of a most splendid waterfall. So I began to suspect that I ought not to go on, but then unfortunately though I could with ease drop down a smooth rock 7 feet high, I could not *climb* it, so go on I must and on I went...

... the next 3 drops were not half a foot, at least not a foot more than my own height, but every drop increased the palsy of my limbs—I shook all over, Heaven knows without the least influence of fear, and now I had only two more to drop down. To return was impossible—but of these two the first was tremendous, it was twice my own height, and the ledge at the bottom was so exceedingly narrow, that if I dropped down upon it I must of necessity have fallen backwards and of course killed myself. My limbs were all in a tremble—I lay upon my back to rest myself, and was beginning according to my custom to laugh at myself for a madman, when the sight of the crags above me on each side, and the impetuous clouds just over them, posting so luridly and so rapidly northward, overawed me. I lay in a state of almost prophetic trance and delight and blessed God aloud, for the powers of reason and the will, which remaining no danger can overpower us! O God, I exclaimed aloud—how calm, how blessed am I now—I know not how to proceed, how to return, but I am calm and fearless and confident—if this reality were a dream, if I were asleep, what agonies had I suffered!'

The modern era of organised rock climbing in England is usually dated back to 1886, when Walter Parry Haskett Smith made the first ever solo ascent of the 70ft Napes Needle on Great Gable to public acclaim—an achievement that Coleridge's unscheduled climb predates by nearly a century.

ROOM OCCUPANCY RATES IN THE LAKE DISTRICT

When is the best time to visit the Lake District? Based on room occupancy rates across Cumbria, the quietest time is January and the busiest is August. Cumbria Tourism's monthly survey of occupancy in serviced accommodation—hotels, B&Bs and guesthouses—is a good indication of how busy the area is, and how difficult it is likely to be to find a room for the night at any given time. Occupancy rates range from

33 per cent in the depths of winter to 71 per cent in the school summer holidays, but accommodation is more than half-full from April through to October. The annual average rate of occupancy in 2006 was 56 per cent.

Month	Room occupancy rate in 2006/%
January	33
February	45
March	44
April	58
May	59
June	63
July	68
August	71
September	69
October	61
November	45
December	41

LITERARY LAKELANDERS – CANON RAWNSLEY

Vicar, writer, philanthropist, inspiration to Beatrix Potter and co-founder of the National Trust—Canon Rawnsley was a hardworking man who did more than most to protect and promote the natural beauty of the Lake District.

Born in 1851, Hardwicke Drummond Rawnsley moved to the Lake District at the age of 26 to take up the post of vicar at Wray Church near Ambleside. He soon involved himself in local activities to protect the local countryside against exploitation and the effects of heavy tourism, forming the Lake District Defence Society with support from intellectual and literary heavyweights like John Ruskin, Lord Alfred Tennyson and Robert Browning. His views also had a lasting effect on Beatrix Potter, whom he met during her holiday to the Lake District aged 16. Rawnsley later encouraged Potter to write and publish her tales of Peter Rabbit.

After five years at Wray, Rawnsley moved on to Keswick, and was appointed an honorary canon of Carlisle Cathedral in 1891. His various philanthropic acts included the setting up of schools, galleries and nursing associations, and he was a prolific writer, penning a staggering 30,000 or so sonnets as well as books about the Lake District and a biography of his friend John Ruskin.

But it is for his work in founding the National Trust that Rawnsley is now best remembered. Together with two other philanthropists, Octavia Hill and Sir Robert Hunter, Rawnsley created the organisation in 1895 with the aim of preserving places of natural and historic interest across the country. Rawnsley was its first secretary and Rupert Potter, Beatrix's father, one of its first members. The Trust campaigned against unsightly development and industrialisation in areas of the Lake District like Borrowdale, and raised money to buy land and property. Many of Rawnsley's own estates were bequeathed to the Trust after his death in Grasmere in 1920.

Though much of its early work was in the south of England, Rawnsley's influence has meant that the National Trust has always been very active in the Lake District. Since Rawnsley's day, it has grown its membership to more than 3.4 million people, and now cares for 600,000 acres of British countryside and 200 buildings and gardens. There is a memorial to Canon Rawnsley by Friars Crag off Derwent Water—a suitable point, since it was the tranquil and spectacular views from places like this that he worked so hard to preserve.

THE LAKE DISTRICT'S BEST AND WORST ASCENTS

Hopegill Head offers the best reward for an uphill slog in the entire Lake District—according to an assessment of all 759 ascents logged by legendary fellwalker Alfred Wainwright.

The 'Index of Quality' was compiled by Peter Linney in his *Official Wainwright Gazetteer* (Michael Joseph). Linney interpreted Wainwright's notes on the ascents in the *Pictorial Guides to the Lakeland Fells* to create a formula that combined the difficulty of the walk, the quality of the summit and the view, and the space devoted to each fell in the books. The end result was a rating for each ascent from 0 to 100—where 0 was the most tedious climb imaginable and 100 the perfect walk, summit and view. By this rating, Linney reckoned the best ascents were of Scafell Pike (95), Blencathra (94) and Great Gable (94), which each received their marks for several different starting points and routes. Two fells—Sheffield Pike and Hart Side—received ratings of just 9, suggesting that these are best avoided.

Linney then used these scores to produce a 'Value for Effort' index to work out which of the ascents were the most rewarding relative to the time spent on them by the average walker. His painstaking number-crunching produces a top ten of the climbs that give Lakeland walkers the best return for their exertions.

1 Hopegill Head, from Coeldale Hause via Hobcarton Crag
('Value for Effort': 40)
2= Hopegill Head, from Coeldale Hause via Sand Hill (31)
2= Great Gable, from Sty Head (31)
4 Haystacks, from Black Sail Youth Hostel (29)
5= Ill Bell, from Kentmere Reservoir (28)
5= Red Screes, from Kirkstone Pass (28)
7= Green Gable, from Styhead Gill via Aaron Slack (27)
7= Green Gable, from Styhead Gill via Mitchell Cove (27)
9= Eel Crag, from Coledale Hause via the pools (25)
9= Grange Fell, from Watendlath via Brund Fell (25)

And the ascent that gives the least value for effort? Choose from Caudale Moor, Hart Side, Sheffield Pike, Tarn Crag and Wether Hill, which each receive a rating of just 2 for various different routes of ascent.

These ratings are based on one man's interpretations of the *Pictorial Guides*, of course—but they do chime with Wainwright's own opinions. He called Hopegill Head 'a delightful top, fashioned for the accommodation of solitary walkers,' while of one of the duds, Sheffield Pike, he said: 'Even on a sunny summer day the top of the fell seems a dismal, cheerless place.'

CUMBRIA INDUSTRIES – COPPER

Copper was a major industry for the Lake District in the 19th century, and although it is no longer mined, signs of its importance can be seen around the fells and towns.

There is evidence that the Romans used the copper they found in the Lake District, but retrieval of it began in earnest with the arrival of German miners in the 16th century. They called the best mine in the area Gottesgab—God's gift—and this soon became corrupted into Goldscope, the name by which it was known locally. Mining areas were mostly found in the north of the Lake District, but copper was also in plentiful supply around Coniston in the south.

After sporadic mining over the next few hundred years, it took off in Coniston in the 1820s. The mines proved to be very productive, fuelling the expansion of this and other nearby towns and villages and prompting the building of a branch railway line in the 1850s to transport the copper south. But soon afterwards, supplies began to be exhausted and challenged by cheaper foreign imports. Apart from intermittent retrieval of the remnants, the copper mining industry decayed, leaving behind dozens of vast spoil heaps and old buildings that can still be seen today on the fells around Coniston and elsewhere.

Through most of their history, copper ore was retrieved with the help of only gunpowder and hand drills, and chipping away at the hard volcanic rock was backbreaking work. The Ruskin Museum in Coniston displays some of the tools used along with other artefacts on the copper heritage, and some of the old mines can be explored with expert guidance.

BUILDINGS AT RISK

English Heritage's 'Buildings at Risk' register records all Grade I and Grade II listed buildings and Scheduled Ancient Monuments that are known to be at risk through decay or neglect. Cumbria has 37 such sites.

Arnside Tower
Augill Lead Mine Smelting Mill, Stainmore
Backbarrow Ironworks, Haverthwaite
Brackenhill Tower, Arthuret
Brougham Hall
Burneside Hall Tower
Calder Abbey, Calder Bridge
Cockermouth Castle Towers
Coniston Copper Mines
Cornmill, Warwick Bridge
Crake Trees Tower House, Crosby Ravensworth
Gale Mansion, Whitehaven
Gleaston Castle, Aldingham
Greenside Lead Mine, Glenridding
Hadrian's Wall at Burtholme
Hadrian's Wall, Port Carlisle to Bowness
Haig Pit Engine House, Whitehaven

Hazelslack Tower, Beetham
Heltondale Beck Bridge, Askham
High Head Castle, Skelton
Kirkoswald Castle
Lammerside Castle, Wharton
Lowther Castle
Lowwood Gunpowder Works
Millom Castle
Naworth Castle, Brampton
Newland Blast Furnace, Egton
Petterill Bank, Carlisle
Roachburn Colliery, Carlisle
Rotherhopefell Ore Works
Saltom Pit Engine House
St Michael's Rectory, Workington
Stonehouse Tower, Nicholforest
The Stonehouse, Nether Denton
Triermain Castle, Waterhead
Whitesyke and Bentyfield Lead Mines, Alston Moor
Winster Potash Kiln, Cartmel Fell

TEN LITERARY GRAVES

The final resting places of some of the most famous
literary Lakelanders.

William Wordsworth, **Dorothy Wordsworth** and **Hartley
Coleridge** – St Oswald's Churchyard, Grasmere

Robert Southey – St Kentigern's Church, Crosthwaite, Keswick

John Ruskin – St Andrew's Churchyard, Coniston

Hugh Walpole – St John's Churchyard, Keswick

Norman Nicholson – St George's Churchyard, Millom

Arthur Ransome – St Paul's Churchyard, Rusland

Beatrix Potter – ashes scattered around Sawrey

Alfred Wainwright – ashes scattered on Haystacks

ROCK CLIMBING GRADES

Rock climbers assess the difficulty of their routes using a series of
grades. Their categories vary from country to country, and there are
alternative systems even within the UK, but the following is usually
accepted as standard. So if you think a 'Hard Very Difficult' climb in the
Lake District might present you with a challenge, then you will be
alarmed to discover that it is only the fifth rating in a series that is
topped by 'Extremely Severe' climbs. The categories are:

Easy	Hard Severe
Moderate	Mild Very Severe
Difficult	Very Severe
Very Difficult	Hard Very Severe
Hard Very Difficult	Extremely Severe
Severe	

The extremely severe category is often broken down into
further sub-grades.

GWENDA MATTHEWS' FAVOURITE LAKE DISTRICT BOOKS...

Gwenda Matthews runs Bookends in Carlisle, one of Cumbria's many excellent independent bookshops. Here, in no particular order, are her personal and professional favourite Lake District books.

Pictorial Guides to the Lakeland Fells Volumes One to Seven by Alfred Wainwright (Frances Lincoln). A meticulously produced labour of love which has opened up the beauty of all the fells to everyone for the past 50 years.

The Tale of Mrs Tiggy-Winkle by Beatrix Potter (Frederick Warne). A favourite bedtime story for my daughter.

The Grasmere and Alfoxden Journals by Dorothy Wordsworth (OUP). A fascinating record of Dorothy's life with her brother at Dove Cottage.

A Dictionary of Lake District Place-Names by Diana Whaley (English Place-Name Society). An accessible, affordable record which is also a great social history of the county.

The Buildings of England: Cumberland and Westmorland by Nikolaus Pevsner (Yale University Press). *The* architectural guide.

The Maid of Buttermere by Melvyn Bragg (Sceptre). The story of Mary Robinson immerses you in 19th century Buttermere and Cumbria with such ease.

The Breeding Birds of Cumbria (Cumbria Bird Club). A complete record and another labour of love, with so much information and so well researched.

Keswick: The Story of a Lake District Town by George Bott (Bookcase). A classic of local history writing, researched and written with a great love of the place.

Traditional Buildings of the Lake District by RW Brunskill (Cassell). Another book on the history of buildings, but you get social history too.

The Silent Traveller in Lakeland by Chiang Yee (Mercat Press). The Lake District from the gentle viewpoint of this Chinese author, with some beautiful, haunting illustrations.

... AND STEVE MATTHEWS' FORGOTTEN LAKE DISTRICT CLASSICS

Gwenda's husband Steve runs Carlisle's Bookcase, a vast second-hand and antiquarian bookshop with the biggest range of out-of-print and rare Cumbrian books to be found anywhere. This is Steve's choice of classic Lake District books through the centuries. Not all of them are in print any more—but Bookcase is the best place to find them.

The History and Antiquities of the Counties of Westmoreland and Cumberland by William Hutchinson (W Strahan and T Caldell, 1777). The first book to tell the full story of the two counties.

The History of the County of Cumberland by William Hutchinson (F Jollie, 1794). A great rag-bag of information—anything and everything on 18th century Cumberland.

A Guide to the Lakes, in Cumberland, Westmorland and Lancashire by Thomas West (B Law, 1778). The man who first showed people where to go and what to see.

The Lake Country by E and WJ Linton (Smith, Elder and Co., 1864). An idiosyncratic account of the Lakes by the first female journalist, with illustrations by her wayward and errant husband.

Rock-Climbing in the English Lake District by Owen Glynne Jones (Abraham and Sons, 1900). The ultimate guide for the early climbers on the crags, with George Abraham's pictures to boot.

Mines and Mining in the English Lake District by John Postlethwaite (WH Moss and Sons, 1913). A new angle on the Lakes and mountains from underneath.

The English Lakes by William Palmer and A Heaton Cooper (A&C Black, 1908). A nostalgic book of the Edwardian Lakes.

Lake District History by WG Collingwood (Titus Wilson, 1928). The best and most elegant of Lake District histories.

The Lakers: The First Tourists by Norman Nicholson (Robert Hale, 1955). The story of how they discovered the Lakes, told by one of the county's most elegant writers.

The Tarns of Lakeland by E Heaton Cooper (Frank Peters, 1983). A personal vision of the high fells.

FARMERS' MARKETS

Farmers' markets have been at the forefront of the recent food revolution in the Lake District. As well as promoting great local food, the markets provide valuable income for farmers and other local producers—money that has been especially needed since the foot-and-mouth crisis of 2001. Cumbria now boasts more than a dozen regular markets, and they are all well worth a visit. Markets generally run from 9 or 10am until early afternoon.

Brampton Last Saturday of every month by the Moot Hall

Brough Third Saturday in the Memorial Hall

Carlisle First Friday in the city centre

Carnforth Fourth Wednesday at the railway station

Cockermouth First Saturday in the Market Place

Egremont Third Friday in the Market Hall

Greenhead Second Sunday in the Village Hall

Harrison & Hetherington Second Saturday at Borderway Mart, Rosehill

High Bentham, near Ingleton First Saturday in the Market Hall

Kendal Last Friday in the Market Place

Orton Second Saturday in the Market Hall

Penrith Third Tuesday in the Market Square

Pooley Bridge Last Sunday behind the Sun Inn and in Rheged during winter

Ulverston Third Saturday outside the Market Hall

LAKE DISTRICT FOOD – RUM BUTTER

Butter has been an important product of Lake District farms over the centuries, and although its production has declined lately, it is generously used in many traditional recipes. Rum and spices, which arrived in to the ports of west Cumbria from the Caribbean, were adopted into cooking too, and there are several different stories about how they came to be mixed with butter. One has it that the recipe was devised by smugglers who, holed up in their caves, improvised it out of their illicit haul of rum, butter and sugar.

Whether it was first made by accident or design, rum butter soon became a firm favourite in Cumbrian society, and a popular luxury among farming communities too. It was traditionally eaten at Lake District christenings, with each of its ingredients carrying a special significance: butter representing the richness of life, sugar its sweetness, rum its spirit and nutmeg its spice. Rum butter is simple to make and is often eaten as a spread on scones, toast, biscuits and crackers. It is also a good accompaniment to Christmas pudding or mince pies.

A recipe for rum butter
100g unsalted butter
200g brown sugar
Half a nutmeg, grated
Pinch of ground cinnamon
80ml rum or to taste

Gently melt the butter. Add the sugar and beat to a cream. Add the nutmeg and cinnamon and then, gradually, the rum, tasting every now and then to check if you have enough. Transfer to pots or dishes and allow to cool and set.

WAINWRIGHT'S BEST RIDGE WALKS

After 13 years compiling his *Pictorial Guides to the Lakeland Fells*, Alfred Wainwright was well placed to judge the best ridges for walking in the Lake District. He chose:

The Fairfield Horseshoe
The High Street range
The Mosedale Horseshoe
Causey Pike to Whiteless Pike
Grisedale Pike to Whiteside
Esk Hause to Wrynose Pass via Bowfell
The Eskdale Horseshoe
Grisedale Pass to Threlkeld on the Helvellyn range
The High Stile ridge
Cat Bells to Scope End via Dale Head and Hindscarth
The Coniston Round from Old Man to Wetherlam

WHERE TO FIND WORDSWORTH'S DAFFODILS

Of all the poems inspired by the Lake District, none is more widely known or loved than William Wordsworth's 'I Wandered Lonely as a Cloud'. It was inspired by a carpet of daffodils seen by Wordsworth and his sister Dorothy by the edge of Ullswater at Gowbarrow Park in 1802, and the connection has generated a tourist industry of its own ever since.

William and Dorothy discovered the daffodils while walking back to their Grasmere home. Dorothy remembered the experience in her diary entry for 15th April 1802. 'When we were in the woods beyond Gowbarrow Park we saw a few daffodils close to the water side. We fancied that the lake had floated the seed ashore and that the little colony had so sprung up. But as we went along there were more and yet more and at last under the boughs of the trees, we saw that there was a long belt of them along the shore, about the breadth of a country turnpike road. I never saw daffodils so beautiful—they grew among the mossy stones about and about them, some rested their heads upon these stones as on a pillow for weariness and the rest tossed and reeled and danced and seemed as if they verily laughed with the wind that blew upon them over the lake. They looked so gay, ever dancing and ever changing.'

Wordsworth wrote his poem two years later, but revised it in the version that is best known today. It begins:

> *I wandered lonely as a Cloud*
> *That floats on high o'er Vales and Hills,*
> *When all at once I saw a crowd*
> *A host of golden daffodils;*
> *Beside the lake, beneath the trees*
> *Fluttering and dancing in the breeze.*

Gowbarrow Park was bought by the National Trust in 1906. Large numbers continue to flock to Ullswater each spring to see the daffodils, and although a busy road now runs past the spot, the sight can still be as spectacular as it was when Wordsworth found it.

SWIMMING ROUND THE LAKE DISTRICT

Even on the warmest of summer days, few of the people who walk past the Lake District's hundreds of tarns fancy dipping in. But for a small group of very hardy people, swimming the tarns is a pleasure and something an obsession.

On a doubtless freezing day in November 1959, two Grasmere men, Colin Dodgson and Timothy Tyson, stepped out of a tarn in Esk Pike to complete one of the Lake District's most spectacular endurance feats of all, in a part of the country that has more than its fair share of them. With this bracing dip, they had completed the extraordinary challenge of swimming in 463 tarns in the Lake District.

Though there is no agreement on the exact number of tarns in the Lakes—some appear in wet winters while others disappear in hot summers—463 was the number that Dodgson and Tyson considered permanent and deep enough to swim in. For good measure, they added probably hundreds more pools, dubs and temporary tarns. The challenge took them eight years to complete, and they swam as many as a dozen tarns in a single outing. Winter didn't put them off, and they sometimes broke ice to get at the water. At other times they had to swim around geese, ducks and swans in the tarns, move sheep and cows to get to them, or slip quietly in to some under the cover of darkness before they were found trespassing on private land. They fitted in their swims around work, often returning to Grasmere before the day's walkers had even laced up their boots.

Dodgson and Tyson were 50 and 76 respectively at the time of their 463rd swim. As if this wasn't enough, Dodgson also climbed every peak over 3,000 feet high in Scotland and Ireland; every one over 2,000 feet in England; and every one over 2,500 feet in Wales. He and Tyson never publicised their achievements, and talked about them only reluctantly. Nowadays swimming in Cumbria's lakes is quite popular, and there are companies specialising in organised tours of several of them—but the achievement of Dodgson and Tyson is not likely to be surpassed.

COUNTING SHEEP THE LAKE DISTRICT WAY

Yan Tan Tethera is a shepherd's system of counting sheep that was once widely used across the Lake District. When counting heads of sheep at morning or night, or before transporting, shearing or dipping, shepherds would use the system of words instead of numbers. The rhythmic system is thought by some to have prompted the method of counting sheep as a way to lull oneself to sleep.

The vocabulary derives from a strain of Celtic language, and provides words for one to 20. Though the system is now virtually out of use, it is still occasionally taught to children as an aid to counting, and *yan* or *tan* will sometimes be used by farmers instead of one or two. The words for each number have corrupted and varied over the years from region to region, and even from valley to valley within the Lake District. The following is just one version.

Yan	Yan-a-Dick
Tan	Tyan-a-Dick
Tethera	Tethera-Dick
Methera	Methera-Dick
Pimp	Bumfit
Sethera	Yan-a-bumfit
Lethera	Tyan-a-bumfit
Hovera	Tethera bumfit
Dovera	Methera bumfit
Dick	Giggot

Beyond 20, the words are repeated; 21, for instance, would be one score and *yan*.

THE LAKE DISTRICT'S NUMBER ONE POSTMAN

Although the television and book adventures of Postman Pat are set in a fictional Yorkshire village, the popular children's character actually has his roots firmly over the border in Cumbria. His creator, John Cunliffe, lived in Kendal for six years, during which time he conceived and wrote many of the adventures of his rural postman.

Cunliffe's inspiration for Postman Pat was fuelled by regular chats with a friendly Kendal shopkeeper and postmaster, who relayed stories of delivering the mail in the country. Friends introduced Cunliffe to farmers and other local people, who all helped to provide material for his stories. Postman Pat's fictional home of Greendale is based firmly on the Longsleddale valley close to Kendal, as the narrow, winding lanes, surrounding hills and copious numbers of sheep shared by both make clear. Some Longsleddale residents can see clear traces of themselves in their animated counterparts.

Created in 1981, Postman Pat has since become one of the most enduringly popular of all children's characters, prompting numerous spin-off TV series, ranges of books and merchandise. Longsleddale's role in the success was such that the Museum of Lakeland Life in Kendal gave Cunliffe the honour of an exhibition for many years, though it has now closed. Also gone is the post office that inspired him—a victim of the pressures of commercial competition common to many rural sub post offices.

A VIOLENT LANGUAGE

Perhaps because of the popularity of wrestling, or simply because the Lake District has received violent visits from the Vikings and Scots over the centuries, the Cumbrian dialect has a particularly large range of words for beating or striking. One 19th century dictionary—William Dickinson's *Dialect of Cumberland*—lists well over one hundred, meaning that Cumbrians are never short of vocabulary for a fight. Here are 50 of the more original words.

bang	dander	larrop	pelt	towel
bat	dang	lash	pum	trim
batter	doose	ledder	quilt	trounce
bensal	drub	lig at	rozzel	twilt
bezzel	floor	lounder	scop	warm
clink	hide	mash	settle	weft
clonk	kange	nap	shelp	whap
cloot	kelk	pay	switch	whelk
clowe	knap	peg	tan	whop
cob	lam	pelk	targe	whump

THE RECKLESS BISHOP OF BARF

Drivers on the A66 to the western shores of Bassenthwaite Lake will be able to see to their left a prominent whitewashed rock on the slopes of Barf fell, a local landmark for more than two centuries.

The rock is a tribute to the Bishop of Derry, who broke his journey to Whitehaven in 1783 at the Swan Inn in the nearby village of Thornthwaite. Energised by a few drinks at the hotel, he struck a bet that he could ride his pony all the way to the top of Barf. He didn't make it. The pony slipped on the steep slopes, plunging both itself and the Bishop to their deaths. They were buried at the foot of the slopes, but it is the rock on which they perished that has become a lasting tribute to the Bishop and his foolhardy challenge. The landlord of the Swan Hotel paid locals in money and beer to whitewash the ten feet high rock in memory of the Bishop—and, perhaps, to warn others against attempting something similar. The rock is now known as the Bishop of Barf and noted on Ordnance Survey maps. The Swan continues the tradition of whitewashing it each year.

ON THE FELLS WITH CHARLES DICKENS

Like all self-respecting literary types of the 19th century, Charles Dickens was a visitor to the Lake District. He seems to have made the journey there only once—and to judge by his account of climbing on his holiday, he had no desire to go back.

Dickens toured the northern Lakes in 1857 with his friend and fellow novelist Wilkie Collins, and as part of their trip the pair climbed Carrock Fell, a mountain of around 2,200 feet north-east of Keswick that Dickens had read about. The pair's account of their experiences later appeared in 'The Lazy Tour of Two Idle Apprentices', a thinly fictionalised story of two Londoners who escape their employer and head to the Lake District. The characters of Thomas Idle and Francis Goodchild are taken up Carrock Fell by the landlord of their inn—and the frustrations they experience along the way will be familiar to many walkers.

'The sides of Carrock looked fearfully steep, and the top of Carrock was hidden in mist. The rain was falling faster and faster. The knees of Mr Idle—always weak on walking excursions—shivered and shook with fear and damp. The wet was already penetrating through the young man's outer coat to a brand-new shooting-jacket, for which he had reluctantly paid the large sum of two guineas on leaving town; he had no stimulating refreshments about him but a small packet of clammy gingerbread nuts; he had nobody to give him an arm, nobody to pull him up tenderly in front, nobody to speak to who really felt the difficulties of the ascent, the dampness of the rain, the denseness of the mist, and the unutterable folly of climbing, undriven, up any steep place in the world, when there is level ground within reach to walk on instead. Was it for this that Thomas had left London? London, where there are nice short walks in level public gardens, with benches of repose set up at convenient distances for weary travellers—London, where rugged stone is humanely pounded into little lumps for the road, and intelligently shaped into smooth slabs for the pavement! No! It was not for the laborious ascent of the crags of Carrock that Idle had left his native city and travelled to Cumberland. Never did he feel more disastrously convinced that he had committed a very grave error in judgment than when he found himself standing in the rain at the bottom of a steep mountain, and knew that the responsibility rested on his weak shoulders of actually getting to the top of it...

*.... Carrock is but a trumpery little mountain of fifteen
hundred feet, and it presumes to have false tops, and even
precipices, as if it were Mont Blanc. No matter: Goodchild
enjoys it, and will go on; and Idle, who is afraid of being left
behind by himself, must follow. On entering the edge of the
mist, the landlord stops, and says he hopes that it will not get
any thicker. It is twenty years since he last ascended Carrock,
and it is barely possible, if the mist increases, that the party
may be lost of the mountain. Goodchild hears this dreadful
intimation, and is not in the least impressed by it. He
marches for the top that is never to be found, as if he were
the Wandering Jew, bound to go on forever, in defiance of
everything. The landlord faithfully accompanies him. The
two, to the dim eye of Idle, far below, look in the exaggerative
mist, like a pair of friendly giants, mounting the steps of
some invisible castle together. Up and up, and then down a
little, and then up, and then along a strip of level ground,
and then up again. The wind, a wind unknown in the happy
valley, blows keen and strong; the rain-mist gets impenetrable;
a dreary little cairn of stones appears. The landlord adds one
to the heap, first walking all around the cairn as if he were
about to perform an incantation, then dropping the stone on
to the top of the heap with the gesture of a magician adding
an ingredient to a cauldron in full bubble. Goodchild sits
down by the cairn as if it were his study-table at home; Idle,
drenched and panting, stands up with his back to the wind,
ascertains distinctly that this is the top at last, looks round
with all the little curiosity that is left in him, and gets in
return, a magnificent view of—Nothing!'*

FROM *THE LAZY TOUR OF TWO IDLE APPRENTICES*
BY CHARLES DICKENS

LITERARY LAKELANDERS –
ARTHUR RANSOME

Like many literary heroes of the Lake District, Arthur Ransome got
to know the area during childhood holidays. Born in Leeds in 1884,
he spent many summers at Nibthwaite near Coniston Water, and as a
young adult built a friendship with artist WG Collingwood and his
family. Starting work in publishing, he soon became an author in his
own right. After visiting Russia on a writing commission, he moved

there to live, causing some consternation in Britain about his political allegiances. Ransome remained in the country after the Russian Revolution and there met his second wife, a secretary to Leon Trotsky. He then spent several years travelling around Russia and the Baltic states as a journalist.

Ransome didn't settle in the Lake District until he was 41, when he bought a house at Low Ludderburn in the Cartmel Fell valley. Here he wrote his most famous book, *Swallows and Amazons*, which was followed by several more in the same vein, mostly set in the Lake District. *Swallows and Amazons* was based on Ransome's own childhood and on his time spent teaching the children of a family friend to sail on Coniston Water. Although the books were not immediately successful, they have become children's classics that still sell heavily today.

Ransome lived in the Lake District for most of his remaining years, for a while settling in Coniston before retiring to Haverthwaite. He died in 1967, and is buried with his wife at St Paul's Church in Rusland, between Windermere and Coniston Water. The Arthur Ransome Society was founded in 1990 to celebrate the author's life and works, and is based at the Museum of Lakeland Life at Abbot Hall in Kendal. The museum has a permanent display dedicated to Ransome and *Swallows and Amazons*.

SOME CUMBRIAN PLACE NAMES IN DIALECT

Pronunciation of Cumbria's dialect varies from region to region and even village to village, but here are some places as some locals pronounce them.

Ambleside = *Amelsed*	Hawkshead = *Aakseyd*
Barrow-in-Furness = *Barra*	Millom = *Millum*
Bassenthwaite = *Bassenthat*	Penrith = *Peerith*
Carlisle = *Carel*	Ulpha = *Oofer*
Cockermouth = *Cockermuth*	Ulverston = *Oostan*
Crosthwaite = *Crosthat*	Sedbergh = *Sebba*
Egremont = *Eggermunt*	Staveley = *Steevla*
Grasmere = *Gersma*	Workington = *Wukkit'n*

THE LAKE DISTRICT LOVESTONE

A one-tonne slab of Lake District slate at Fell Foot Park near the south end of Windermere makes up the Lake District Lovestone—the result of a Cumbria Tourist Board initiative to find the country's most romantic message. It is inscribed with the winning lines following the competition, which was run around Valentine's Day in an effort to promote the Lake District as a romantic destination for weddings and holidays. Written by Andy Rayfield from Kent, it reads:

> *'To Nikki, you make my heart soar across the water,*
> *you fill my soul with love fresher than the mountain air,*
> *you are my world...'*

LAKE DISTRICT FOOD – WESTMORLAND DAMSONS

Damsons were originally imported into Britain from Damascus in Syria during the Crusades, but the combination of the relatively mild but damp climate and the calcareous soils means they have since grown very well in the Lyth Valley in the southern Lake District.

A member of the plum family, damsons have been a significant export for farmers since they were first established in the valley, probably in the 18th century. At the height of their popularity before the Second World War, hundreds of tons of the fruit would be exported on 'Damson Saturday', held in its picking season each autumn, with much of the fruit going to jam-makers in neighbouring Lancashire. The war and sugar shortages afterwards meant sales have since declined, but it is still a popular fruit locally and is now mostly sold direct to customers from farms' roadside stalls.

The tradition of an annual festival of damsons continues with Damson Day, now staged each April to coincide with the spectacular white blossoming of the damson trees. Most of the damson producers in the Lyth Valley put on displays, and there are cooking and craft demonstrations and guided walks around the orchards. Damson Day is organized by the Westmorland Damson Association, which helps to protect the orchards in the Lake District and promotes its damsons as the best-tasting of all home-grown varieties. More information about its work can be found at www.lythdamsons.org.uk.

Damsons can be eaten raw, but are more commonly cooked or preserved. The fruit is a versatile ingredient that has been used in pickles, chutneys, pies and sausages, and in desserts including ice cream and chocolates. It is good under a crumble topping, as a base for bread-and-butter pudding, with yoghurt and muesli at breakfast or with roast pork or gammon at dinner. Among its most popular uses are in jam and gin, and it has been used to flavour wine and beer too. Damsons were also used as a natural dye in the textiles industry in Lancashire.

A recipe for damson gin
250g damsons
125g white sugar
300ml or so of good gin

Destalk and wash the damsons. Prick each one a couple of times with the point of a sharp knife or a needle. Half fill sterilized bottles or jars with the damsons, and add the sugar. Fill to the top with gin. Cork the bottles tightly and leave them on their sides for three months, turning every few days so that the sugar dissolves in the liquor. When you're ready to decant the gin, taste to see if it needs any more sugar, then strain it through muslin or filter paper into bottles. The gin continues to improve with age. Damson gin is great before or after dinner, mixed with tonic or lemonade, or as a pick-me-up from a hipflask on the fells.

THE LAKE DISTRICT'S WOODLAND CRAFTS

The coppices across Cumbria have produced numerous products and sources of employment over the centuries, and although some crafts have died out, others are still practised by dedicated specialists.

Charcoal. Made from the carefully controlled burning of dry coppice poles. Still made in some coppiced woods, though now in metal kilns rather than man-made stacks.

Bobbins. Produced from coppiced birch for the cotton mills of Lancashire during the manufacturing boom. Stott Park Bobbin Mill near Newby Bridge has the last remaining working bobbin machinery in the country.

Swill baskets. Thin coppice oak is fashioned to make these versatile baskets that are still produced by some artisans.

Besoms. Traditional brooms, made from birch twigs bound with bark.

Barrels. Once a major Lakeland industry, supplying nearby gunpowder mills and other manufacturers requiring packaging.

Clog soles. Usually made from birch, beech or sycamore, fashioned by specialist clog makers.

Hurdles. Made from coppiced hazel and used by farmers for enclosures.

Tool handles. Usually made from ash.

THE TALES OF BEATRIX POTTER

Many of Beatrix Potter's stories, characters and settings were influenced by the Lake District, where she spent childhood holidays and later lived. Her 23 original Peter Rabbit tales, with their year of first publication, are:

The Tale of Peter Rabbit (1902)
The Tale of Squirrel Nutkin (1903)
The Tailor of Gloucester (1903)
The Tale of Benjamin Bunny (1904)
The Tale of Two Bad Mice (1904)
The Tale of Mrs Tiggy-Winkle (1905)
The Tale of the Pie and the Patty-Pan (1905)
The Tale of Mr Jeremy Fisher (1906)
The Story of a Fierce Bad Rabbit (1906)
The Story of Miss Moppet (1906)
The Tale of Tom Kitten (1907)
The Tale of Jemima Puddle-Duck (1908)
The Tale of Samuel Whiskers *or* The Roly-Poly Pudding (1908)
The Tale of the Flopsy Bunnies (1909)
The Tale of Ginger and Pickles (1909)
The Tale of Mrs Tittlemouse (1910)
The Tale of Timmy Tiptoes (1911)
The Tale of Mr Tod (1912)
The Tale of Pigling Bland (1913)
Appley Dapply's Nursery Rhymes (1917)
The Tale of Johnny Town-Mouse (1918)
Cecily Parsley's Nursery Rhymes (1922)
The Tale of Little Pig Robinson (1930)

LAKE DISTRICT POEMS – FROM 'REFLECTIONS ON HAVING LEFT A PLACE OF RETIREMENT' BY SAMUEL TAYLOR COLERIDGE

But the time, when first
From that low Dell, steep up the stony Mount
I climb'd with perilous toil and reach'd the top,
Oh! What a goodly scene! Here the bleak mount,
The bare bleak mountain speckled thin with sheep;
Grey clouds, that shadowing spot the sunny fields;
And river, now with bushy rocks o'er-brow'd,
Now winding bright and full, with naked banks;
And seats, and lawns, the Abbey and the wood,
And cots, and hamlets, and faint city-spire;
The Channel there, the Islands and white sails,
Dim coasts, and cloud-like hills, and shoreless Ocean—
It seem'd like omnipresence! God, methought,
Had built him there a Temple; the whole World
Seem'd imag'd in its vast circumference:
No wish profan'd my overwhelmed heart.
Blest hour! It was a luxury,—to be!

HOW TO HAVE AN ACCIDENT IN THE FELLS

Walkers, runners and cyclists in the Lake District find all sorts of ways to get themselves into trouble. The Lake District Search and Mountain Rescue Association records the reasons for each of the incidents its teams attend, of which there have been close to 6,000 between 1991 and 2006, and the results reveal the common causes of distress. More than half of the incidents were due to a slip or a fall, and getting lost or failing to return from a walk at the expected time are other frequently cited reasons for call-outs. Around one incident a month on average is due to walkers becoming cragfast—stuck on crags or rocks with no way of getting off—and several groups a year are caught out by the fast fall of darkness in the fells. There have been nine injuries due to avalanches, though none since 1999.

This list shows the causes of the call-outs logged by mountain rescue teams between 1991 and 2006. Not all of the teams' call-outs had a genuine cause, and some had more than one, such as a slip due to exhaustion.

Cause	Number of citations	Cause	Number of citations
Slip	1,607	Separated	137
Fall	1,381	Lights reported	135
Overdue	706	Severe weather	92
Lost	644	Shouts heard	59
Collapse	448	Exhaustion	40
Cragfast	237	In difficulty	39
Benighted	182	Belay/runner failure	32
Trip or stumble	164	Avalanche	9

WORDSWORTH ON... THE BEST TIME TO VISIT

'Mr West, in his well-known Guide to the Lakes, recommends, as the best season for visiting this country, the interval from the beginning of June to the end of August; and, the two latter months being a time of vacation and leisure, it is almost exclusively in these that strangers resort hither. But that season is by no means the best; the colouring of the mountains and woods, unless where they are diversified by rocks, is of too unvaried a green; and, as a large portion of the vallies is allotted to hay-grass, some want of variety is found there also. The meadows, however, are sufficiently enlivened after hay-making begins, which is much later than in the southern part of the island. A stronger objection is rainy weather, setting in sometimes at this period with a vigour, and continuing with a perseverance, that may remind the disappointed and dejected traveller of those deluges of rain which fall among the Abyssinian mountains, for the annual supply of the Nile. The months of September and October (particularly October) are generally attended with much finer weather; and the scenery is then, beyond comparison, more diversified, more splendid, and beautiful; but, on the other hand, short days prevent long excursions, and sharp and chill gales are unfavourable to parties of pleasure out of doors. Nevertheless, to the sincere admirer of nature, who is in good health and spirits, and at liberty to make a choice, the six weeks following the first of September may be recommended in preference to July and August.'

FROM *GUIDE TO THE LAKES* BY WILLIAM WORDSWORTH

TEN LAKE DISTRICT CAMPSITES

Campsites offer some of the most picturesque accommodation in the Lake District and are a great base for walking in the fells above. Here are ten of the best.

Castlerigg Farm, near Keswick. Quiet, elevated site with great views over Derwent Water. Tel 017687 72479.

Fisherground Farm, Eskdale. Peaceful, family-oriented site in Eskdale. Tel 01946 723349.

Great Langdale. Popular National Trust site at the head of the Langdale valley close to the distinctive Langdale Pikes. Tel 015394 37668.

Hoathwaite Farm, Torver. Basic facilities but a great, tranquil location just off Coniston Water. Tel 015394 41349.

Low Wray, Ambleside. Busy but nicely located site on the shores of Windermere. Run by the National Trust. Tel 015394 32810.

Side Farm, Patterdale. Handy for Helvellyn and close to Patterdale and Glenridding. Tel 017684 82337.

Stonethwaite. Basic but beautiful site by the river and between the steep fells of Borrowdale. Tel 017687 77602.

Syke Farm, Buttermere. Positioned between Buttermere and Crummock Water. Tel 017687 70222.

Wasdale. A National Trust-run site at the foot of the Scafell range, popular with rock climbers in particular. Tel 019467 26220.

Waterside House, Pooley Bridge. Just off Ullswater and a good base for walking. Tel 017684 86332.

IN SEARCH OF WITHNAIL AND I

'Withnail and I' is probably the best known of all the films featuring the Lake District. Bruce Robinson's movie about two unemployed actors visiting a remote Lakeland cottage for a rejuvenating holiday has developed a large cult following since its release in 1986, and many fans have hunted down its Lake District locations. Here are some of them.

Crow Crag, the holiday cottage owned by Uncle Monty, is actually **Sleddale Hall** alongside the Wet Sleddale Reservoir near Shap. The cottage has been largely untouched since filming, and is now in a semi-ruinous state. Walls and doors are daubed with fans' quotes from the film. The lake around which the two walk, scene of Withnail's 'I'm going to be a star' quote, is **Haweswater**, seen from Whiteacre Crag on the eastern shore. Withnail phones his agent from the red phone box in **Bampton**, and the scene featuring a charging bull was also filmed on a footpath nearby. The farmhouse where Withnail and Marwood seek food is **Tailbert Farm** near Shap, now privately owned. Film fans seeking the Penrith Tea Rooms will be disappointed to learn that scenes set here were actually filmed in the village of Stony Stratford in Buckinghamshire.

CAMRA'S FAVOURITE CUMBRIAN BEERS

There are few people better placed to judge the best beers in Cumbria than the local members of the Campaign for Real Ale.

CAMRA was founded in 1971 by a band of real ale enthusiasts committed to reversing the decline in locally brewed beers and the closure of many small breweries unable to compete with their larger counterparts. It has been a great success and currently boats over 84,000 members. There are now well over 600 locally run breweries in Britain, producing more 2,000 varieties of beer.

In Cumbria the Campaign is supported by four branches—Furness, Solway, Westmorland, and West Cumbria & Western Lakes—with over 600 members. Cumbria has more than 20 active breweries, one cidermaker and nearly 600 pubs, hotels and other outlets offering real ales, many of which are brewed in the county, making it a beer drinkers' paradise. CAMRA's Cumbria Branches publish a *Cumbria Real Ale Guide* (*CRAG*), essential reading for real ale enthusiasts in the county. CAMRA's main annual publication, *The Good Beer Guide*, details more than 4,500 of Britain's top real ale pubs, as surveyed and nominated by CAMRA branches. More than 80 of these are located in Cumbria.

The following 'favourite' choices from each brewery in Cumbria and accompanying tasting notes have been made by CAMRA Branch Officers from across the county. BLO refers to a Brewery Liaison Officer, appointed by CAMRA to act as a link between the brewery and the Campaign.

Abraham Thompson – **Letargion** – 'A vinous, 9% dark Barley wine. Initial sweetness gives rise to a dark malt, roasted body with mellow, fruity flavours. Surprisingly bitter finish encourages another sip but beware of the strength.' *Graham Donning, Chairman, Furness Branch*

Barngates – **K9** – 'A terrific ale, light golden in colour but with a twist and bags of character. Grapefruit aroma and a delicate citrus taste on the palate.' *'Lou' Lewis, BLO*

Beckstones – **Bitta Clout** – 'A truly "premium" bitter. What it lacks in colour, it makes up for in strength and taste.' *Jim Chapple, Editor, CRAG*

Bitter End – **Tempest Fugit** – 'An occasional ale, well-balanced and very drinkable with a pleasant finish.' *Bob Johnston, BLO*

Coniston – **Bluebird Bitter** – 'A truly Champion beer in flavour, balance and drinkability.' *Jim Chapple*

Cumbrian Legendary Ales – **Wicked Jimmy** – 'One of their first brews, a very flavoursome session beer. Goes down a treat.' *Jim Chapple*

Dent – **Kamikaze** – 'Really hits the spot. One to end the evening with. Gutsy, amber, hoppy, flavourful beer.' *Jenny Turner, Secretary, Westmorland Branch*

Derwent – **Derwent Spring Time** – 'A seasonal beer with subtle flavours and easy drinking. Light in colour, bringing to mind warm summer days.' *Ian MacCartney, BLO*

Foxfield – **Brief Encounter** – 'Superb fruity session beer. Improves with each pint quaffed.' *Jim Chapple*

Geltsdale – **Tarn Monath Bitter** – 'Has a fruity, slightly sweet initial flavour but with a more bitter aftertaste. Refreshing, easy on the palate, golden bitter.' *Dawy Edwards, BLO*

Great Gable – **Yewbarrow** – 'Dark, rich, fruity and well worth savouring.' *Russell Forster, BLO*

Hardknott – **Woolpacker** – 'An excellent example of a full-flavoured session bitter. Well worth seeking out.' *Jim Chapple*

Hawkshead – **Hawkshead Bitter** – 'Excellent session beer full of hoppy and bitter flavours and a lingering bitter finish. One of the best session bitters available in the north-west.' *Graham Donning, BLO*

Hesket Newmarket – **Skiddaw Special Bitter** – 'A true session bitter; largely Maris Otter pale ale malt with just enough crystal malt to round the flavour. Classic combination of hops provides the bitterness, finished with a hint of Styrian Goldings.' *Paul Claringbold, BLO*

Jennings – **Bitter** – 'An excellent session beer, full of flavour and unique taste and only 3.5%. Very moreish.' *Richard Watson, BLO*

Keswick – **Thirst Pitch** – 'A bitter with a twist. Mid-brown, hoppy with a good balance of coloured malts. A complex flavour and easy drinking.' *Alan Dunn, BLO*

Loweswater – **Kirkstile Gold** – 'Pale lager-style beer. Lovely to drink on a hot day after a walk on the fells. Refreshing with a hint of tropical flavour.' *Pat Spencer, BLO*

Tirril – **Old Faithful** – 'Golden, hoppy, well rounded beer with a good aftertaste.' *Jenny Turner*

Ulverston – **Laughing Gravy** – 'A full-flavoured copper-coloured beer in the "best bitter" tradition. Juicy malty flavour with a hint of caramel and a thirst-quenching aftertaste.' *'Lou' Lewis*

Watermill – **Collie Wobbles** – 'Light, fragrant, very slightly citrus with a good aftertaste.' – *Jenny Turner*

Yates – **Sun Goddess** – 'A light, golden brew with loads of flavour and aroma and refreshing aftertaste. Very drinkable.' *Jim Chapple*

THE GREAT GABLE WAR MEMORIAL

Great Gable is home to the highest war memorial in the country—and perhaps the most stunningly located.

In remembrance of the 20 members who were killed in the First World War, the Fell and Rock Climbing Club of the Lake District purchased 1,200 acres of land on and around Great Gable, and handed it to the National Trust for safe keeping in 1923. Its intention was to remember the war dead and to preserve access to the fells to everyone in perpetuity. The following June, a bronze war memorial tablet was installed on rocks around the summit, and dedicated at a special service attended by more than 500 people.

One of the speakers at the dedication was Geoffrey Winthrop Young, a poet and climber who lost a leg during the war. He said: 'Upon this rock are set the names of men—our brothers, and our comrades upon these cliffs—who held, with us, that there is no freedom of the soil where the spirit of man is in bondage; and who surrendered their part in the fellowship of hill and wind and sunshine, that the freedom of this land, the freedom of our spirit, should endure.'

A non-denominational memorial service is still held on Great Gable each Remembrance Sunday when, regardless of the weather, hundreds of people climb the fell from Seathwaite, Wasdale and Honister to lay wreaths and remember those who lost their lives at war.

SOME OF CUMBRIA'S TWIN TOWNS

Town	Twin	Country
Brampton	Berry Bouy	France
Carlisle	Flensburg	Germany
	Slupsk	Poland
Cockermouth	Marvejols	France
Coniston	Illiers-Combray	France
Cumbria County	Rheinisch-Bergischer	Germany
Kendal	Rinteln	Germany
Sedbergh	Zrece	Slovenia
Ulverston	Albert	France
Windermere	Diessen-am-Ammersee	Germany
Workington	Selm	Germany

AN 18TH CENTURY HIKE

Although the fells look much the same today as they did to Wordsworth and Coleridge in the late 18th century, a walking tour was a far more ambitious undertaking in their day. By modern standards, a walk of 137 miles in a week and a half is something to be done only by the well-prepared, fit walker during the long days of summer; but to Wordsworth and Coleridge it was nothing out of the ordinary. This was their itinerary:

Day	From / to	Mileage
1	Temple Sowerby to Bampton	18.5
2	Bampton to Kentmere	11.25
3	Kentmere to Hawkshead	11.75
4	Hawkshead to Grasmere	8
5	Grasmere to Keswick	14.5
6	Keswick to Ouse Bridge	8.75
7	Ouse Bridge to Buttermere	12.5
8	Buttermere to Wasdale Head	15
9	Wasdale Head to Threlkeld	16
10	Threlkeld to Patterdale	11.5
11	Patterdale to Pooley Bridge	9.5
	TOTAL	**137.25**

WINDERMERE'S LEGENDARY CREATURES

The lake and shores of Windermere are home to two famous creatures—both rarely spotted but famous enough to keep the area in curious tourists and postcard sales over the years.

The so-called Beast of Bowness was first spotted in 1900 by a Windermere boatman, who claimed it had the body of a hedgehog, the tail of a squirrel and a pair of bee-like wings. His sighting and subsequent stories inspired locals and visitors to search the shores of Windermere for the creature, though attempts to catch what he christened the tizzie-wizzie have always proved strangely elusive. Somewhat suspicious photographs emerged in 1906, and although the creature has not been found since, the legend persists. Whether the tizzie-wizzie was mistaken for a type of bat or was a complete fabrication, it earned the boatman plenty of drinks from fascinated tourists eager to hear the story.

Another mysterious species is meanwhile said to inhabit the waters of Windermere. The creature seen rising to the surface from time to time has been variously described as resembling an eel, serpent or the Loch Ness Monster, and as measuring up to 20 feet in length. In 2006 a team of scientists from the Centre for Fortean Zoology began an observation of the lake in an attempt to identify the creature, but more rational fish experts suggest that the creature could be a catfish, which can grow to a similar length and weigh up to 300kg.

BRITAIN'S BEST WALK

The Coast to Coast walk devised by Alfred Wainwright was voted the best walk in Britain by an expert panel for *Country Walking* magazine—and the second best in the world.

The walk stretches for 190 miles (304km) between England's west and east coasts. Walkers usually set off from St Bees Head near Whitehaven on the western coast, and pass through Ennerdale, Borrowdale, Grasmere, Patterdale and Haweswater, as well as crossing several Lake District peaks, before leaving Cumbria. The path then takes in two more National Parks—the Yorkshire Dales and the North York Moors—before ending at Robin Hood's Bay in Yorkshire. The scenery is mostly hilly but very varied, and it showcases the best of the northern countryside. Wainwright's route is not prescriptive: he encouraged walkers to find their own variations on it, and several new guidebooks have been written to take account of changes to paths and roads since he devised it in 1973.

Wainwright suggested that walkers embarking on the walk dip their boots into the Irish Sea at St Bees, and dip their bare feet in the North Sea at Robin Hood's Bay. It takes the average walker about two weeks to complete the trek, although inevitably the route has challenged people to complete it as quickly as possible. Lake District fell running legend Joss Naylor ran the route in a superhuman 41 hours in 1976.

The walk has proved extremely popular since its launch, and tens of thousands of people follow part of all of it each year. Some stretches can be busy at weekends, and paths are now being eroded in places. The route has not yet been designated a national trail and is not signposted for its whole length, so walkers have to navigate their way across the country—although the Wainwright Society is campaigning for it to be given official status.

Wainwright's Coast to Coast walk was voted ahead of famous routes in the Himalayas and Alps in *Country Walking*'s poll of guidebook authors and walking experts. Anyone wanting a better stroll than this will have to travel to New Zealand, where the 33 mile (54km) Milford Track was voted the best walk in the world.

TEN ANIMAL ATTRACTIONS

Ten of the best places to go to see animals both native and new to the Lake District.

The Aquarium of the Lakes, Newby Bridge. Follows the water life of the Lake District from the tops of the mountains down to Morecambe Bay. Sited on the south shore of Windermere. Tel 015395 30153 or online at www.aquariumofthelakes.co.uk.

Ducky's Park Farm, Flookburgh. Visitor centre that introduces children to farming animals and methods. Tel 015395 59293 or online at www.duckysparkfarm.co.uk.

Holme Open Farm, Sedbergh. Working farm with tours and chances to see the shearing, marking and lambing of sheep, plus pigs, ducks and geese. Tel 015396 20654 or online at www.holmeopenfarm.co.uk.

Keswick Sheepdog Demonstrations. Weekly demonstrations of sheepdogs' skills by a local farmer, Derek Scrimgeour, who has represented England at the world sheep dog championships. Tel 017687 79603.

The Lakeland Bird of Prey Centre, Lowther. Eagles, falcons, hawks and owls are all flown daily in the estate of Lowther Castle. Tel 01931 712746.

The Lakeland Sheep and Wool Centre, Cockermouth. Demonstrations of 19 breeds of Lakeland sheep, plus sheepdogs and a wool shop. Tel 01900 822673 or online at www.sheep-woolcentre.co.uk.

The Lake District Osprey Project, Whinlatter Centre. Viewpoint for birds of prey, run by the Forestry Commission, Lake District National Park Authority and the RSPB, and an accompanying exhibition. Tel 017687 78469 or online at www.ospreywatch.co.uk.

The Owl Centre, Muncaster Castle. The world's largest collection of owls, with flying and feeding sessions. The centre is also home to the World Owl Trust. Tel 01229 717614 or online at www.muncaster.co.uk.

South Lakes Wild Animal Park, Dalton-in-Furness. The Lake District's only zoological park, home to some rare breeds. Tel 01229 466086 or online at www.wildanimalpark.co.uk.

Trotters World of Animals, near Keswick. 25 acres featuring hundreds of different animals, with demonstrations and conservation projects. Tel 017687 76239 or online at www.trottersworld.com.

DONALD CAMPBELL AND CONISTON WATER

Coniston Water is one of the most picturesque lakes in the Lake District, but it is probably best known for its association with Donald Campbell and his fateful attempt on the world water-speed record.

Campbell was born in 1921, the son of Sir Malcolm Campbell, who set numerous world speed records on land and sea in the 1920s and 1930s. When his father died of natural causes in 1948, Donald continued his quest for greater and greater speed. After a 170mph crash on Coniston Water in 1951, Campbell developed a new boat, in which he soon set and repeatedly broke the world water-speed records, reaching a peak of 276mph on a run in western Australia in 1964. Campbell also pursued records on dry land, and despite a high-speed crash on the Utah salt flats in the US, he went on to break 400mph, also in 1964.

Campbell then set about extending his water record beyond 300mph, modifying his Bluebird K7 for more speed and practising on Coniston Water. Early in January 1967, he reached 298mph on a run from the north end of the lake to the south, and began a return run while the water was still choppy from the turbulence. As he reached 320mph, the boat started to wobble, before flipping up at a 45 degree angle from the water. The boat somersaulted and hit the lake nose first, before cartwheeling across the water and sinking. Campbell was killed instantly.

After much debate over whether the remains of Campbell and his boat should be left at the bottom of Coniston Water, they were recovered by divers in 2001. Campbell was buried at St Andrew's Churchyard in Coniston later that year. The village's Ruskin Museum now houses an exhibition about his life as well as photos and memorabilia from his speed record attempts, and a project is now underway to completely restore Bluebird K7 from its wreckage before returning her to Coniston. Coniston Water hosts a Records Week each year, during which attempts are made on speed records in various classes of powerboat.

LAKE DISTRICT FOOD – BORROWDALE TEA BREAD

Afternoon tea is an important part of the day in Lake District hotels and tea-rooms, especially if you've just finished a long walk in the fells. This tea bread may once have been a speciality of Borrowdale, but it can now be found served with sandwiches, scones and cakes in many corners of the Lake District.

450g dried mixed fruit – currants, raisins, sultanas and so on
250g plain flour
175g brown sugar
25g butter
1 egg
Large mug of strong black tea
Half a teaspoon of bicarbonate of soda
Pinch of salt

Put the mixed fruit in a bowl, pour the tea over it and stir well. Leave for several hours, ideally overnight. Transfer to a large mixing bowl and stir in the sugar. Beat the egg and melt the butter before adding both to the mixture. Sift the flour, salt and bicarbonate of soda and fold that in too. Mix thoroughly. Spoon the mixture into a greased, medium-sized loaf tin and bake in a low to moderate oven (gas mark 4) for about 1 hour 20 minutes or until firm. Cool on a wire rack. Serve in buttered slices with, of course, a cup of tea.

LITERARY LAKELANDERS – HUGH WALPOLE

Hugh Walpole was a prolific writer of novels, short stories, non-fiction and memoirs, but he is best remembered now for The Herries Chronicle, a series of historical novels about several generations of the same Cumberland family.

Walpole was born in New Zealand in 1884, but was brought to England aged five. He worked as a teacher before devoting himself full-time to writing, and his early work met with critical and popular acclaim. Some of it was based on his experiences of the First World War, during which he served time in Russia.

Walpole moved to the Lake District in 1924, settling at Brackenburn on the slopes of Cat Bells and overlooking Derwent Water. It was here that he wrote The Herries Chronicle, a series of four books—*Rogue Herries*, *Judith Paris*, *The Fortress* and *Vanessa*—all set in the Lake District and celebrating its people and landscape. Walpole wanted the books to cement his literary reputation, and they were well received nationally as well as in Cumbria. He said in 1935: 'Fifty years from now I think the Lake stories will still be read locally, otherwise I shall be mentioned in a small footnote to my period in literary history.'

Walpole lived at Brackenburn until his death in 1941, having been knighted three years earlier. He is buried in St John's Churchyard in Keswick. The house, which he extended substantially to house his library of 30,000 books and collection of paintings, is now privately owned, though the gardens are occasionally open to the public. A good place to find out more about Walpole is the Keswick Museum and Art Gallery, which houses his diaries and manuscripts.

THE LAKE DISTRICT'S BEST MODERN BUILDINGS

A 2006 survey by the Lake District National Park Authority set out to find the best buildings constructed or renovated since its foundation in 1951. The top three in the 'Slate Idol' poll were:

1 Priest's Mill, Caldbeck. An 18th century watermill carefully restored in 1986 to house a small museum, shop, café and offices.

2 Lakeland Limited, Windermere. Flagship store of the kitchenware chain, housed in a strikingly bright, airy glass-fronted building near Windermere Station, built in 2004.

3 Shelter, Aira Force Car Park. Pretty 1995 shelter extension near one of the Lake District's most popular landmarks.

❧❧❧❧❧❧❧❧❧❧❧❧❧❧

CUMBRIA AND THE SLAVE TRADE

Cumbria's coastline and history of trading mean it has closer links than many counties to slavery in the British Empire—but it was also influential in the abolition of the trade.

Although its traffic was small compared to larger hubs like Liverpool, Whitehaven was a busy port throughout the 18th century trade in slaves, and grand houses around the town are evidence of the profits made by merchants during this time. Ship owners across Cumbria, and particularly on the Furness peninsula, were also involved in the 'golden triangle' of slave trade between Britain, Africa and the Caribbean. John Bolton, a merchant from Ulverston, spent much of his slave profits extending Storrs Hall near Windermere, now a luxury hotel. Some other important Cumbrian families used slave labour on their plantations in the Caribbean, and Barbados place-names like Carlisle Bay and Kendal Point are reminders of the island's connections with the county. There is also evidence from the registers that some slaves even settled in Cumbria en route from Africa to the Caribbean, acting as family servants with questionable levels of freedom.

But Cumbria was also home to many supporters of the abolition of slavery, both prominent and unsung. William Wilberforce, the MP who led the campaign against the slave trade, took frequent trips to the Lake District and used to row out to the islands on Windermere to quietly contemplate his anti-slavery legislation. Wilberforce's campaign was supported by his friend William Wordsworth, who denounced slavery in several poems, and by Thomas Clarkson, who owned a house near Ullswater. It was on his way back from a visit to Clarkson that William and Dorothy Wordsworth saw the host of daffodils that inspired one of the most famous poems of all time—'I Wandered Lonely as a Cloud'. Wordsworth remained in touch with both Wilberforce and Clarkson after their campaign prompted an act preventing the trade of slaves in 1807. Wilberforce died a month before another law was passed to emancipate all slaves in the British Empire.

Evidence of the slave trade and its profits can still be seen in places across Cumbria, and the bicentenary of the abolition act in 2007 prompted fresh interest in its history. Whitehaven's Rum Story and Beacon museums both have excellent exhibitions about the trade and the ships that transported slaves across the seas, and display evidence of support for abolition within the town.

LAKE DISTRICT POEMS – FROM 'MOUNTAIN TARNS' BY FREDERICK WILLIAM FABER

There is a power to bless
In hill-side loneliness,
In tarns and dreary places,
A virtue in the brook,
A freshness in the look
Of mountains' joyless faces.

And I would have my heart
From littleness apart,
A love-anointed thing,
Be set above my kind,
In my unfettered mind
A veritable king.

And so when life is dull,
Or when my heart is full
Because my coy loves have frowned,
I wander up the rills
To stones and tarns and hills,—
I go there to be crowned.

WORDSWORTH'S PARTING STONE

A stone near Grisedale Tarn between the fells of Fairfield and Dollywaggon Pike marks the spot where William and Dorothy saw their brother John for the last time in September 1800. John was drowned at sea shortly afterwards.

The Brothers Parting Stone replaces words that William originally etched into a rock, although the inscription is now very hard to make out on the weather-beaten tablet. A rusty metal sign perched on top of the rock marks the spot, which is easily missed from the footpaths. The stone reads:

Here did we stop; and here looked round
While each into himself descends,
For that last thought of parting Friends
That is not to be found.

Brother and friend, if verse of mine
Have power to make thy virtues known,
Here let a monumental Stone
Stand sacred as a Shrine.

THE SEVEN NEWBIGGINS

Rather confusingly, Cumbria has seven places called Newbiggin. They are:

Newbiggin, near Stainton, just west of Penrith
Newbiggin, near Temple Sowerby, about seven miles east of Penrith
Newbiggin, near Croglin, ten miles south-east of Carlisle
Newbiggin, on Morecambe Bay, just east of Barrow-in-Furness
Newbiggin, just south of Ravenglass on the west coast
Newbiggin-on-Lune, on the edge of the Howgills between
Tebay and Kirkby Stephen
Newbiggin, near Burton-in-Kendal. Nearby are Newbiggin Crags.

There are even more Newbiggins in the neighbouring counties of
Durham, Northumberland and North Yorkshire. Newbiggin means
simply 'new building', from the Old English *biggin*.

CUMBRIA INDUSTRIES – IRON

The rich source of haematite iron ore in the limestone layers of western
Cumbria has been tapped since Roman times, but it wasn't until the
1830s that it was mined in a concerted way. It quickly become one of
the county's great industries.

As the iron industry thrived in the late 19th and early 20th centuries,
works developed at towns including Workington, Millom, Barrow and
Maryport, many of them large mining complexes. The industry also spread
inland, although mining in the Lake District fells produced more sporadic
returns. The boom years made a handful of people very rich, but conditions for the vast majority of miners were unpleasant and dangerous.
Iron also brought to Cumbria a wave of people who wanted to mine the
area—from Europe as well as elsewhere in Britain. And it accelerated
the building of railways and roads to transport the iron; examples include
the Ravenglass and Eskdale Railway, built in 1873 to take the ore from
the Eskdale workings to the mainline railway and coast at Ravenglass.

Falling reserves and cheap foreign imports led to a decline in the industry as the 20th century wore on. Cumbria's iron heritage is now best preserved at the Florence Mine at Egremont, the last deep iron mine in western Europe and where workers were known as the 'red men' from the bright colour of the ore they mined. Though iron is still retrieved here, Florence is now best-known for its excellent Heritage Centre, with a mining museum, mineral room and tours of the underground mines. The Millom Folk Museum also has displays relating to west Cumbria's mining, and there is an 18-mile, signposted Haematite Trail that explores its iron heritage, starting and finishing in Barrow.

THE LAKE DISTRICT'S MOST FAMOUS SONG

John Peel was a legendary Cumberland farmer and huntsman, immortalised in the song 'D'ye ken John Peel?'

Peel was born around 1776 near Caldbeck. After marrying well and acquiring land nearby, he began to spend less of his time farming and more of it hunting. He became a champion huntsman of foxes in particular, and struck up friendships with wealthy landowners and mill owners from towns across northern England who built or bought country estates in Cumbria. Hunting dominated Peel's life, and led him into some debts in later life, though he was usually rescued from these by friends. One of them, John Woodcock Graves, remembered 'I believe he would not have left the drag of a fox on the impending death of a child or any other earthly event.' Peel died in 1854, and is now remembered very fondly by many as an archetypal Cumbrian character, immensely proud of his rural way of life. He has also been adopted as a hero of the pro-hunting movement opposed to recent bans on their activities.

Peel's fame beyond the Lake District was fuelled by the song, first written by Graves in 1829. It was composed in Cumberland dialect to an existing Scottish tune, and after a few recitals in London became a firm favourite among Victorian society. People loved the rural English idyll it brought to mind, and as it spread around the British Empire, the cult of Peel's personality grew and grew.

The song has had numerous variations in lyrics and tune over the years. Here is a popular non-dialect version.

D'ye ken John Peel with his coat so grey,
D'ye ken John Peel at the break of day,
D'ye ken John Peel when he's far, far away,
With his hounds and his horn in the morning?

Chorus
For the sound of his horn brought me from my bed,
And the cry of his hounds which he oft-times led,
For Peel's 'View halloo' could awaken the dead
Or the fox from his lair in the morning.

Yes, I ken John Peel and Ruby too,
Ranter and Ringwood, Bellman and True,
From a find to a check, from a check to a view,
From a view to a death in the morning.

Then here's to John Peel from my heart and soul,
Let's drink to his health, let's finish the bowl,
We'll follow John Peel through fair and through foul,
If we want a good hunt in the morning.

D'ye ken John Peel with his coat so grey?
He lived at Troutbeck once on a day,
Now he has gone far, far away,
We shall ne'er hear his voice in the morning.

John Peel's grave can be found at St Kentigern's Churchyard in Caldbeck. The Tullie House Museum in Carlisle has a large collection of his possessions and various recordings of the song.

INJURIES ON THE FELLS

What's the most common accident on the fells? Figures from the Lake District Search and Mountain Rescue Association suggest it's a damaged ankle, usually twisted or turned on the uneven fell ground. LDSAMRA's records of its mountain rescue casualties between 1991 and 2006 contain no fewer than 887 incidents affecting people's ankles—an average of more than one a week. These are the ten most common sites of injury according to LDSAMRA's statistics.

Ankle 887	Hand and wrist 184
Lower leg 457	Arm 164
Head 409	Chest 145
Knee 258	Shoulder girdle 115
Spine 219	Upper leg and hip 80

WORKING IN CUMBRIA

Employment in the Lake District has changed a great deal over the last half-century. While their ancestors might have worked predominantly in farming or heavy industries such as mining or shipbuilding, workers today are far more likely to be employed in tourism or local services. Across the county of Cumbria, 2005 figures show that more than a quarter of the workforce is connected with the tourist trade, while just 1.5 per cent now work in agriculture or fishing. Unemployment in the county as a percentage of the population is below the national average at around 2 per cent.

Sector	Workforce	% of total
Distribution, hotels and restaurants	63,020	29.2
Public administration	51,633	23.9
Manufacturing	36,755	17.0
Banking, finance and insurance	24,286	11.3
Construction	10,588	4.9
Transport and communications	10,094	4.7
Agriculture and fishing	3,398	1.5
Energy and water	1,409	0.7
Other	14,609	6.8

RON KENYON'S FAVOURITE LAKE DISTRICT ROCK CLIMBS

The Fell and Rock Climbing Club is the leading climbing club in the UK and celebrated its centenary in 2006. It produces definitive guides to climbing in all areas of the Lake District, and its guidebooks secretary is Ron Kenyon, who has massive experience and an encyclopaedic knowledge of the area's climbs. These are Ron's ten personal favourite climbs, together with their difficulty ratings—from easy to the various sub-grades of extremely severe—and notes on their ascent.

'**Capella**', Pavey Ark, Langdale; Extremely Severe E1. This is one of the excellent routes from the little black book of Colin Read, one of the legends of Lake District climbing. First climbed in 1997, it takes a line just to the left of Arcturus on the crag below Jacks Rake on Pavey Ark. It contains two long pitches, each of which starts steeply but leads to immaculate slab climbing on wonderful rock. A modern classic.

'Eliminate A', Dow Crag; Very Severe. What makes a classic climb—straight, direct lines or a route that weaves around to find the easiest way up? This falls into the second category. Dow Crag is a fantastic crag, made up of a series of buttresses looking out over the corrie, and Eliminate A starts up just left of Great Gully. Traverses, blind moves and scrambles take you to the summit and a view over the South Lakes and beyond.

'The Fang', Swindale; Mild Very Severe. Swindale, adjacent to Haweswater, has been a popular valley for climbers in Penrith for many years. A steep crack leads to moves leftwards onto the face and a ledge below another corner. Some worrying moves up this lead to a spacious ledge, then a tricky move gains a crack. A finish above leads to the top and a feeling of satisfaction looking down on this pleasant vale.

'Grooved Arete', Pikes Crag, Scafell Pike; Very Difficult. This 120m route offers a great way to the summit of Scafell Pike. The line makes its way up the right-hand side to end on top of a buttress, Pulpit Rock, slightly detached from the mountain. This necessitates a climb down, or abseil, to finish—from where a short walk takes you to the top of England.

'Humdrum', Esk Buttress, Eskdale; Extremely Severe E3. Eskdale is a fantastic valley with the great crag of Esk Buttress looming above its floor. Facing south with usually clean rock, this crag contains a wide spread of excellent routes covering most of the grades, and in the middle is the Humdrum, taking a fine intricate line on superb rock.

'Lord of the Rings', East Buttress, Scafell; Extremely Severe E2. This girdle traverse is 342m long, taking in some of the best rock in the Lakes and maintained at a good standard for its length.

'Overhanging Bastion', Castle Rock of Trierman, Thirlmere; Very Severe. The Birkett family has left its mark on the Lakes, and the first line up this impressive face was made by Jim Birkett in the 1930s. A short introductory pitch is followed by a steep corner, leading to a ledge in the middle of the crag. A steep gangway above leads to the top of a small pinnacle below a further gangway, the climbing of which is exhilarating.

'Praying Mantis', Goat Crag, Borrowdale; Extremely Severe E1. This weaving way up the crag was discovered by Les Brown in the 1960s. The first pitch follows an ominous crackline, and moves left leading to what I think are the hardest moves up to gain the belay. Easier climbing scuttles up leftwards to a short corner. The final moves round a rib gain the wall, and an abseil down is an apt finish to a marvellous route.

'**Tophet Wall**', The Napes, Great Gable; Hard Severe. This is a spectacular route up the Napes, starting in the centre and finishing rightwards. The end of the route is not the end of the climbing, as you must scramble up the ridge above to just below Westmorland Crag, near the summit of Great Gable. It makes for a great mountaineering day.

'**Troutdale Pinnacle**', Black Crag, Borrowdale; Severe. One of the most popular routes in the valley, this weaves up the buttress for 105m. The initial pitches are not too interesting, but as height is gained it improves. The pinnacle that gave the route its name when it was first climbed back in 1914 is now long gone.

THE STORY OF DUNMAIL RAISE

As with many characters of his era, it is unclear where history ends and legend begins with Dunmail, a 10th century king of Cumberland. But the story of his last and most famous battle certainly endures, albeit in numerous different versions, and it gives its name to one of the most frequently used mountain passes in the Lake District.

According to the legend, Dunmail took on the combined forces of Saxon king Edmund I and Malcolm I, king of Scotland, after they assumed control of the area. After retreating into the fells, Dunmail's men met their opponents on the mountain pass that separates the lakes of Grasmere and Thirlmere in 945. A furious battle ended with Dunmail killed, and his body was buried beneath a pile of rocks on the pass that can still be seen.

Some versions of the story have it that Dunmail's crown was then thrown by his surviving men into Grisedale Tarn near Helvellyn to keep it from the Saxons. Various theories link the character of Dunmail to different rulers of the era, and there is also disagreement over the precise location of the battle and whether Dunmail was even actually killed in it. But there has been enough in the story for it to give its name to the road that now runs over the fells—the Dunmail Raise.

WAINWRIGHT'S FIRST FELL

Alfred Wainwright climbed every fell in the Lake District many times over—but like most hikers, he started his walking career rather modestly. His first ascent was of Orrest Head, a short ascent of 780 feet

(240m) close to Windermere. Although brief, the climb gives lovely views across the lake and the fells beyond, and there are benches and notes on the view at the top. Orrest Head has been many people's introduction to the Lake District since William Wordsworth first made it popular as a viewpoint, and its proximity to Windermere makes it ideal for day-trippers. Wainwright immediately fell in love with the Lake District as he climbed it in 1930.

CUMBRIA'S TOP TEN BIRDS

Cumbria's most common bird is the house sparrow, followed by the chaffinch. The findings come from the RSPB's annual 'Big Garden Birdwatch', based on a snapshot of birds seen in 236,000 gardens across the UK on two days in 2007. The full top ten for the county is:

1 House sparrow	6 Great tit
2 Chaffinch	7 Goldfinch
3 Blue tit	8 Robin
4 Blackbird	9 Jackdaw
5 Starling	10 Collared dove

LITERARY LAKELANDERS – SAMUEL TAYLOR COLERIDGE

After Wordsworth, Coleridge is often one of the first names to spring to mind when thinking of the Lake Poets and the romantic movement of poetry—but his connections with the area were mostly a result of his friendship with Wordsworth.

Coleridge was born in Devon in 1772, educated at a boarding school and the University of Cambridge, and read voraciously from an early age. After befriending Robert Southey, the pair married two sisters, though Coleridge's marriage was a generally unhappy one. Around the same time he also met Wordsworth and struck up a close friendship, embarking on a tour of the Lake District together. While living in Somerset he wrote two of his most famous poems, 'The Rime of the Ancient Mariner' and 'Kubla Khan', and in 1798 he and Wordsworth published their famous joint *Lyrical Ballads*.

It wasn't until 1800 that Coleridge followed Wordsworth up to the Lake District to live. He settled at Greta Hall in Keswick, but pressures of work, an addiction to opium and an infatuation with Wordsworth's sister-in-law led to tensions between the two, and in 1812 he moved from the Lakes back to London. Though he was inspired by the Lake District and was a keen walker, he did not have quite the devoted attachment to it as did Wordsworth, and his work is not so rooted in the area as other poets. His son Hartley Coleridge, also a renowned writer, lived much of his adult life at Grasmere and Rydal.

TEN ALTERNATIVE OUTDOOR ACTIVITIES

There's much more to do in the Lake District besides walking. For anyone wanting a little more excitement, here are ten activities on land, on water and in the air.

Caving. The old mines of west Cumbria and the limestone hill caves in the east make for some great underground exploring. The British Caving Association can help you get started at www.trycaving.co.uk.

Diving. Scuba companies will help you explore lakes and tarns across Cumbria. See www.freshwaterdiver.com.

Fell running. Why walk when you can run? Learn more about this lunatic sport at www.fellrunner.org.uk.

Hang-gliding or **paragliding.** For the perfect bird's eye view of the fells and valleys. The Cumbria Soaring Club has advice on take-off and landing sites at www.cumbriasoaringclub.co.uk.

Mountain biking. There are trails across the Lake District, and this is becoming a popular activity on the fells and in the forests, to the consternation of some walkers. A good source of routes and more information is www.cyclingcumbria.co.uk.

Offroad driving. For those who don't want to get out of the car, companies including Kankku—www.kankku.co.uk—organise 4x4 motor trails through the fells.

Rock climbing. Another way up the fells. There are plenty of companies catering for beginners to experts. The Fell and Rock Climbing Club has everything you need to know at www.frcc.co.uk.

Ski-ing. After a decent snowfall, the Lake District offers the best ski-ing in England. The Lake District Ski Club can be found on the slopes of Raise, and online at www.ldscsnowski.co.uk.

Swimming. Dipping into any of the lakes will soon wake you up and get you moving. Charities and clubs including the British Long Distance

Swimming Association—www.bldsa.org.uk—organise swims in many of the large lakes.

Windsurfing. An invigorating way to explore the lakes. Coniston Water, Derwent Water, Windermere and Ullswater are all popular windsurfing locations. The UK Windsurfing Association has information at www.ukwindsurfing.com.

THE MAID OF BUTTERMERE

Just as guidebooks' endorsements today can send holiday-makers flocking to a particular hotel or restaurant, so an 18th century guide caused a rush on the inn at Buttermere—to see one of its residents in particular.

In his 1792 book 'A Fortnight's Ramble in the Lakes in Westmorland, Lancashire and Cumberland', author Joseph Budworth found himself particularly drawn to Mary Robinson, the daughter of the landlord at what is now the Fish Hotel in Buttermere. He noted that 'Her hair was thick and long, her face was a fine oval, with full eyes, and lips as red as vermillion.'

Palmer's gushing description prompted curious readers to seek out the girl, who quickly became known as the 'Maid of Buttermere' or the 'Beauty of Buttermere'. Her reputation reached Romantic poets including William Wordsworth, who wrote of her in his 'Prelude' as an 'artless daughter of the hills', living a simple but happy life at one with nature.

In 1802, Mary fell victim to a notorious fraudster of the times, John Hatfield, who falsely presented himself as an aristocrat and wooed her despite having been previously married. When the deception was uncovered soon afterwards, Hatfield fled but was eventually tracked down and hung for this and other crimes. Mary was distraught to have been caught up in the scandal, but it only served to emphasise her innocent nature and she won widespread sympathy. As her fame continued to spread, much of her previously simple way of life was lost, although the story has a happy ending: she married a local farmer and lived contentedly with him and their children in Buttermere and Caldbeck.

The story of Mary Robinson and the marriage fraud has continued to inspire many artists and writers, including Melvyn Bragg, whose novel *The Maid of Buttermere* is still in print.

LAKE DISTRICT POEMS –
'A MEMORY OF GRASMERE' BY FELICIA DOROTHEA HEMANS

O vale and lake, within your mountain-urn
Smiling tranquilly, and set so deep!
Oft doth your dreamy loveliness return,
Colouring the tender shadows of my sleep
With light Elysian; for the hues that steep
Your shores in melting lustre, seem to float
On golden clouds from spirit-lands remote,
Isles of the blest; and in our memory keep
Their place with holiest harmonies, Fair scene,
Most loved by evening and her dewy star!
Oh! Ne'er may man, with touch unhallowed jar
The perfect music of thy charm serene!
Still, still unchanged, may one sweet region wear
Smiles that subdue the soul to love, and tears, and prayer.

LAKE DISTRICT FOOD –
CUMBERLAND SAUCE

Cumberland sauce is a popular fruity accompaniment to most meats, and especially pork, gammon, game and goose. It is a thin, pouring sauce that is sometimes used warm or as a glaze for joints, but more often served cold, perhaps splashed over Christmas leftovers or as a piquant accompaniment to barbequed sausages, spare ribs or lamb cutlets. Variations on the basic Cumberland sauce include the addition of pepper, ginger, cayenne pepper or vinegar, but this is a simple, classic version.

100g redcurrant jelly
100ml port or to taste
1 lemon
1 orange
1 teaspoon mustard
Salt

Grate or peel the lemon and orange into fine slices. Drop the zest into boiling water for a few minutes to reduce its bitterness, and strain. Juice the fruit. Place the jelly and port in a pan over a low heat. Bring to the boil, whisking to help break up the jelly, and simmer until it is reduced by about a quarter. Add the mustard, whisking to incorporate it, then add a pinch of salt and the juice and zest of the lemon and orange. Bring to the boil again and simmer gently for five minutes, stirring regularly. Once cooled, the sauce will keep in the fridge for two weeks or so.

FLORA AND FAUNA IN LAKE DISTRICT PLACE NAMES

A dozen of the many places in the Lake District that owe their names to the nature around them.

Applethwaite	Fir Island
Beech Grove	Grasmere
Birch How	Ivy Crag
Borrowdale Yews	Ling Mell
Brackenrigg	Oakhowe Crag
Cherry Holm	Thorn Crag

THE DAFFODILS RAP

It's fair to say that the Lake District is better known for its poetry than its hip-hop, but a rap version of its most famous verse is trying to update the area's image among young people.

The adaptation of William Wordsworth's 'I Wandered Lonely as a Cloud' was devised by Cumbria Tourism to mark the 200th anniversary of the poem in 2007 and to make the poet more relevant to youngsters. The rap's authors say that it brings the poem into the 21st century while keeping true to the sentiments of the original—though some scholars might question whether Wordsworth would have penned the line 'I never knew in advance but they were tossing up their heads like a pogo dance.' The full rap reads:

I wandered lonely along as if I was a cloud
That floats on high over vales and hills
When all at once I looked down and saw a crowd
And in my path there was a host of golden daffodils—so check it.

The kind of sight that puts your mind at ease
I saw beside the lake and beneath the tress
And they moved me like they were based on the keys.
They were fluttering and dancing inside the breeze and seemed
infinite
Just like the stars that shine up in the belt of Orion across to the
Milky Way
They stretched along the coast in a never-ending line
All across the water, marching across the golden silky bay.

Must have been 10,000 I saw in my retina
No more than a glance then I register they're beautiful etcetera
I never knew in advance but they were tossing up their heads like a
pogo dance.

In a contrast to the plants, there were waves beside them
The way they crashed and sparkled added to the marvel
And the writer couldn't help but feeling bright like sunbeam
'Cos the flowers and the waves they were quite something, yeah!
Across the spot just lost the plot—just watched and watched all the
yellow and green
And at the time I didn't need to pay them no mind but when I think
back to the day it was a hell of a scene.

So often when I'm on my couch just sitting
In a vacant mood or idle position
With nothing to do my face screwed, time ticking
I gotta rewind to my vision
I get a flashback in my minds eye
Feel the bliss of solitude from the hindsight
My heart fills up until the pleasure has spilled, yeah
I'm taking back to dancing with the daffodils… daffodils… daffodils.

THE ULTIMATE LAKE DISTRICT PICNIC

Storrs Hall Hotel on the shores of Windermere has devised what it claims to be the ultimate picnic in the ultimate location. Its hamper replaces sandwiches and biscuits with foie gras and gold leaf chocolate shavings as well as plenty of Lake District specialities, and costs a hefty £1,566.60 for two. For those of more limited means, Storrs Hall also provides picnic boxes from £17.95 per person. The Ultimate Picnic Hamper contains:

French goose foie gras and Sauternes terrine
English asparagus and Périgord truffle salad

~

Smoked quails' breasts
Smoked loin of Holker venison
Bresaola of British rare white beef
Waberthwaite air-dried ham

~

Marinated hand-dived Scottish scallops
Smoked wild Lune Valley salmon
Lock Fyne oysters on crushed ice
Beluga caviar and buckwheat blini
Poached Scottish lobster

~

Jersey Royal potato & rock chive salad
Red and yellow plum cherry tomato, balsamic and feta salad
Violet artichoke and Queen olive salad
Mixed continental leaf salad with saffron and gold leaf dressing

~

Breads: French Fougasse, English oat and rye, Italian sun-dried tomato
and parmesan
Cheeses: Wigmoore, Coulton Basset Stilton, Pont L'Eveque,
Chardonnay grapes and celery

~

Wild strawberries and Jersey cream
Exotic fruit trifle with gold leaf Valrhona chocolate shavings
Scones with semi-dried raisins, Cornish clotted cream and strawberry
preserve

~

Louis Roederer Cristal, 1999
Chateau Lafite-Rothschild, 1981
Lakeland Willow Water

LAKELAND'S MINERAL WATER

All mineral waters make grand claims about their purity, but Lakeland
Willow Water at Flookburgh near Grange-over-Sands claims to have
some extra-special qualities.

The water's source is at the foot of Cartmel Fell, where layers of
limestone make it rich in calcium. Layers of peat, formed by the remains
of prehistoric white willow trees, meanwhile add salicin and give the
water its name. Willow bark has been renowned for centuries for its

therapeutic qualities, and chemically is closely related to aspirin. Manufacturers of Willow Water say it helps to build and maintain strong bones and well-being—though evidence so far is anecdotal rather than scientific.

CONSTABLE AND TURNER IN THE LAKE DISTRICT

It's not just writers who have been inspired by the Lake District. Among the artists who have been stirred by the countryside are John Constable and JMW Turner, who both found their skills advanced by their visits.

Constable was 30 when he arrived in the Lake District in 1806. He stayed at the home of his uncle—Storrs Hall on the shores of Winderemere, now a hotel—and toured around the towns and valleys of the Lake District, spending several weeks in Borrowdale. His visit produced nearly 100 sketches and watercolours, capturing fells including Great Gable, Skiddaw, Blencathra and the Langdale Pikes, and waterfalls including the Lodore Falls and the Upper and Lower Falls at Rydal. The trip helped to further Constable's mastery of landscape, and improved his ability to capture shifting weather and atmosphere in particular. He is thought to have enjoyed the majesty of the Lake District scenery, although his friend and biographer CR Leslie later claimed that he found the solitude of the area oppressing. His love of nature and romantic sensibilities made him an artistic contemporary of poets like William Wordsworth—whom he met—but his Lake District sketches and drawings contrasted with much of his other work, which tended to focus on the flatter and sunnier agricultural idylls of southern England.

Just as the Lake District was an essential stopping point for literary tourists of the time, so it was for youthful and aspiring artists. It was one of several places visited by Turner as he sought to improve his painting on a sketching tour of northern England in 1797, aged 22. He returned four years later on his way back to London from Scotland, professing great admiration of the dramatic fells and valleys. His work from the Lake District includes several paintings of the Coniston fells and a famous scene of a stormy sky over Buttermere that shows how the landscape helped him to master light and shade. Turner's work was championed during his lifetime by John Ruskin, who collected his paintings and sketches at Brantwood, his home in Coniston. Turner's watercolour of Ullswater, painted from sketches from his 1797 visit, is now housed in the Wordsworth Museum at Dove Cottage in Grasmere, which also has other pieces by key artists either living in the Lake District or visiting it.

THE LAKES AND TARNS: LARGEST, SMALLEST, LONGEST AND DEEPEST

Of the Lake District's 18 waters usually classified as lakes, Windermere is by some distance the biggest. Running about 10.6 miles or 17km from its northern tip near Ambleside to its southernmost point near Newby Bridge, it has a perimeter that stretches close enough to 26.2 miles to have made the Windermere Marathon a popular event for many years. Its surface area of 5.7 square miles (14.8 square kilometres) also makes it the largest natural lake in England. Brothers Water, which stretches only around 500m at its widest, is usually accepted as the smallest lake in the Lake District.

The deepest lake in the Lake District, and also in England, is Wastwater, which reaches a depth of 258 feet or 79 metres. The deepest tarn is Blea Water near Haweswater, which reaches 223 feet or 68 metres down, while the largest tarn is Devoke Water, which runs 0.8 miles or 1.2km from its easternmost point to its westernmost. Its proximity to the Sellafield nuclear power station also gives Devoke Water the unfortunate reputation of having the most radioactive fish in England.

AN AMERICAN PRESIDENT IN THE LAKE DISTRICT

The Lake District receives thousands of American visitors a year, and its connections across the Atlantic stretch right into the White House.

Although he was born in Virginia, Woodrow Wilson had Cumbrian heritage from his Carlisle-born mother, and he retained close and highly affectionate links with the county even after he became the 28th president of the US. He first visited in 1896, aged 39 and while a professor at Princeton University, and was immediately enraptured by the area. 'There is no spot in the world in which I am so completely at rest and peace as in the lake country,' he wrote in one of many letters to his wife back home.

Wilson's trip was part of a cycling holiday that included a ride from Keswick to Rydal, which he called '16 enchanting miles'. He returned on another cycle tour with a friend three years later, riding from Penrith down the length of Ullswater, along what he judged to be 'the most beautiful road in the world.' He explored Keswick and Cockermouth, looking for places associated with William Wordsworth, and went on to the poet's home at Dove Cottage.

Wilson returned with his wife in 1903, spending a week in the Lake District as part of a two-month tour of Britain and Europe. He came back again in 1906, this time with his daughters, and noted: 'It has rained a great deal, but very gently and sweetly, and the whole countryside is kept fresh for the bright days.' On this visit he became friends with local artist Fred Yates and National Trust co-founder Canon Hardwicke Rawnsley, and he kept up an affectionate correspondence with the Yates family in particular for the rest of his life. In 1908 he spent the whole summer in the Lakes, searching for his mother's birthplace in Carlisle and exploring the valleys and fells on the western side of the Lake District by bike.

Back in the US, Wilson was elected governor of New Jersey and then, in 1913, President. Yates, in the country at the time, attended the inauguration and came back to Rydal with the gift of the huge American flag on which Wilson had sworn his oath. It was draped from the Yates' Rydal home on special occasions such as American Independence Day on 4th July for years afterwards.

Wilson made one more visit to Cumbria at the end of the First World War, attending events in Carlisle put on in his honour. He had hoped to make another trip to the Lake District after his presidency ended in 1921, but ill health prevented him from leaving the US again. When he died in 1924, flags flew at half-mast in Carlisle and Lake District newspapers carried lengthy news reports and obituaries.

Presidential suites—some of the Lake District hotels stayed in by Woodrow Wilson

The Wordsworth Hotel in Grasmere
(Wilson visited it as the Rothay Hotel)
The George Hotel, Keswick
The White Lion Inn, Patterdale
The White Lion Hotel, Ambleside
The Keswick Hotel, Keswick
The Crown and Mitre Hotel, Carlisle
Wilson and his family also stayed at **Loughrigg Cottage** in Rydal,
still available as a self-catering holiday cottage.

THE COUNTY OF DOODLESHIRE

The ancient counties of Cumberland and Westmorland are important parts of Cumbria's heritage—but less well known is the independent territory of Doodleshire.

After fighting for Richard I in the crusades, legend has it that the king sent Dickie Doodle to Kendal in the 12th century to set up a mayoralty. After getting drunk on his arrival and upsetting some locals, he was apparently chased across the River Kent, to the patch of town now known as Gooseholme. Here, perhaps emboldened by drink, he decided to set up his own county of Doodleshire, and put himself in charge of it.

Doodle has been remembered intermittently in Kendal ever since, with fairs, processions, races and events in his honour in the part of town he made his own. Successors to the title of Mayor of Doodleshire are also voted in, with a special requirement that the incumbent honours Doodle's reputation for hard drinking and keeps a close eye on all the pubs in the area. A Doodleshire festival was part of the 400th anniversary celebrations of Kendal's town charter proper in 1974, and there are plans to revive the event on an annual basis. A live music bar in the town also carries his name.

J B PRIESTLEY ON THE LAKE DISTRICT

'Here, concentrated in a single area, known as the Lake District, are the hardest of the English rocks, the highest of the English summits, and the loveliest settings of English scenery — made up of a rich blend of estuary, woodland, river, lake and mountain.'

THE BEAUTY OF BRITAIN 1935

SOME MOUNTAIN NAMES AND THEIR MEANINGS

Black Combe The dark crested mountain, from the Old English *blaec* and *camb*.

Blencathra The chair-shaped mountain, from the Welsh *blaen* for summit and *cateir* for chair. Blencathra is so shaped from many angles, and in the 18th century was given a second name, Saddleback, by which it is now sometimes known.

Bowfell This is likely to be derived from its obvious bow-shaped appearance, but some theories link it to 13th century men called Bowe or Bowes.

Castle Crag The rocky peak with a fortification.

Cat Bells The wild cats' den. From Middle English *belde* for shelter.

Catstye Cam The ridge with the wild cat's path. Cam means the crest of the hill.

Glaramara The mountain with the hut by the ravines. From the Old Norse *hovedgleuermerhe*: *hoved* meaning mass of fell; *gleuerm* meaning by the ravines and *erhe* meaning a mountain hut.

Great Cockup Derived from the valley where woodcock are found, rather than from any misadventure on the fell.

Great Gable Referring to the shape of the fell, which from some angles looks like the gable of a house.

Grisedale Pike The peak above the valley of the pigs, from the Old Norse *griss* meaning pigs.

Hardknott Rough, difficult, craggy fell. From the the Old Norse *harror* meaning rocky peak.

Harter Fell The hart's mountain.

Haystacks Probably derived from its appearance, though it could be linked to the Old Norse *har stakkr*, meaning high rocks.

Helvellyn There is no agreement about the source of this name. One theory was that it was known to early inhabitants as El-Velin or the Hill of Baal, another that it once belonged to someone called Vellin or Willan.

High Spy Perhaps named after an old look-out post or fort.

High Street The modern name refers to a Roman road that runs over and along the summit ridge. It linked Roman forts in the north and south of the Lake District.

Ill Bell The treacherous, bell-shaped hill

Kirk Fell The fell above the church. From the Old Norse *kirkja* meaning church. Kirk Fell overlooks St Olaf's church at Wasdale Head.

Latterbarrow The hill where animals had their lair, from the Old Norse *latr* and *berg* meaning lair and hill.

Coniston Old Man An evocative name derived from the dialect word man, meaning cairn on a summit.

Orrest Head Hill on which a battle was fought. The date and details of the battle are not known. From the Old Norse *orrusta* meaning battle.

Pike O'Stickle The pike with the sharp summit.

Pillar Takes its name from the large and famous pillar-shaped rock nearby.

Raise From the Old Norse *hreysi* and subsequent dialect word meaning pile of stones.

Robinson One of the many mountains named after Lake District landowners. A Richard Robinson purchased surrounding land in the reign of Henry VIII.

Sail From the Old Norse *seyla* meaning swampy hill.

Scafell and **Scafell Pike** Either the fell with the shieling or the fell with the bare summit. From the Old Norse *skali* or *skalli* meaning shieling or bare summit respectively, and *fjall* meaning fell.

Skiddaw There has been plenty of disagreement about the origins of this fell's name. Suggestions have included the archer's hill, the hill with the craggy ridge and the hill where wood is found, based on the Old Norse words *skyti*, *skuti* and *skith*, meaning archer, craggy ridge and firewood respectively.

Wetherlam The home of the castrated ram. From the Old Norse *vethr*, meaning castrated ram.

Yewbarrow The hill where ewes graze.

SOME LAKE DISTRICT LIMERICKS

The following were among the Cumbrian entries to a limerick competition run by the BBC's RaW scheme to get people reading and writing.

> There was a young maid at Far Sawrey,
> Who wrote a most wonderful story.
> Peter Rabbit and Co
> Were the stars of the show
> And the rest of the tale is history!

> Said a wise Mountain Rescue man, 'Stop it.
> On Helvellyn you're likely to cop it.
> That vertiginous ledge
> That is called Striding Edge
> Is no place for a novice, so hop it.'

An old Herdwick sheep once heard tell
That young Jobby his sheep soon would sell,
So she gathered her mates
Said 'there's no time to waste'
And they took off up Brackenthwaite Fell.

An agile young Ambleside lass
Acrobatically climbed Kirkstone Pass.
Somersaulting 'The Struggle'
Three Herdwicks she'd juggle
And wrestlers in Grasmere outclass.

By Ullswater once I did roam,
Just me and the clouds all alone.
The daffs looked so sprightly,
I think of them nightly
When sprawled on the sofa at home.

TEN LONG-DISTANCE WALKS

As well as plenty of short fell walks, Cumbria is home to some of the finest long-distance trails in the country, either wholly within the county or just passing through. In descending order of distance, here are ten of the best-loved walks, ways and paths of 80 miles or more.

The Pennine Way. A National Trail, from Edale in Derbyshire to Kirk Yetholm on the Scottish borders – 270 miles.

Wainwright's Coast to Coast Walk. From St Bees on the west coast to Robin Hood's Bay in Yorkshire on the east – 190 miles.

The Cumbria Coastal Way. From Silverdale to Gretna – 150 miles.

The Thirlmere Way. From Greater Manchester to the source of its water at Thirlmere Reservoir – 130 miles.

Lady Anne's Way. From Skipton to Penrith – 100 miles.

The Wainwright Memorial Walk. A circular route from Windermere, taking in Wainwright's favourite places – 100 miles.

The Westmorland Way. From Appleby to Morecambe Bay – 95 miles.

Hadrian's Wall Path. From Bowness-on-Solway on the west coast to Wallsend on the east – 85 miles.

The Cumberland Way. From Ravenglass to Appleby – 80 miles.

The Dales Way. From Ilkley in Yorkshire to the shores of Windermere – 80 miles.

ARTS AND CRAFTS IN THE LAKE DISTRICT

The Arts and Crafts movement of the late 19th century and its 20th century legacy form an important part of the heritage and culture of the Lake District. Here are ten places to find out more.

Abbot Hall, Kendal. Gallery of art including watercolours by Ruskin, and examples of Lakeland furniture and textiles of the last 250 years. Tel 015397 22464 or online at www.lakelandmuseum.org.uk.

Blackwell, near Bowness. Showcase home for arts and crafts, built in 1900 and mixing Victorian and modern design. Tel 015394 46139 or online at www.blackwell.org.uk.

Brantwood, Coniston. John Ruskin's realisation of 'organic architecture' and filled with his work. Tel 015394 41396 or online at www.brantwood.org.uk.

Broadleys, Windermere. House designed by Charles Voysey and now home to the Windermere Motor Boat Racing Club. Tel 015394 43284 or online at www.wmbrc.co.uk.

Fairfield Mill, Sedbergh. Arts and heritage centre on the edge of the Yorkshire Dales. Tel 015396 21958 or online at www.fairfieldmill.org.

Hutton-in-the-Forest, Penrith. Classic country house with William Morris wallpaper and William de Morgan ceramics. Tel 017684 84449 or online at www.hutton-in-the-forest.co.uk.

Keswick Museum and Art Gallery. Purpose-built museum, constructed in the Arts and Crafts style and featuring items from the Keswick School of Industrial Arts. Tel 017687 73263 or online at www.allerdale.gov.uk/keswick-museum.

Ruskin Museum, Coniston. Tribute to Ruskin's work, plus local linen and lace. Tel 015394 41164 or online at www.ruskinmuseum.com.

Tullie House Museum and Art Gallery, Carlisle. Includes about 5,000 fine and decorative art items and 7,000 items of clothing and textiles. Tel 01228 534781 or online at www.tulliehouse.co.uk.

Lickbarrow Lodge, Windermere. Arts and Crafts house, built in 1912 and now renovated as a bed and breakfast. Tel 015394 45252.

CUMBRIA INDUSTRIES - NUCLEAR

The nuclear energy facilities in west Cumbria have been the subject of enormous controversy ever since they were built—and continue to be even as they are decommissioned.

The two-square-mile site just north of Seascale comprises around 200 nuclear facilities, and since 1981 has been known by the umbrella name of Sellafield. The site grew out of Royal Ordnance factories that were first used to develop Britain's nuclear capabilities after the Second World War, and then to build the world's first civil and commercial nuclear power station, Calder Hall. It opened in 1956.

With its useful life now at an end, Calder Hall and other Sellafield facilities have been in a decommissioning phase since the early 1980s as the Nuclear Decommissioning Authority seeks to clean up the site and land ready for other uses. Dismantling the site has big implications for Cumbria, since it is the county's biggest single employer with around 10,000 staff and indirectly supports many more workers nearby. The decommissioning process is expected to take up to 50 years, so job losses will be gradual.

A fire in one of the nuclear reactors in 1957 and ongoing disquiet about radioactive discharges from Sellafield have fuelled controversy about whether nuclear energy can ever be entirely safe. Local pressure groups continue to campaign against it, and there have also been concerns about the way potentially dangerous materials are transported to and from the facilities.

The Sellafield complex now includes a large visitor centre with information about its work and hands-on activities for children. The Core Cumbria pressure group has its own 'Alternative Tour of Sellafield' outlining what it claims are problems ignored by the site's owners at www.corecumbria.co.uk.

LITERARY LAKELANDERS - NORMAN NICHOLSON

While William Wordsworth and Samuel Taylor Coleridge are among the literary champions of the Lake District proper, no-one has chronicled life on the western side of Cumbria better than Norman Nicholson.

Nicholson lived his whole life in the house where he was born in 1914, in Millom, a small industrial town north of Barrow-in-Furness along Cumbria's coast. He developed tuberculosis of the lungs and larynx at the age of 16, and while recuperating in a sanatorium, was forbidden to speak in anything above a whisper for nearly two years in order to rest his larynx. He read voraciously and began writing in earnest during this time.

Nicholson's poems were often written in west Cumbrian vernacular, and were inspired by the mining and iron activities of the area. While the Romantic poets rejoiced in the dramatic landscape of the Lake District, Nicholson was more taken by Cumbria's roots, industries and people. He covers the dramatic demise of the industries that helped to build Millom and its surrounding towns in 'On the Closing of Millom Ironworks', and was acutely aware of its devastating effect on the area. He became a committed Christian in adult life, and his obituary in the *Times* called him 'the most gifted Christian poet of the century.'

Because his work was so centred on his locale and he did not follow any particular poetic tradition, Nicholson did not receive the wider critical acclaim that he deserved during his lifetime. Much of his work is now out of print, although his high-profile supporters included Seamus Heaney, and he received both the Queen's Medal for Poetry and the OBE. His thoughtful prose—including novels, an autobiography and several anthologies, including the classic *Portrait of the Lakes*—helped to bring him to the attention of a wider audience than his poetry had reached.

Nicholson died in 1987 and is buried in St George's churchyard in Millom. The church has a stained glass window inspired by Nicholson's life and work, with stories from his poems incorporated into the design. The town's Folk Museum has a permanent exhibition about him and collections of his work, and his old house on St George's Terrace in the town has a commemorative plaque outside. A Norman Nicholson Society exists to celebrate and promote his work. Nicholson's reputation has continued to grow since his death, and he is now generally agreed to be Cumbria's finest poet of the modern era.

THE SWALLOWS AND AMAZONS LAKE

Arthur Ransome's classic children's adventure story *Swallows and Amazons* was inspired by the Lake District. The book's setting is referred to only as 'that great lake in the North', but Ransome had Coniston Water firmly in his mind when he wrote the story, and elements of the lake and its shoreline are also reminiscent of Windermere. Wild Cat Island is based on Peel Island on Coniston Water, though it might also have been partly inspired by Windermere's network of islands, and Kanchenjunga's real-life equivalent is the Old Man of Coniston.

SMALL IS BEAUTIFUL

As well as boasting England's tallest mountain—Scafell Pike—and deepest lake—Wast Water—the western fells of the Lake District also claim the country's smallest parish church. St Olaf's at Wasdale Head reckons to seat a maximum of 40 people uncomfortably, though more have crammed into the narrow and low-beamed building on occasions.

The first reference to the church was made in 1550, but it is likely that it dates to well before the Reformation, and the roof is thought to have been formed from a Viking longboat. The graveyard has memorials to many walkers and climbers killed on the surrounding fells.

St Olaf's claim to be the smallest church in Britain has been challenged recently by several others, including Bremilham Church in Wiltshire, which is now listed by the *Guinness Book of Records*—though this is a relative newcomer, having been built in the 1800s. And if other churches can challenge it for size, then its position with steep fells on all sides mean that it is without doubt one of England's most spectacularly located.

WORDSWORTH ON... LAKE DISTRICT LIFE IN THE PAST

'Towards the head of these Dales was found a perfect Republic of Shepherds and Agriculturalists, among whom the plough of each man was confined to the maintenance of his own family, or to the occasional accommodation of his neighbour. Two or three cows furnished each family with milk and cheese. The chapel was the only edifice that presided over these dwellings, the supreme head of this pure Commonwealth; the members of which existed in the midst of a powerful empire like an ideal society or an organized community, whose constitution had been imposed and regulated by the mountains which protected it. Neither high-born nobleman, knight, nor esquire was here; but many of these humble sons of the hills had a consciousness that the land, which they walked over and tilled, had for more than five hundred years been possessed by men of their name and blood.'

FROM *GUIDE TO THE LAKES* BY WILLIAM WORDSWORTH

THE LIGHTER SIDE OF MOUNTAIN RESCUE

The roll-call of incidents in the annual reports of the Lake District Search and Mountain Rescue Association can make for unsettling reading. Fortunately for readers—and infuriatingly for the rescue teams involved—not every incident is serious. Here are some of the more eye-catching entries from the LDSAMRA's journals of call-outs in 2005 and 2006.

19 April, 2005, 13.55, Forest Head, Brampton. 'Unattended bike found chained to post for 24 hours; police were concerned for owner. Search concluded when subject returned to collect bike. Questioned and advised of good practice.'

23 April 2005, 21.05, Helton, Penrith. 'Report from various members of the public of flares sighted over Helton, Shap and Loadpot Hill. Investigations found that fireworks had been discharged from party at forest holiday resort in the Eden valley.'

26 June 2005, 18.05, Scafell. 'Subject called her mother to tell her she was "slipping down a rock". When phone resumed contact one hour later, she was found to be safe and well.'

30 August 2005, 01.20, Flookburgh. 'Subject reported missing from campsite in Flookburgh. Subject was located in Manchester while the team was mobilising.'

27 December 2005, 16.48, Castle Crag, Borrowdale. 'Dog called Lucky chased a robin on the summit and became separated from her owners, falling over the summit crag onto a ledge 60 feet below. Her barks alerted a passing walker just before nightfall. Retrieved without loss or injury.'

6 April 2006, 15.25, Angle Tarn. 'Party of ten women from Thailand overcome by cold. Eight evacuated by passing walkers to Borrowdale. Two given shelter by school group in tent. No injuries.'

23 April 2006, 14.45, Loadpot Hill. 'Team member spotted military shell exposed on footpath. Police requested team help and bomb squad were taken to site. Shell was disposed of by Army Bomb Squad.'

29 April 2006, 17.12, Swarth Fell. 'Person reported a parascender laying still for a long time and became concerned that he may have fallen. Team investigated and found man waiting for updraft. False alarm, good intent.'

22 May 2006, 19.40, White Moss, Rydal. 'Man reported collapsed. Turned out to be drunk and sleeping.'

2 June 2006, 23.43, Langdale Pikes. 'Party reported overdue after leaving intended route with friend by phone. Located in bed in hotel after check revealed that route was for previous day.'

10 June 2006, 07.00, Loughrigg Fell. 'Subject reported missing by friends after becoming separated when going to watch sunrise. Alcohol may have contributed to general confusion. Turned up at 10am unhurt but unable to give account of movements.'

12 June 2006, 18.29, Blakerigg, Great Langdale. 'Subject became separated from friends. Lost glasses. Walked over edge of crag. Landed on small ledge after short fall. Further fall of 70m next option. No injuries reported.'

23 September 2006, 17.40, Loughrigg. 'Subject reported she couldn't find her way off the hill because the ground was steep and rough. She was eventually located in a very large, overgrown private garden, 50 metres above the road. Unhurt.'

SOME LAKE DISTRICT TOWNS AROUND THE WORLD

The spread of the Commonwealth and British settlers means that names of some Lake District towns pop up in some far-flung corners of the world. Here are some of the other Conistons, Kendals, Keswicks and Windermeres.

Coniston
New South Wales, Australia
Northern Territory, Australia
Ontario, Canada
Murray, Georgia, US
Yolo, California, US

Keswick
Adelaide, Australia
Ontario, Canada
Keokuk, Iowa, US
Albemarle, Virginia, US
Shasta, California, US
Leelanau, Michigan, US
New Brunswick, Canada

Kendal
New South Wales, Australia
Stann Creek, Belize
Saskatchewan, Canada
Jawa Tengah, Indonesia
Mpumalanga, South Africa

Windermere
Tasmania, Australia
Victoria, Australia
British Columbia, Canada
Waldo, Maine, US
Tolland, Connecticut, US
Orange County, Florida, US
Montgomery, Tennessee, US
Seattle, Washington, US

WAINWRIGHT'S SIX BEST SUMMITS

As chosen in Alfred Wainwright's conclusion to his seventh and final *Pictorial Guide to the Lakeland Fells*.

Dow Crag
Harter Fell in Eskdale
Helm Crag
Eagle Crag
Slight Side on Scafell
Steeple

ARTISAN FOOD'S FAVOURITE FOODIE PLACES

Artisan Food is an online guide to the best food and drink in Cumbria, with information about the best restaurants, retailers, farmers' markets and events, plus ideas, recipes and profiles of the people behind the food. It promotes producers of all shapes and sizes, and celebrates the wealth of fantastic food that the Lake District has to offer. Artisan Food can be found at www.artisan-food.com. Here are the favourite foodie places of the site's founders, Cecilia and Martin Campbell.

The Jumble Room, Grasmere. This is our favourite restaurant in the Lakes—in fact it's our favourite eating place full stop. Andy and Chrissy Hill run it with passion, care and flair, and the food matches the mood. Small, cosy and welcoming with dishes prepared from top local ingredients, often organic, always seasonal, and always full of amazing flavours.

Lucy's Deli, Ambleside. Fantastic shop in Ambleside, with loads of local produce and pretty much anything a gourmet cook could wish for from the four corners of the world. It's run by Lucy Nicholson, who is something of a food ambassador for Cumbria, and who also has a restaurant in the village. Her latest venture is Lucy Cooks, a cooking school in Staveley.

Teza Indian Canteen, Carlisle. There isn't a great deal of good ethnic food in the Lakes, but this modern Indian restaurant in Carlisle has great, flavourful food and is incredible value for money, particularly at lunchtime. The evening menu contains both contemporary and traditional food, and has a good selection of mouthwatering vegetarian offerings.

Yanwath Gate Inn, near Penrith. This pub is a cut above the rest—gastropubs as well as pubs. The menu is unusual and interesting—not just goats' cheese tartlets and wild mushroom risotto—and there is amazing seafood, bought in fresh from Scotland.

Orton Farmers' Market. There are several good farmers' markets around the county, including Pooley Bridge, Cockermouth and Kendal, but Orton is the best. It's a bit out of the way, but attracts plenty of top producers. It's held on Orton's market square and there are no high street shops to detract from the event.

Linthwaite House, Windermere. This lovely hotel has a three-rosette restaurant, and is our choice for what is popularly known as 'fine dining'. Chef Simon Bolsover is a very cool customer with a great passion for what he does, and the food lives up to expectations. Simon is also an avid supporter of local produce.

The Village Bakery, Melmerby and **the Watermill**, Little Salkeld. These two businesses may be owned and run by different people, but together they make a great day out. The Watermill in Little Salkeld makes amazing stone-ground flour and you can have a tour of the mill as well as a snack at the little café by the stream. Down the road in Melmerby is the Village Bakery with a very good shop and a restaurant with great fresh food. Upstairs is a beautiful gallery that usually has a nice exhibition on.

Low Sizergh Barn, near Kendal. One of the best-stocked farm shops in the county. There's a cheese and charcuterie counter with loads of Cumbrian products as well as stuff from further afield. Upstairs and downstairs are craft shops, and there's also a café, from where you can watch the cows being milked—great for children! On a sunny day, follow the farm trail around the grounds and through the woods.

The Queen's Head, Troutbeck. This pub in the extraordinarily picturesque village of Troutbeck is an old favourite of ours. The food is great—it's not the pub to visit for a bowl of chips—and the bar is made from a four-poster bed. There are log fires inside, and outdoor seating for warm days. A great place for Sunday lunch.

Airey's Farm Shop, Grange-over-Sands. Really high quality meat. The animals they sell are raised either on their own farm as naturally as possible, or at local Cumbrian farms with similar high standards of animal welfare. They stock a wide selection of rare and traditional breeds of animals as they have more fat and marbling and a better flavour. Animals are properly finished, slaughtered on the premises, and left to hang to mature properly. In short: quality, traceable meat treated properly.

TEN LAKE DISTRICT NOVELS

Ten old and new stories set in and around the Lake District.

Swallows and Amazons by Arthur Ransome (Red Fox). Classic story of innocent childhood adventures on a lake. Many of Ransome's subsequent stories were also set in Lakeland.

The Tales of Peter Rabbit by Beatrix Potter (Frederick Warne, various editions). Potter's books, inspired by Lake District creatures and locations, have become an industry of their own.

Haweswater by Sarah Hall (Faber). Set among the communities of the Mardale valley as it is flooded to create the Haweswater reservoir.

The Cumbrian Trilogy by Melvyn Bragg (Sceptre). Three volumes tracing four generations of a Cumbrian family, among the many books by Bragg on his home county.

The Herries Chronicle by Hugh Walpole (various). Epic series of books following different generations of a Lakeland clan.

The Grave Tattoo by Val McDermid (HarperCollins). A Wordsworth expert investigates a corpse found on a Lake District hillside.

Hazard's Way by Roger Hubank (Ernest Press). A young mountain climber's adventures at Wasdale Head at the turn of the 19th century.

The Coffin Trail by Martin Edwards (Allison & Busby). A peaceful Lake District valley is the backdrop to this crime thriller.

All Quiet on the Orient Express by Magnus Mills (HarperCollins). An outsider finds himself pulled into life among the Lakeland fells. Sinister, strange, evocative and moving.

Fell of Dark by Reginald Hill (HarperCollins). More murder on the mountains. Hill grew up in Cumbria and has set several of his books there.

THE BOB GRAHAM ROUND

The Bob Graham Round is not just the pinnacle of fell-running and the most physically demanding challenge that the Lake District has to offer—it is just about the biggest test for athletes or mountaineers anywhere in the UK.

'Rounds' of various Lake District peaks have been popular for many years, but the name for this route was coined after Bob Graham completed a circuit of 42 Lake District peaks within 24 hours on 13th and 14th June 1932. Graham, a former gardener and Keswick guesthouse owner, modestly called his route 'a long walk' after he finished it at the age of 42; he chose the number of peaks to match his years. Graham ran in tennis shoes, baggy shorts and a shirt, and ate bread and butter, boiled eggs, fruit and sweets to keep his energy levels up. After finishing in the early hours of 14th June, he was back up at his guesthouse to prepare breakfast by 6am.

Bob Graham's route started and finished at the Moot Hall in Keswick and covered 72 miles and around 28,000 feet of climbing—nearly equivalent to scaling Mount Everest from sea level. His time of 23 hours 39 minutes was not surpassed for more than 28 years, and his achievement had been nearly forgotten until a newspaper article by Lake District writer A Harry Griffin inspired a new generation of fell-runners to take up the challenge of the round. Alan Heaton, a local runner, took nearly an hour off the record, which has since been repeatedly broken again. It now stands at a barely comprehensible 13 hours 53 minutes, set by Billy Bland in 1982.

As more and more runners attempted the round, the Bob Graham 24 Hour Club was set up in 1971. More than 1,300 people have now received the club's certificate for completing the same circuit or a route that is similarly arduous—and plenty of the members have seen attempts end in painful failure before finally succeeding.

The Bob Graham Round has inspired fell runners to set ever more extreme records. In 1962 Alan Heaton racked up 54 peaks in 24 hours, beating a previous record of 51 set by his brother Ken. Another fell-running legend, Joss Naylor, stretched the record to 61 in 1971, and then, a year later, to 63 during 24 hours of appalling wind and rain. In 1975 he extended it to 72 peaks covering 37,000 feet of ascent, a record broken most recently by Mark Hartell, who notched up 77 in 24 hours.

Jean Dawes became the first woman to complete the round in 1977. As the bar was raised, runners completed double rounds, running first clockwise and then, after a short break, returning anti-clockwise. The round is hard enough during midsummer daylight and warmth, but in 1986 four runners completed it in mid-winter, when two-thirds of the time is spent in the dark and all of it in the cold. The youngest and oldest members of the Bob Graham 24 Hour Club completed their rounds at the equally remarkable ages of 13 and 66. And in 1994 a paraplegic, Andrew Chamings, completed the circuit with the aid of crutches and callipers in a little over three days. Hi-tech equipment, pacemakers and support vehicles have all helped to make the route a lot more accessible than it was to Bob Graham in 1932, but it remains an enormous challenge for body and mind, and an achievement for the very few.

The 42 peaks on the Bob Graham Round, ascended in either a clockwise or anti-clockwise direction from Keswick, are:

Skiddaw (3,054 feet)	Pike o' Stickle (2,323)
Great Calva (2,265)	Rossett Pike (2,136)
Blencathra (2,848)	Bowfell (2,959)
Clough Head (2,382)	Esk Pike (2,904)
Great Dodd (2,807)	Great End (2,986)
Watson's Dodd (2,584)	Ill Crag (3,068)
Stybarrow Dodd (2,756)	Broad Crag (3,064)
Raise (2,897)	Scafell Pike (3,209)
White Side (2,832)	Scafell (3,163)
Helvellyn Lower Man (3,035)	Yewbarrow (2,058)
Helvellyn (3,117)	Red Pike (2,629)
Nethermost Pike (2,923)	Steeple (2,687)
Dollywaggon Pike (2,810)	Pillar (2,926)
Fairfield (2,864)	Kirk Fell (2,630)
Seat Sandal (2,415)	Great Gable (2,949)
Steel Fell (1,811)	Green Gable (2,628)
Calf Crag (1,762)	Brandreth (2,344)
High Raise (2,500)	Grey Knotts (2,287)
Sergeant Man (2,414)	Dale Head (2,473)
Thunacar Knott (2,351)	Hindscarth (2,385)
Harrison Stickle (2,415)	Robinson (2,417)

LAKE DISTRICT FOOD – STICKY TOFFEE PUDDING

Of all the Lake District's famous rich desserts, none is more widely known than the sticky toffee pudding. Several hotels and restaurants claim to be its originator, but one of the strongest claims is from Sharrow Bay country house hotel near Ullswater, whose former chef Francis Coulson introduced it to his menu as 'icky sticky toffee pudding' in the 1970s. There is some evidence of versions well before this, but Sharrow Bay certainly advanced its popularity, and continues to serve what it claims is the original and best sticky toffee pudding in the world.

That claim is also made by the Cartmel Village Shop, which now employs 35 people to make and sell its sticky toffee pudding. Its mail order business sends the dessert all over the world, and it is especially popular in the US, where it is produced locally and fondly regarded as the quintessential British pudding. Made with chopped dates and drenched in a toffee sauce, it is a suitably rich and filling pudding after a long day's walk in the fells.

A recipe for sticky toffee pudding

Competition for the best sticky toffee pudding recipe is fierce, and there are plenty of variations on the theme—but this is a classic and delicious version.

225g plain flour
175g white sugar
175g stoned dates
50g butter
275ml boiling water
1 egg
1 teaspoon baking powder
1 teaspoon bicarbonate of soda
1 teaspoon vanilla essence

For the topping:
120g brown sugar
80g butter
4 tablespoons double cream

Cream the butter and sugar together. Sift the flour and baking powder and add a little of it to the creamed mixture. Whisk the egg and beat that in too, before adding the rest of the flour. Chop the dates finely, dust them with flour and pour the boiling water over them. Add the bicarbonate of soda and vanilla essence to them. Combine this mixture with your creamed mix of butter, sugar, flour and egg, and blend well. Pour it all into a buttered cake tin or dish and bake in a moderate oven (gas mark 4) for about 40 minutes.

For the toffee topping, heat the brown sugar, butter and cream and simmer for three minutes. When the pudding is done, pour the topping over it and place under a hot grill for a few minutes until it bubbles. Serve hot with cream or ice cream.

THE BOATS OF THE LAKE DISTRICT

Rowing, sailing, yachting, windsurfing, canoeing and kayaking—from the 17th century fishing vessels to modern powercrafts, there is a long history of boating on Cumbria's lakes.

On a busy summer's day, commercial and private boats can take tens of thousands of people out onto larger lakes like Windermere, Derwent Water and Coniston Water. There are echoes of the past in the traditional boats catching charr on Windermere, used by fishermen to keep their deep-sunk metallic lures moving in the water. And many of the ferries carrying tourists across the lakes have been doing so for well over a hundred years—the Ullswater Steamers company uses steamers that have been cruising there since the 19th century.

Perhaps the Lake District's most famous boat is Coniston's Gondola, one of the oldest steam yachts in Britain. Built in the 1850s as a hybrid of Venice gondola and Victorian steamer, it was once a popular tourist attraction, but fell out of public use in the 1930s. Painstakingly rebuilt by the National Trust in the 1970s, 'The Lady of the Lake' now cruises around Coniston Water every day during the summer.

LAKE DISTRICT WEBCAMS

Internet webcams help those far away from the Lake District to enjoy the scenery from their desktops, and allow walkers to check the local weather—rather than the forecast, which can often be somewhat different—before they lace up their boots. Here are ten of the best Lake District webcams.

www.lakelandwebs.co.uk - Constantly updated views of the fells and villages from Buttermere, Coniston, Eskdale, Langdale and Wasdale

www.bbc.co.uk/cumbria/in_pictures/webcams - The BBC has more than a dozen webcams around the Lake District, including several monitoring the wildlife of the area

www.thelakedistrictguide.com - Collected webcams from Keswick, Coniston, Glenridding and Carlisle

www.eldergrove.co.uk/webcam - The latest views over Ambleside and the Fairfield Horseshoe, from the Elder Grove hotel

www.highfieldkeswick.co.uk/webcam - Views down the Borrowdale valley from the Highfield Hotel in Keswick, updated every minute

www.214fells.com/webcam - Live views of Scafell Pike and its surrounding fells

www.ullswater-steamers.co.uk/webcam.htm - Images of Ullswater from the lake's ferry company www.ospreywatch.co.uk/webcam.htm - Updates every ten minutes from the osprey nest on the edge of Bassenthwaite Lake

www.churchstile.com/webcam.htm - Check the weather before you pitch your tent with this view from the Church Stile farm and campsite in Wasdale

www.lakelandcam.co.uk - Not strictly a webcam, but Tony Richards updates his site every day with wonderful photos from his latest walks across the Lake District.

LAKE DISTRICT POEMS – FROM 'THE EXCURSION' BY WILLIAM WORDSWORTH

We scaled, without a track to ease our steps,
A steep ascent; and reached a dreary plain,
With a tumultuous waste of huge hill-tops
Before us, savage region! which I paced
Dispirited: when, all at once, behold!
Beneath our feet, a little lowly vale,
A lowly vale, and yet uplifted high
Among the mountains…
Urn-like it was in shape, deep as an urn;
With rocks encompassed, save that to the south
Was one small opening, where a heath-clad ridge
Supplied a boundary less abrupt and close;
A quiet treeless nook, with two green fields,
A liquid pool that glittered in the sun,
And one bare dwelling…
Full many a spot
Of hidden beauty have I chanced to espy
Among the mountains; never one like this
So lonesome, and so perfectly secure;
Not melancholy—no, for it is green
And bright and fertile…
In rugged arms how softly does it lie.
How tenderly protected! Were this
Man's only dwelling, sole appointed seat,
First, last, and single in the breathing world.
It could not be more quiet: peace is here
Or nowhere.

ALISDAIR AIRD'S FAVOURITE
LAKE DISTRICT PUBS

Alisdair Aird earns his living by going to pubs. He has been editor of *The Good Pub Guide* since its very first edition in 1983, during which time the book has become an indispensable companion for pub-goers across the UK. *The Good Pub Guide* is published each autumn by Ebury Press. Few people know the Lake District's pubs as well as Alisdair—here are his ten favourites.

The Pheasant, Bassenthwaite Lake Actually a beautifully placed hotel, but its charmingly old-fashioned and pubby bar is delightfully welcoming to all.

White Hart, Booth Cheerful old place with a real Lakeland flavour, and lovely surrounding walks.

Punch Bowl, Crosthwaite A place for a special meal, yet with all the proper pubby virtues too, and nice bedrooms.

Britannia, Elterwater Beautiful outside, handsomely traditional inside—no wonder it's heaving with visitors in summer.

Dog & Gun, Keswick Those magnificent old mountain photographs by G P Abrahams would make me thoroughly happy here anyway—but this bustling town pub has good honest food and drink too.

Strickland Arms, Levens Recently reopened and a model of how to bring a foodie pub up to date while keeping plenty of character.

Tower Bank Arms, Near Sawrey Still recognisably as illustrated in *The Tale of Jemima Puddleduck*, with plenty of rustic charm—just right if you're on the Beatrix Potter trail.

Newfield Inn, Seathwaite Interesting 16th-century Newlands Valley pub, very hospitable, with good simple food all day—and getting there, whether on foot or by car, is a joy.

Queens Head, Troutbeck Great individuality, which I value really highly in a pub, and top-notch for just a drink, for a meal, or even to stay in.

Gate Inn, Yanwath My current Lakeland favourite for a really good imaginative meal—yet unlike so many so-called 'gastropubs' this is at heart a proper pub, warm, relaxed and informal.

ACKNOWLEDGEMENTS

This book owes much to the ideas and expertise of other people, and I am hugely grateful to everyone who helped in its compilation. I am especially indebted to all those individuals in the Lake District and beyond who took the time to contribute lists and provide material for entries: to Alisdair Aird, David Baxter, Peter Burgess, Cecilia and Martin Campbell, Jim Chapple and all his fellow members of CAMRA in Cumbria, Barry Colam, Ron Kenyon, Gwenda and Steve Matthews, Sean McMahon, Lucy Nicholson, Tony Rogers and Peter Wilde.

Thanks are due to the wonderful libraries and librarians of Cumbria, and in particular the staff at Kendal, who patiently helped me with what must have seemed like endless requests. I gratefully acknowledge the assistance of the staff, publications and websites of the Lake District National Park Authority, Cumbria County Council and the six district councils in the county, Cumbria Tourism, the Lake District Search and Mountain Rescue Association and its member teams, the Fell and Rock Climbing Club, the Cumbria Fells and Dales Leader Programme and Made in Cumbria. Information and assistance was also received with thanks from the Ordnance Survey, the Office for National Statistics, Visit Britain, the Meteorological Office, the Department for Environment, Food and Rural Affairs, Natural England, the Ramblers Association, the National Trust, English Heritage and the Royal Society for the Protection of Birds.

I also thank my family and friends for their contributions and advice throughout the writing of this book. Above all, and as ever, I thank my amazing wife Ceri, for constant support and love.

BIBLIOGRAPHY

A miscellany like this inevitably borrows heavily from the research and books that came before it. The Lake District has a rich literary heritage, and I have been lucky to draw on so much wonderful writing. The following is a selection of some of the books consulted during research for this one, and all of them are warmly recommended for further reading on the Lake District.

Poems of Lakeland: An Anthology ed Ashley Abraham (Frederick Warne)
Feet in the Clouds: A Tale of Fell-Running and Obsession by Richard Askwith (Aurum Press)

The William Wordsworth Way by Howard Beck (Mainstream)

Dry Stone Walling Techniques and Traditions by David Bellamy (Dry Stone Walling Association)

Lakeland's Greatest Pioneers: 100 Years of Rock Climbing by Bill Birkett (Robert Hale)

Cumbria in Verse ed Melvyn Bragg (Secker & Warburg)

The Maid of Buttermere by Melvyn Bragg (Sceptre)

The Rough Guide to the Lake District by Jules Brown (Rough Guides)

A Fortnight's Ramble to the Lakes by Joseph Budworth (Preston Publishing)

Cumbria Real Ale Guide ed Jim Chapple (CAMRA)

The Lazy Tour of Two Idle Apprentices by Wilkie Collins and Charles Dickens (The Echo Library)

Hound Trailing: A History of the Sport in Cumbria by John Coughlan (Frank Peters)

The Eddie Stobart Story by Hunter Davies (HarperCollins)

The Good Guide to the Lakes by Hunter Davies (Century)

A Tour Through the Whole Island of Great Britain by Daniel Defoe (Yale University Press)

Millican Dalton: A Search for Romance and Freedom by MD Entwistle (Mountainmere)

Lake District Place Names by Robert Gambles (Dalesman)

Home Grown in Cumbria by Annette Gibbons (Zymurgy Publishing)

Cumbria: Lake District Life ed Hilary Gray (Pelham Books)

Favourite Lakeland Recipes by Carole Gregory (Salmon)

The Westmorland Gazette Book of the 20th Century ed Peter Holme (The Westmorland Gazette)

Haweswater by Sarah Hall (Faber)

The Regular Re-invention of Sporting Tradition and Identity: Cumberland and Westmorland Wrestling 1800-2001 by Mike Huggins (St Martin's College, Ambleside, research paper)

The Tale of Beatrix Potter by Margaret Lane (Frederick Warne)

A Literary Guide to the Lake District by Grevel Lindop (Sigma Press)

Official Wainwright Gazetteer by Peter Linney (Michael Joseph)

The Lake District: The Official National Park Guide by Terry Marsh (Pevensey Guides)

Joss Naylor MBE Was Here: A Personal Account of the Complete Traverse of the Wainwright Lakeland Peaks by Joss Naylor (self-published)

The Lake District: An Anthology ed Norman Nicholson (Penguin)

Norman Nicholson's Lakeland: A Prose Anthology by Norman Nicholson (Robert Hale)

Portrait of the Lakes by Norman Nicholson (Robert Hale)

Highest Mountains: The Mountains of England and Wales Volume 2: England by John and Anne Nuttall (Cicerone Press)

The Complete Tales of Peter Rabbit by Beatrix Potter (Frederick Warne)

Geology Explained in the Lake District by Robert Prosser (Fineleaf Editions)

Recollections of the Lakes and the Lake Poets by Thomas de Quincey (Penguin)

The English Lakes: Tales from History, Legend and Folklore by David Ramshaw (P3 Publications)

The Lake District: The Ultimate Guide by Gordon Readyhough (Hayloft)

The Cumbrian Dictionary of Dialect, Tradition and Folklore by William Rollinson (Smith Settle)

The Lake District Life and Traditions by William Rollinson (Weidenfeld & Nicolson)

The Bob Graham Round by Roger Smith (self-published, copies available at £3 from Pete Bland Sports, 34a Kirkland, Kendal, Cumbria, LA9 5AD).

Prisoner of War Camps 1939-1948: 20th Century Military Recording Project by Roger Thomas (English Heritage report)

A Pictorial Guide to the Lakeland Fells Volumes 1 to 7 by Alfred Wainwright (Frances Lincoln)

Wordsworth and Coleridge: Tour of the Lake District 1799 ed Dave and Kerry Walker (David Walker)

Guide to the Lakes in Cumberland, Westmorland and Lancashire by Thomas West (Woodstock Books)

A Dictionary of Lake District Place-Names by Diana Whaley (English Place-Name Society)

An American President's Love Affair with the English Lake District by Andrew Wilson (Lakeland Press Agency)

The Grasmere Journals by Dorothy Wordsworth, edited by Pamela Woof (Oxford University Press)

Guide to the Lakes by William Wordsworth (Frances Lincoln)

Agricultural and Horticultural Census 2005 (Department for Environment, Food and Rural Affairs)

Cumbria Facts and Figures 2006 (Cumbria County Council factsheet)

Foot-and-mouth Disease 2001: Inquiry Report (The Stationery Office)

Mountain Accidents 2005 and *2006* (Lake District Search and Mountain Rescue Association)

Notes on Building a Cairn: A Leaflet for the Working Waller or Dyker (Dry Stone Walling Association of Great Britain)

INDEX

afternoon tea 29–30
animal attractions 161–162
artists 89
arts festivals 123–124

beer 156–158
birds
   most common 173
   ospreys and golden eagles
     107–108
Blamire, Susanna
   life 81–82
   'Wey, Ned, Man!' 125–126
boats 198–199
books
   Lakeland books of the year
     86–87
   novels set in the Lake
     District 195
   Steve and Gwenda Matthews'
     favourites 139–140
Border wars 93
breweries 101–103
Brontë, Bramwell 86
Brontë, Charlotte 5
buildings
   at risk 137
   best modern 164–165

cairns 41–42
Campbell, Donald 162–163
campsites 155
Casson, Edmund 63
castles
   best 111
   haunted 122–123
churches
   best 47
   smallest 190
Clinton, Bill and Hillary 76
Coleridge, Samuel Taylor
   'A Thought Suggested By a
     View of Saddleback' 36

life 173–174
   'Reflections on Having
     Left a Place of Retirement'
     153
   rock-climbing exploits
     132–133
Constable, John 180
constituencies 36
Countryside Code 49
county towns 37
crafts 187
creatures 87–88, 160
Crier of Claife 129–130

Dalton, John 43
De Quincey, Thomas 67
Defoe, Daniel 121–122
dialect
   glossary of 127–128
   place names in 149
   violent synonyms 146
Dickens, Charles 147–148
Doodleshire 182–183
driving 25
dry stone walls
   how to build 57–58
   length 7
Dunmail Raise 172

employment 170

Faber, Frederick William 166
famous residents 131–132
farming
   farmers' markets 141
   figures 27–28
   impact of foot-and-mouth
     disease 112–113
   year in sheep farming 58
fell-running
   Bob Graham Round
     195–197
   history 40–41

fells
    214 Wainwrights 82–84
    best and worst ascents
        135–136
    glossary of terms 23–25
    highest 6
    name meanings 183–185
    Sean McMahon's favourite
        59–60
    steepest 63
    Wainwright's favourite
        summits 193
    Wainwright's favourite 10
    Wainwright's first 172–173
    well-dressed ghost of 112
    Wordsworth on 13
ferries 25
film, Lake District on 117–118,
    155–156
fish 56
food
    an 18th century dinner 80
    Artisan Food's favourite foodie
        places 193–194
    Borrowdale tea bread 163
    Cumberland sauce 176–177
    Cumberland sausages 44–45
    Grasmere gingerbread 78–79
    heroes 68–70
    Kendal Mint Cake 26
    Lucy Nicholson's favourite
        120–121
    Morecambe Bay shrimps and
        cockles 114–115
    rum butter 141–142
    sticky toffee pudding
        197–198
    tatie pot 60–61
    ultimate picnic 178–179
    Westmorland damsons
        150–151
foot-and-mouth disease
    112–113

gardens 94–95
ghosts 112, 122–123, 129–130
Graham, Bob 195–197

guidebook, the Lake District's
    first 11
gurning 51

Hadrian's Wall 37
Hemans, Felicia Dorothea 176
hermits 49–50
hound trailing 99–101

industries
    coal 30–31
    copper 136–137
    iron 167–168
    lead 105
    nuclear 188
    slate 16
islands 66

Keats, John 44

Lake District, christening of 27
lakes
    drowned villages under 104
    islands of 66
    largest, smallest, longest and
        deepest 181
    meanings of names 109–110
    of the Lake District 11
    speed limit on Windermere
        98–99
land breakdown 29
land ownership 12
liars, the world's biggest 7–8
limericks 185–186
literary associations
    graves 138
    homes 12
local news 130–131
Long Meg and Her Daughters
    73–74

Maid of Buttermere 175
Martineau, Harriet 98
memorials
    across the Lake District 38
    on Great Gable 158
    on Helvellyn 95

mineral water 179–180
mountain rescue
   advice 92–93
   causes of call–outs 153–154
   first 13–14
   history and call-out statistics
      39
   lighter side of 191–192
   types of injury 169
museums
   curiosities at Keswick 94
   unusual 63–64

National Park, the Lake District
   history and compared to
      others 18
   in figures 5
National Trust
   history 134–135
   properties 53
   properties bequeathed by
      Beatrix Potter 105–107
nature reserves 88
Newbiggin 167
Nicholson, Norman 188–189

old counties 16–17, 81
outdoor activities 174–175

passes 85
Peel, John 168–169
pencils 119
place names
   animals in 122
   flora and fauna in 177
   in dialect 149
   longest and shortest 107
   meanings 31–32
population 20
Postman Pat 145
Potter, Beatrix
   life 17–18
   property bequeathed to
      the National Trust
      105–107
   tales of 152
   trail 62–63

Priestley, JB 183
prisoner-of-war camps 129
pubs
   Alisdair Aird's favourite 201
   highest 97

racing 85
railways
   lost 54–55
   reclaimed 126–127
Ransome, Arthur
   inspiration for 'Swallows and
      Amazons' 189
   life 148–149
Rawnsley, Canon Hardwicke
   life 134–135
   'Skating on Derwent Water
      104–105
restaurants
   Best 193–194
   Michelin-starred 46
roads
   best drive 25
   steepest 67
rock-climbing
   grades 138
   history 42–43, 132–133
   Ron Kenyon's best 170–172
rocks 22–23
Roman remains 79–80
romantic places 108, 150
rushbearing 55–56
Ruskin, John
   involvement in first mountain
      rescue 13–14
   life 119–120
   'Yearning for the Lakes' 76

Scott, Walter 113–114
sheep
   counting 144–145
   Herdwicks 18–20
   year in farming 58
sheepdog trials 91–92
shows 74–76
ski-ing 68
slave trade 165

Smith, Elizabeth 29
Smith, Walter Parry Haskett 42–43
smuggling 35–36
sounds 14–15
Southey, Robert
  life 108–109
  'The Wanderer Returns' 15
squirrels 60
stately homes 21–22
Stobart, Eddie 115–116
swimming 143–144

television, Lake District on
  116–117
Three Peaks Challenge 48–49
tourism
  accommodation types 48
  in figures 61, 133–134
  questions asked 65
  top attractions 32–33
towns around the world 192
tree, tallest 35
Turner, JMW 180
twin towns 159

views
  best 28
  Georgian-style 46

Wainwright, Alfred
the 214 fells 82–84
  book dedications 40
  favourite fells 10
  favourite places 90
  favourite ridge walks 142
  favourite summits 193
  first fell 172–173
  life 33–35
walking
  an 18th century hike 159
  the 18th and 21st century
    walkers 22
  best in the Lake District 43–44
  Britain's best 160–161

  footpaths 70
  long-distance routes 186–187
  Naismith's Rule 110
  steepest climb 63
  Wainwright's favourite ridge
    walks 142
Walpole, Hugh 164
watercourses 8–9
waterfalls 96–97
weather
  advice for the fellwalker
    77–78
  Beaufort wind scale 115
  wettest place in England 6–7
  wild 65
  Wordsworth on 101
  working out the wind chill
    factor 90
  the year in 52
webcams 199–200
wildlife
  best place in Britain 15
  best in the Lake District 70–73
  in place names 177
Wilson, John 50–51
Wilson, Woodrow 181–182
Withnail and I 155–156
woodland crafts 151–152
Wordsworth, Dorothy 52–53
Wordsworth, William
  'The Excursion' 200
  'I Wandered Lonely as a Cloud'
    143, 177–178
  life 9–10
  on climbing mountains 55
  on the best time to visit 154
  on the fells 13
  on the past 190
  on the weather 101
  Parting Stone 166–167
  'The Prelude, Book IV'
    118–119
  trail 80–81
wrestling 124–125